Diary of a Barking Mad Dog Owner

Jackie McGuinness

Published by Dolman Scott Ltd

ISBN 978-1-909204-07-2

Dolman Scott
www.dolmanscott.com

This book is dedicated to my sister Lex, who encouraged me to put the stories I told her into a book so other people could enjoy them.

I'd like to thank Maureen Scott of AireCanada Airedale Rescue Network for her help editing the book and Andrea Denning for saving all the early emails I shared with the Airedale Rescue Network.

My thanks also go to artist Inez Smillie for the wonderful drawings, which are reproduced here with the permission of AireCanada Airedale Rescue Network, who own the originals.

Elle and Mahri running away

Prologue

'Well, call me mad – stark raving bonkers even!'

Breaking news!

My husband, Len, had been muttering about getting an Airedale pup for a while now. Mr Mac, my sort-of rescued Airedale, had been ignoring him when I was in the house and Annie, the resident Airedale, was turning into a right grand old duchess; she mostly ate and slept and only really graced us with her company if a special treat was on offer. If we took too long to put Mr Mac's lead on to go for a walk, she would return to bed rather than wait around for us. Len wanted a dog to sit by his side and be his pal.

When Mr Mac's breeders told us in April of 2006 they had a litter of seven pups, then two weeks old, and a handful, up and running around already, Len wanted one and was brimming with excitement at the prospect. I'd already said I would consider a small pup, like a Poodle or a Welsh Terrier, for instance; less work to groom and bathe, I thought. Because of Len's accident, he could no longer do all the training, walking and grooming and, most importantly, playing and socialising. I was concerned that a young pup would get lonely and bored. Doubtless this might lead to non-food things being chewed. The pup would be safe in its pen, so destruction of our existing dogs, Mr Mac and Annie, and our possessions would be limited; but there was the distinct possibility of impending boredom and the mischief it would bring with it. There was a solution, however! Two pups!

I must have been mad, stark raving bonkers even, because I agreed to have both an Airedale Terrier pup and a Welsh Terrier pup. Welsh pups were expected to be born on 24 May 2006, so the pups would be only two to three weeks apart and good company for each other – in theory, anyway! Len wanted to train the Airedale as his helper dog and I was going to train the Welsh pup in obedience and agility, along with Mr Mac. I thought Mr Mac would be happy with this plan, as he was used to being a pack-dog at the breeder's home and he desperately wanted a doggy friend to play with. He was positively clueless when it came to playing with toys or humans.

Still being in a state of shock, I couldn't even decide whether it was me or Len who'd made the decision to buy both pups.

I'm not sure why I did agree to it, but I did, and I was more than a little excited about the new arrivals. It could only have been the sight of the puppies at training school that had melted my resolve like ice cream on a hot day. My thoughts were laden with all sorts of scenarios. Annie likes Welsh rarebit; what's to say she wouldn't wonder whether a bit of Welsh Terrier would taste just as good? How long would it be before Mr Mac started wanting to play chase? How many pairs of slippers did I need to keep on standby?

I already thought raising Mr Mac was hard work, and he was two-and-a-half years old. He was a piece of cake compared to our first night with a nine-week-old pup. If people ever wondered why they should pick a mature rescue rather than a pup, I suggest that they ask me. I shall tell them more than a tale or two.

Introduction

A Bit of Background

MacIain joined us in December 1995, a bold little pup that had made the journey from Belfast to Luton by plane. Two weeks later, Annie joined us, making the same trip, but that did not go quite as smoothly and the airline lost her for several hours. She was called Annie because by the time we got her she was like a little lost soul crying for her mum, a warm meal and a cuddle. Len always insisted he called her after my mother. It was one of his little jokes and, as my mother had recently passed away, he thought it was a nice way to remember her.

The two pups quickly grew and got up to all sorts of mischief; but this was in the days before computers and digital cameras, so, in their early years, their stories were not recorded in the same way. Well, they were not recorded at all unless you count being stored on God's original hard drive, 'The Brain', and it has proved to be no more trustworthy than the computerised versions.

The two dogs went everywhere with us, hiking over hill and moor, as we took frequent breaks in our caravan. We bought the caravan to coincide with the arrival of the pups so we could have lots of holidays together. The years passed and computers and emails became available to everyone.

I joined an internet forum of Airedale lovers and would recount the odd tale or two of my dog's antics. I would also send the stories to my sisters to amuse them, because they lived in Scotland and I could not visit them as often as I would have liked. My younger sister always said I should put the stories into a book to share with other dog lovers.

Thanks to the internet, a lot of the little original emails had been saved, so the decision was made for me. All I had to do was get them printed, or so I thought; but that is another story. This book is a collection of short anecdotes about the dogs and people that have filled my life, lifted my spirits when I've been down and kept me sane when life conspired against me.

30 August 2005

We have had a glorious August bank holiday weekend; as most people in England know, bank holidays usually equal rain, low temperatures and wind. This year we had been lucky and it had rained a week early. Because we'd had that week of heavy rain, everything in the garden had grown in leaps and bounds – well, grass and weeds to be precise – so I set about getting it back under control. Instead of using the strimmer, a heavy duty petrol

Chilli MacIain

engine one, which is a bit big for me, I decided just to spray some weedkiller round the base of the trees. One of the reasons I didn't want to use the strimmer was that, the last time I used it, I didn't notice a small frog in the long grass and managed to strim it all the way to the next life. The part of that memory I'd most rather forget was that I had bits of frog all over me; my glasses, my face, my clothes, everywhere! It was extremely unpleasant. Almost like a scene from a Kermit horror movie.

So there I was, enjoying the peace and quiet of Sunday morning − birds singing, dogs snoozing, bees humming − when I spotted something staring at me from under a tree. Eeeek!

A python? I told myself not to be silly, remembering that I was in England after all. Perhaps I should think quickly, as much as I could think for the dilemma I was in!

Quick, hide the dogs, hide me and then jump up and down and panic … my first thoughts were merely a representation of the panic I was in. I thought about spraying it and then decided against the unkindly action. Then I questioned whether, if the roles were reversed, it would think it unkind to bite me? I tried to reassure myself. *Calm down. Breathe in and out. In, out. Try it again, but slower this time. That's better; look at it again.*

After taking another look and concluding that it wasn't a python after all, I decided that it actually looked more like a baby adder. This thing was black with brown markings and a flat skull with big black eyes. It actually looked a bit cute, like a cartoon, and it almost appeared to be smiling − how cute can a creepy-crawly be? It was four inches long and fatter than my thumb − *that's a <u>BIG</u> creepy-crawly* −

with what looked like a hook on its tail-end curving over its back.

At that moment, I saw Fred across the road. Fred looked like an old sea captain. Fred was seventy-one and had worked on the land since he was seven. He told wonderful stories of ploughing and harvesting with horse-drawn machinery and how they used to hand-scythe fields and bale the straw.

"Fred, come here quick!" I shouted. "I've got a funny snake in the garden."

He strolled over, smiled a toothless smile, and in a strong country accent he said, "Weelll, mee beooty, wot aave we eere?"

He was talking to the snake, not me.

"Ah," he said. "This is a black hawk moth caterpillar."

He picked it up to show me that the snake appearance was to fool the birds, and its eyes and fangs were on the flat end of its face. It was like something from *Alien* and I had to fight the urge to run off and throw up. I was brought up in the city and not used to the unusual creatures roaming around my garden.

Bitey Face

7

"So it won't bite my dog and make her sick then?"

"Nope. It only eats leaves."

"Well, all I can say is, I hope none of those moths ever gets in the house."

My next job was to dig up some potatoes: a nice safe job, I thought. First, I was eaten by ants and then a big frog leapt out of the undergrowth at me. This was the definitive signal: time for a cup of tea, I thought … and maybe a rest from the wildlife of the suburban jungle that was my garden.

I was sitting, drinking my tea and chatting to Len, when Annie, who had been sleeping all morning, jumped up and headed towards the stable. She stopped short and stared at the door. I walked over to see what she was looking at. She was so funny. Her body seemed to be backing up towards me, while her head and neck were extending to see and sniff at something. As I got close, I realised it was the big frog that I had disturbed and I told her so. She looked at me in relief and skipped round behind me. Len had now joined us to see what was so interesting.

"Pick it up," he said.

"No way!" I responded.

"Put your gloves on, then," he said.

"There is no way, even with gloves on, that I could pick a frog up."

I decided to be really brave and got a big piece of cardboard, folded it up at each side, and placed it in front of the frog so it would hop on to it and I could move it into the flowerbeds. When I put the cardboard in front of it, the frog sat up on its back legs and puffed itself up to intimidate me. It worked! As soon as it dropped on to the card, I grabbed the sides and turned, heading for the flowerbed, six feet or less away from me; but the frog started to run up the cardboard towards me! With a scream, I threw the card with the frog attached into the flowers. Whoever said gardening was relaxing?

MacIain lifted his head from his recumbent position in the shadow of one of the trees and glared. *"Keep the noise down. I'm snoozing."*

Annie was sitting by Len, looking up at him with that "my hero, you saved me" look. Len was laughing at me for being scared of a frog. And me? I just wanted to go back to the peace and tranquillity of my office. Roll on Tuesday.

Jackie: "It's hard being the man about the house."
Annie: *"I've never seen a frog before."*
MacIain: *"I'm cool ... zzzzzzzz"*

In early October, 2005, my special boy MacIain managed to swallow a hide chew that he'd been playing with. He never let on that he was in any pain and I never knew anything was wrong till one day he was so ill that even a drink of water made him vomit. I took him to the vet, who transferred him to a specialist. They did some x-rays and found what they thought to be a piece of bicycle tyre in his oesophagus. It was at this point we realised it was the chew. It had softened and dropped down, blocking the entrance to his stomach. He was a very sick dog with aspirated pneumonia along with the damage to his oesophagus. The vet was hesitant to suggest that he would last the night. We left with heavy hearts. The following day, the vet called us to let us know MacIain was responding to the medication and his prospects looked a little better. He was still on the danger list and would have to spend a few more days in the doggy hospital intensive care unit.

21 October 2005

The vet phoned us last night: the news was still good. MacIain had eaten some boiled chicken and had a drink. His gag reflex had returned to normal and the food and water had stayed down. They called him their little trooper and were not worried about pneumonia any more, but they still needed to keep an eye on him to make sure the oesophagus didn't rupture. It was going to be Friday before he could come home. The drive to The Small Animal Hospital to collect him won't seem as long as it did that first day.

The dogs commented:

Annie: *"So that's where our chew disappeared to."*
MacIain: *"Well, I thought it was a good hiding place and nobody would ever find it."*

24 October 2005

MacIain came home on Friday night with a sack full of meds and a long list of instructions. Although he was tired and weak, he still managed to jump out of the car; he ran up to me with a wagging tail and nearly pushed me over. After that, he went into the house and straight to his bed.

I had to give him 5 ml of one medicine with a syringe, dripping it down his throat thirty minutes before his food and then he was allowed two spoonfuls of boiled chicken and pasta; he was to get five meals a day. The medicine relaxed and lubricated his oesophagus, so the food would slide down easily. He also had to get antibiotics and painkillers three times a day, while I had to try to conceal all his pills in this tiny amount of food.

On Sunday, MacIain was much improved. He found a spider and chewed its legs off. Later, when I let him out in the garden, Annie ran after something and he joined in the chase. Ironically, I was supposed to be keeping him quiet.

MacIain was watching me preparing his dinner; suddenly he ran across the room and was staring at the wall, swaying ever so slightly. What's up now? I thought, trying not to panic. Then he lunged at the wall, his teeth making a crunching sound. I realised then that he thought a little black mark was a spider and he meant to have it.

Since he'd got home, Annie was a bit put out. She was happy to have him home, but not happy that he was getting all this special food. So every time he got fed, I gave her a spoonful of his special food – she normally had a prescription diet for pancreatitis – or a bit of raw carrot while I was preparing our lunch.

Every time I took the cheese out of the fridge, MacIain appeared at my side. He loved cheese, so I cut up tiny bits and he ate them all. I also gave Annie some and then I made up a pot of chicken pasta for MacIain's next set of meals. Annie sat in front of the microwave, watching it cook.

Len and I sat out in the autumn sun and ate our lunch. Len also gave the two dogs some cheese. It started to rain just as we finished lunch, so I cleared up, thinking Len was watching the dogs. Needless to say, he wasn't. I came out of the house and there was Annie, standing over a puddle of vomit.

"Arrghhhh! MacIain's been sick … quick, where is he?" I ran round the house like a headless chicken, calling and searching for him. Annie had run off in search of Len.

Len arrived at the scene of the crime and MacIain came trotting up the garden. Annie was now beside Len.

"Are you sure it was MacIain?" he asked.

I wasn't sure at all, because Len was meant to be watching him. We examined the content of the puddle. Aha! Cheese! They both had cheese. Carrot! MacIain never had carrot.

"Smell her breath," Len told me.

"It smells cheesy," I replied.

"Well, smell his breath then."

"It smells cheesy too."

We eventually decided that it was definitely Annie who was sick. Too much cheese, I expect. That was her dinner scrapped for the evening. MacIain went for a sleep and Annie stayed close to Len, staring at him as if he had stolen something from her. She usually reserved this action for telling us she was ill or in a lot of pain.

Len asked her if she wanted 'out', 'dinner', 'car ride', 'bath' and everything else he could think of. He didn't get any response, but as soon as I went to the kitchen she followed me, looking at the chicken pasta pot, and touching my hand ever so lightly.

I gave in and when MacIain got his next meal, she got two spoonfuls of his dinner, which she ate in an instant, and had to check the plate several times in case she missed a bit. After that, she was off to bed for a sleep, quite happy that she'd got what she wanted.

I think the little monkey threw up deliberately and pretended she was ill to get some fresh chicken.

MacIain continued to do well and he was starting to object to the medicine − a sure sign that he thought he had recovered. He will go back on Wednesday for a lung scan and a check on his oesophagus, because they were still worried the scar tissue could cause a stricture. He wouldn't be on a normal diet for six weeks and could only have short walks off-lead in the garden, as we couldn't allow him to pull on a lead and put pressure on his throat.

Nevertheless, I was so pleased that my boy was home at my side.

27 October 2005

MacIain returned to The Small Animal Hospital for his check-up yesterday. The vet was really pleased to see him looking so perky. They took him off and x-rayed his chest and are claiming his recovery to be a miracle. It was the miracle of all the Airedale love around the world reaching out to him.

They showed Len the first x-ray taken on 17 October, where there was a huge white patch over MacIain's lung and a very cartoon-like oesophagus, reminiscent of Tom and Jerry cartoons when they swallow something large. The new images featured completely clear lungs and a straight oesophagus. The vet said he could not believe how well MacIain had healed and how well behaved he was.

They'd only had to tell him to lie down and he was in position for the x-ray machine, letting them take as many as they needed. They said that this was the first Airedale they'd come across that had done this. Some vets can be a bit wary of Airedales because they can be a bit exuberant, but no more that any other large young bouncy dog. They said they were pleased to meet such a well-mannered dog and they complimented us on our training. Obviously, the vet didn't realise that MacIain was on his best behaviour. He might have thought differently if he'd heard me shouting, "Are your ears ornamental?" down the garden while being completely ignored.

MacIain had still been sick a couple of times, but we still thought he was feeling better … and hungry. He had been eating his food so quickly sometimes, I think the food didn't know it had left the plate and came straight back up. We'd clean up and give him some more, hoping it stayed down. The vet had suggested liquidising his food for a week, then slowly making it not so smooth.

Because poor MacIain continued to have trouble with his food, we took him back to The Small Animal Hospital for a check-up. The news this time was not so good: MacIain had developed some scar tissue and this was constricting the oesophagus. The vet decided that the best course of action would be to put a feeding tube into his stomach and use some sort of balloon every day to stretch the oesophagus. This also meant that my poor boy would have to stay at The Small Animal Hospital for at least a week. The procedure did not work as well as the vet had hoped. Every time they thought they had fixed the problem, more scar tissue formed. It had become clear that the oesophagus could not be stretched any more. The vet would have to think up a cunning new plan to save my boy.

Annie: *"Give me some. I want some. I'll be sick if I don't get any."*
MacIain: *"Mmmm, chicken pasta."*

14 November 2005

We went to visit MacIain yesterday. He looked like a pot roast with his little body in a sort of white fishnet stocking. He was really happy to see me for two minutes, but this tired him out very quickly. We were allowed to take him for a very short walk, but he was exhausted and just wanted to go back to his bed.

He had a feeding tube in his side. I was surprised at how tiny it was. The vet told us that the stricture caused by the scar tissue had formed just where the oesophagus entered the stomach. This was good in one sense, they said, although I failed to understand why it was good. They were going to try the balloon again to stretch the oesophagus. If it went well, we could have him home for ten days, after which they will have another look. If there was no improvement, they would try it again, and if there was still no change we could continue to tube feed him for as long as his health held up.

The vet said that we had to understand the risks and side effects of long-term tube feeding. If MacIain didn't improve, we would be left with two options. Major surgery would have meant cracking his chest open, pulling the stomach up over the damaged part and hoping that this in turn didn't create a further stricture. But there was only a 50/50 chance of this procedure working and him surviving the operation. It was a huge decision to make on a nine-year-old dog whose health was already compromised by arthritis, an under-active thyroid and the recent month's problems. There was also the aftercare to consider following such a big operation. We didn't know whether MacIain would be able to cope or if it would simply leave him in greater discomfort, all to gain a few more months of his company.

Then there was the question of whether we would be putting him through all of this for our benefit or his, or for the improvement to the vet's bank balance. So far, the insurance had paid out £5500, and the next operation was going to be the same amount again.

We talked long and hard about this dilemma and both Len and I cried till we had no tears left. I loved my boy, but I had to make a decision. We decided that we would try as much dilation as possible to stretch the oesophagus, but we would not, could not, put him through the next operation. So it was a matter of time now whether he was going to recover enough to have some quality of life for a little while longer or whether one of the dilations was going to push him over the edge to the point of no return. I decided to enjoy what quality time I had left with him and to learn about tube feeding.

MacIain was put on the DNR (do not resuscitate) list. It was the end of an era, because he was part of Len's mobile life; even if we gave a home to another dog, it could never be part of that life. Annie was devastated and moped about the house. If we went out, she thought that we had gone to get MacIain and, when he was not in the car on our return, Annie glared at me and threw herself on to her bed with a sigh.

The vet told us that, when MacIain was allowed home, we would have to put a soft muzzle on him, as he could not be allowed anything by mouth and, of course, he couldn't be permitted to run free. He'd be confined to short walks in a harness so we didn't pull on his neck.

17 November 2005

My special boy came home last night with twelve different medications to be given twice a day and sachets of food for use with the feeding tube. I'd had my lessons and felt confident. I gave him one meal last night and one this morning and had no problems. My friend and neighbour, who walked the dogs for me every day, said she would help me out today and Friday by giving him his 11.00am and 3.00pm feed. She used to be a theatre nurse, so was quite confident about using the syringe and feeding tube.

Amy phoned me to say he'd had his morning feed; there had been one or two little problems, but he was fine now. The problem was that she'd tried to make him lie down and he growled at her. He has never been known to growl at anyone, but then it transpired that she was trying to make him lie on his side. Nobody could make him lie on his side if he didn't want to. Not even me. I told her that he had to be fed standing up and that it had never occurred to me that anyone would think otherwise. I understood where the confusion had arisen when she said that most of her patients were lying down when she fed them.

When Amy gave MacIain his afternoon feed, she put the tube back inside the net body stocking, but in a position where he could get to it and he chewed the non-return valve off. I only hope he didn't try to swallow any of the bits. Between Len and Amy, they managed to use bits from one of his spare catheter valves and make a new valve and put the tube high up towards his neck so he couldn't chew it. He was still a little monkey, even though he was a very sick dog. He just didn't know he was sick. The only thing that concerned him was that he couldn't have cheese and biscuits any more.

The specialist vet gave me food for only two days and meds for five days. I asked him what I would do when the food ran out and he told me to go to my local vet and, if that wasn't possible, I could use baby food. He said there'd be enough meds. I never picked up on the importance of what he was saying to me at the time, and a few hours later the penny dropped. MacIain could only drink water, as anything else choked him and the scarring was still forming and getting worse. I think the vet knew he was unlikely to survive the weekend and was trying to let me down gently.

20 November 2005

On the Saturday, we had a few more problems feeding MacIain through the tube; he would only take 80ml at one feed, then 50ml, then 30ml. He was supposed to be on six portions of 100ml per day. Now you may wonder how we knew to stop feeding MacIain, and the answer is he would fidget and try to walk away. As soon as we stopped, he would calm down. The vet had told us to expect this and, as he did not appear to be in pain, we decided to let him rest and see if his appetite returned. Later that day, he seemed a bit brighter and wanted to play and go for a walk. I took him for a stroll round the garden, and he visited all his favourite places, but he tired very quickly. When we came in, he took a little drink of water, which he was allowed, but the vet had warned us that as the scarring continued to grow this too would become a problem. As soon as he finished the drink, he wanted to be sick; this was not a good sign, but it passed and he seemed fine, choosing to sleep by my side rather than his basket. At 8.00am on Sunday, after his breakfast feed, he wanted to be sick again. We knew this was very bad and called the vet, who told us he would come to our house.

MacIain said it was time because he was very tired now. He wanted a nice long sleep. MacIain was helped to cross the 'Bridge', where he joined Carrie and McGregor, our first two Airedales. For MacIain, it was very peaceful, in his own home and bed. He was buried at the bottom of our garden near a Scots Pine tree, next to McGregor. I thought calling the vet was hard, but walking that green mile with my spade to the bottom of the garden was one of the hardest things I've ever done. We put him in the back of my car and drove it slowly down the garden. He loved being in my car, so it was right that he should make his final journey in it.

MacIain – 8 September 1996 to 20 November 2005

MacIain had been a very sick boy and, although the vets had done everything they could for him, it was all in vain. My friends sent hugs across the airwaves to help me come to terms with my sadness. I should explain at this point what is meant by the 'Bridge'. A lot of pet owners believe that their pets will join them in heaven and to do this the pets must wait at a place they call Rainbow Bridge. When the owner dies, they are met by their pets and they can cross the bridge into heaven together. Someone back in the 1980s wrote a poem about this place, but the details of the author have been lost in the mists of time. There are several websites that refer to this bridge and some suggest that the idea dates back to Norse legend. Many pet bereavement counsellors use the story, as most religions do not appear to cater for the spiritual needs of the bereaved pet owner.

The Rainbow Bridge

Just this side of heaven is a place called The Rainbow Bridge.

When an animal dies that has been especially close to someone here, that pet goes across the Rainbow Bridge. There are meadows and hills for all of our special friends so they can run and play together. There is plenty of food, water and sunshine, and our friends are warm and comfortable.

All the animals who had been ill and old are restored to health and vigour. Those who were hurt or maimed are made whole and strong again, just as we remember them in our dreams of days and times gone by. The animals are happy and content, except for one small thing: they each miss someone very special to them who had to be left behind.

They all run and play together, but the day comes when one suddenly stops and looks into the distance. His bright eyes are intent. His eager body quivers. Suddenly, he begins to run from the group, flying over the green grass, his legs carrying him faster and faster.

You have been spotted, and when you and

your special friend finally meet, you cling together in joyous reunion, never to be parted again.

The happy kisses rain upon your face; your hands again caress the beloved head, and you look once more into the trusting eyes of your pet, so long gone from your life, but never absent from your heart.

Then you cross Rainbow Bridge together ...

Author unknown

30 November 2005

I missed MacIain this weekend and, while remembering lots of funny things he got up to over the years, this poem just came into my head. Everyone's kind thoughts and wishes have helped me through this sad period and now I can smile – most times – when I think of my special boy.

EMPTY SPACE

There's an empty space beside my knee
Where MacIain's head would be
There's an empty space beside my feet
Where he would sit and wait for treats

He'd talk to me in a grumbly mumble
He'd shove my knees and make me tumble
He'd steal my socks and underwear
He'd sit and howl if I tugged his hair

He'd catch the flies and bugs and bees
And once or twice he brought home fleas
He'd dance and prance, his aim to please
Then surprise! Surprise! he'd steal the cheese

He's gone from me for a little while
And left his memories to make me smile
We'll meet again at that heavenly gate
Until that day he'll sit and wait

CT: An Airedale looking for a new home

On 19 December 2005, I was given a gift of a handsome two-and-a-half-year-old show Airedale that had become a little bit wary of other dogs – but only in enclosed halls, where most shows took place – so was being retired. His name was CT.

The breeders knew I would give him a safe, loving home for the rest of his years. He didn't appear to know how to play with toys, sit, lie down or stay; or, if he did, he never let on. He was brilliant on the grooming table, though, and would stand for hours. It was clear from the way he stayed close to me that he was very much a 'lady's dog'.

It wasn't love at first sight on either side, but we have subsequently grown to love each other. I think I loved his handsome looks a lot more than he liked mine. He was named CT when we got him from Belfast, but he ignored us every time we called him. We decided it was our accent; we just could not say "CT" the way the Irish could, and discussed changing his name, but had trouble coming up with something suitable. One day, Len forgot and spoke to

CT as if he was MacIain "Mr Mac, poor boy, are you sad?" 'Mr Mac' had been a pet name we used when talking to MacIain. We were really surprised when CT trotted over to Len and sat by his side. That was it then; he had chosen his new name to go with his new home.

His previous owners had paid us a visit shortly after Mr Mac/CT joined our family. When they were leaving, they asked CT to get in the car with them. He turned away from their car and walked over to where I was standing, making it clear that he was staying with me. This, I felt, was the start of a special bond between us.

3 March 2006

Mr Mac had only been with us for a few months, but it felt as if he had been with us a lot longer. He had settled in very well and we could tell he just loved us to pieces. Over the months his character had unfolded bit by bit and we became best of friends. I wrote this poem for him. I had lost MacIain and found Mr Mac.

Love − lost and found

It was a cold and damp winter's day
When Mr Mac he came to stay;
In the show ring, he'd made his name,
But he really didn't like that game.

A handsome boy for all to see,
Tall and proud, he looked at me;

So well groomed, he'd stand and show,
But how to sit he didn't know.

Now home with us, he has such fun,
Playing chase with his new chum;
Stealing hats an' socks an' gloves,
Rearranging beds and rugs.

We start our walks at a steady pace,
But soon, he thinks he's in a race;
First to reach the tree, the gate,
Then off again; he doesn't wait.

Things to do and things to see;
Oops! He missed another tree!
Back and forth and up and down,
His big wet nose stays on the ground.

When Mr Mac first came to stay we had a couple of issues with him snapping at Len, but only if Len touched his ear. He never did it with me and the vet could find nothing wrong with his ears. He would happily place his front paws on the arm of Len's wheelchair or on his bed. Once he even tried to climb on the bed beside Len, but there was not enough room for both of them. Len could fuss over Mr Mac as much as he wanted, but if he stretched out and touched the edge of his ear, even gently, Mr Mac would snap at him.

Yesterday, we suddenly realised what the problem was. Static electricity shocks! When Len was in his wheelchair, if I touched him, I would sometimes get a shock. Once, when we were in a hotel with thick carpet on the floors, the shock was large enough to see the blue arc from the chair to my finger and hear the bang. It came with slightly more than a modicum of pain as well. The first time Len tried to pet Mr Mac, we had been rolling along carpeted corridors in a huge exhibition centre. The poor dog must have got a jolt right on the point of his ear and he either remembered that and it put him off Len and his chair, or it had happened several times and we hadn't realised. As a result, Len tried to make sure he touched his back first, as it did not appear to be so sensitive.

Mr Mac had lost three kilos after coming to stay with us because he had been off his food. We took him to the vet, who was concerned but could find nothing wrong with him and thought he was stressed by the move, and maybe a bit homesick. Eventually, he put the weight back on and just wanted to play all day.

Yesterday, he decided to rearrange the house, starting with the rugs. He picked up the rugs and moved them from the hall to the sitting room, then emptied all the fleeces from Annie's basket in the kitchen and put them in the sitting room too. He regularly stole Len's clothes and hid them in his bed.

He wanted to play chase and 'bitey face' with Annie, but she had gone off Mr Mac after about a week because he was so boisterous and big. She wasn't used to being shoved around; she was more accustomed to doing the shoving. When Mr Mac wasn't falling over the way MacIain used to do, she seemed to feel a bit put out. Mr Mac, intellectual that he was, learned that the way to her heart was via her tummy, so he was leaving some of his dinner each day for her. She must have thought, *"Oops. If I don't get on with him, they will send him back and I will lose out on all his scrummy tripe."* So Annie learnt to play a bit rougher with him and would run under his tummy and grab his elbow so he couldn't turn to get her. She loved running into a tight corner because he had a long body and couldn't manoeuvre as quickly. Because he was much taller than Annie, they couldn't play 'bitey face' when he was standing up, so he laid down for her. Bless him. He also worked out that she didn't like to be bitten on the neck, so he grabbed the bit of her collar that stuck out and pulled her around with it. It looked so cute. I tried for ages to get a picture of it, but as soon as I picked up a camera, all play stopped.

Annie: *"He's kinda cute, I suppose."*
Mr Mac: *"Cute! Yeeeuuuk! Try handsome or a hunk."*

I've been wondering all week why I had felt as if I'd gone a round or two with Tyson, and today I remembered that I cut the grass on Sunday before the weather turned to winter. I took Annie out with me to keep me company while I walked up and down poop-scooping, but she thought it was too cold and windy and went back indoors and curled up in her bed.

I realised the grass was fast on its way to becoming unmanageable, so I'd better cut it. We lived on a small farm and there was about two acres of grass to maintain. I had a nice little yellow tractor-type ride-on mower; a normal lawnmower was just not up to the job. I started the mower and trundled up and down, and down and up, and up and down, so very soon the collector was full. I trundled down to my compost heap at the far corner of our little estate, as I liked to call it. I backed up to dump the grass, being very careful not to drive on to the slimy mud at the side of the compost heap. We'd had a lot of rain recently, so any contact with the slimy mud was probably not likely to end well. I dumped the contents and pressed the accelerator to drive away. I remained stationary. Oops! Must have pressed the brake. I pressed harder and still got nothing, so I looked at the pedal and pressed again. It was the correct pedal I was pressing, but still no forward momentum. I checked the pedal again, just to be sure.

I had another look and realised that I'd backed up a little bit lopsided and my right back tyre was spinning silently in the muddy, smelly, slimy, decomposing grass. Yuk! Now I knew what the problem was, I knew I could easily deal with it, so I switched off the engine and went to get a piece of wood from my to-burn pile nearby. I stuck it under the wheel and restarted the tractor. Vroom, vroom! I looked back, checking the wheel, which was still spinning. I tried moving the wood and used a second piece to dig some muck away – all to no avail.

What it needed was a little push to make it bite on to the wood, but there was no-one else around and there was a safety mechanism in place. If the seat was lifted, this caused the engine to cut out. Hmm! I slid across the seat while pushing it down with one hand and ended up standing in the mud. So far so good. The engine was still running. I backed up, positioning myself so I could push the tractor from the back. Now all I had to do was press the accelerator … which was at the front of the vehicle! However, I was thwarted by my diminutive stature; being only five feet tall, I could not reach the accelerator. Arrgghh!

So, picture this. I crouched, pulling down on the seat to keep the engine running, reached forward with my right leg and attempted to press the pedal and lift the back of the mower while simultaneously trying to push it forward. It was a good job I could multi-task!

Despite my best efforts, I was not successful and I gave up the challenge of doing it on my own. I had no option but to hike up to the house and ask Brian, Len's carer, to give me a hand. Brian was six foot plus but walked with a stoop, so he appeared to be shorter than he actually was. We trudged back down the garden to the mower and I told him to climb on at the left side because it was less muddy. After all, I was the one wearing wellies. I told Brian to press the brake pedal to start the engine; then, when I said "Go", he was to press the accelerator and I would push the mower out of the mud.

It never crossed my mind to move the seat back that had been set for my five-foot frame! Brian looked so funny. His knees were up round his ears, and he was bent over the steering wheel. I nearly couldn't push for laughing, but he did manage to start the mower and drive it. All it took was a good shove from me and we were back on terra firma. Brian returned to the house and I cut the rest of the grass, being very careful not to get so close to the mud again.

4 May 2006

Mr Mac went to school last night. I had decided that we needed to work together on obedience first and, when we'd mastered that, we could move on to agility training. He was a young dog, not quite three years old, with a big brain and lots of energy. He was perfect for this activity.

When we arrived at the class, Mr Mac ignored me,

which was a tad frustrating; but then the other three owners present seemed to have similar problems. The trainer said she'd had two classes of fifteen pups and young dogs, so all the smells were probably distracting them. Eventually, they all settled down.

Mr Mac sniffed at a couple of the dogs, greeted them nicely and sat down ready for class. The response to the command 'Sit' was still slow; sometimes he responded to the first command and sometimes to the fifth; sometimes it was, *"Oh well, 'stand' seems good ... but no sausage as a reward?"* Heel work on lead was fine for 30 to 40 minutes, but if there were too many about turns, he got stubborn, or perhaps he was dizzy; he dropped his head and dug his heels in like a puppy on a lead for the first time. He simply would not be pushed or pulled in any direction when he had chosen not to go. With a bit of cajoling, he eventually moved on, but not with any finesse.

The instructor suggested a tag race to make the lesson more interesting: each dog and owner had to weave through some cones and the dog had to sit at the far end. When all the dogs were sitting, you had to weave back through the cones to the start position. The winning team was the one that had taken all the dogs from one end to the other and back again without touching the cones and all the dogs were in the sit position. Because of his show training, Mr Mac would not sit, so he was the only dog that was allowed to stand. Our team was in the lead. Mr Mac was the last to make the weave through the cones and the team were depending on Mr Mac to walk quickly round each cone. We couldn't start the exercise until all the dogs were sitting; the atmosphere was tense – we wanted to win, even though it was just a game.

Mr Mac could sense that something was up. I think he may have felt that he was back in the show ring, as we started to walk towards the first cone. Much to everyone's surprise, instead of walking round the cone, he stopped and stared at it. "Come on, Mr Mac," I said softly, giving the lead a gentle tug just to remind him of the direction we should have been travelling in. He turned and looked me in the eye, walked up to the cone and kicked it out of his way. He then walked in an almost perfect straight line to each cone, kicking them out of his way; and just to add insult to injury, when we reached the other dogs he sat down.

The games were over and now we had two new exercises to practice. We were called forward one at a time; the other dogs were in a 'sit-stay' position. I had to get Mr Mac to stay while I walked backwards away from him. I had to stop at a comfortable distance – about eight to ten feet – and call him to me. This was the first time I had tried this with other dogs close by. I called him to heel and he came straight to me – that was a pleasant surprise. The other exercise was a walkabout with one of the other dogs. We had to stop in a circle, facing outwards, with our dog in the 'sit-stay', and then walk backwards to stand next to a different dog. Mr Mac stayed where I had left him, although, because he was not sitting, he did nose-poke the groin of the man who was standing beside him because the man didn't offer him a biscuit.

The next test was to make him 'sit-stay' and walk round him. He had issues with anything behind him, but tonight I got all the way round. His biggest test was 'sit-stay' and then, from his side, I walked forward four paces, called him and then kept walking, turning, left, right and about. He did it, although he went a bit wide in places. Then it was back towards the other dogs and sit. Yeah!! Mr Mac had never mastered the 'down' command. When this command is given, the dog should lie down with his belly on the floor. There was nothing that would make Mr Mac lie down in a public place, so when all the other dogs were given the command 'down', Mr Mac was told to sit.

Because Mr Mac had been progressing well at the obedience classes, his reward was to start in the agility class. He didn't really have to pass any obedience test; just prove he could follow some basic commands and not pick fights with class mates. Mr Mac had a little game he liked to play. Every time we walked out of the gate after class, he would kick up the bark mulch from the flowerbeds over anyone or any dog walking behind him. The class laughed so much he jumped on to another flowerbed and kicked up some more. What a little monkey!

I thought agility classes on Monday would be interesting; he would probably be scared witless at all the new things. In preparation, I've tried to make him attempt new activities, like standing on the steps to the garden shed or jumping over fallen trees in the forest.

11 May 2006

We were very disappointed on Monday that the agility class was cancelled due to extremely heavy rain and not enough scuba gear to go round; so it was back to obedience class on Wednesday.

Mr Mac was very good by last week's standards. He sat most times on request and his 'sit-stay...come' was the best yet. He still did not like me to be out of sight, so 'sit-stay and walk round your dog' resulted in him either standing up and turning on the spot or shuffling his bum round to watch me. Circling the cones or indeed just heel work was not something at which he excelled. With straight walking, as soon as I began any about turns or left-right turns, he would drop his head and lift his shoulders. He had to be dragged. Treats did not have the desired effect, but we were working on this issue. Every time I took him out for a walk, I added some turns just to keep him concentrating on me.

Next it was time for a new trick. It had taken five months to teach him to come when he was called, and we had just about mastered it; now he has to learn 'away'. I had no idea how to begin teaching him the concept of this command. Four of the cones were used to make a square and then a small mat was placed in the centre. I had to take Mr Mac up to the mat, let him sniff a treat, place the treat on the mat and take him away a few paces and sit him at my side. Then, with a wave of my hand I had to say 'away'.

Apparently, regardless of whether the dog was really intelligent or just plain greedy, it will immediately run to the mat and eat the treat. Sounds simple; however, if you thought that Mr Mac picked this up with no problem, you would be wrong! Mr Mac knew he got treats if he could 'sit-stay'.

"Away!" I shouted, waving my arm in the direction of the mat and jogging towards it. "Mr Mac, come here … away," I shouted somewhat confusingly, trying to demonstrate to him that every time I said 'away' he should walk forward.

He eventually reached the mat and got the treat. We practised three or four times, but he only seemed to get more confused, so we left it for another day. Class over, we stayed behind for a coffee and a chat. Mr Mac was standing by my side, or leaning on my side to be more precise; the perfect little gentleman. You would not believe this was the grumpy, grumbling growler I took there in December – a dog whose demeanour suggested that if you came within a two-foot radius, he would rip your lungs out. In truth, it would more likely have been my shoulders that would have been pulled out of place as he took off in the opposite direction. It was all bravado. He really was a bit shy and nervous of anything new.

18 May 2006

Monday night was damp and cool, so there were some doubts regarding whether the agility class would take place; but we went to find out anyway. By the time we got there, the sun was peeking through the clouds and it looked as though it would be fine. The trainer had arrived and was setting up the equipment in the compound.

There was only one other dog – a little Cocker Spaniel that had been rescued from a puppy farm as a youngster but looked older because of her distended abdomen. She was scared of everything, except Mr Mac.

We started gently showing Mr Mac a jump, stepping over it and encouraging him to follow with the 'over' command. Mr Mac did very well and copied my exact move, stepping one leg over the bar at a time. We progressed the move until I could extend the lead for Mr Mac to go over and I was able to go round the outside. He was a superstar again, carefully stepping over the same way he saw me do it. If only all his training had been watch and repeat the action, I'd have collected all the obedience prizes.

Next was the seesaw. He was scared of it; but, with patience, we had him walking up it and halfway down before jumping off. He started the weave really well, but he has a long body so took it wide until the last one, where, like the cones, he refused to go round it.

Then it was back to the jumps, which were set a little bit higher this time because a Springer Spaniel had also joined the class. The Springer looked at Mr Mac, growled and lunged at him. I worried that all my good work re-training and socialising Mr Mac could be ruined, but Mr Mac stepped back to avoid contact. Well done, Mr Mac, you might think, but as we passed the dog to take our turn at the jumps, Mr Mac gave his low growl – the one that that vibrates up the lead. He puffed himself up and stared at Jerry the Springer. Yes, the owner thought it was an amusing name for his dog.

"I let you off that time … grrrr *… but before you start again …* grrr *… be sure …* grrr*… I won't back away next time …* grr*!"*

With that, he back-kicked some cut grass in the dog's face and trotted by. Now, you might be wondering what I was doing while this exchange took place. Well, I was pulling his lead and trying to distract him so Mr Mac's behaviour didn't become an issue.

The poles were once more increased in height; the Cocker Spaniel could just about clear them. The Springer jumped over and Mr Mac sauntered up and stepped over the bar without changing pace; so, especially for Mr Mac, the pole height went up again and this gave him a bit more of an opportunity to think about what he was doing. He ambled up to the first jump, where the pole was just about level with his chin, he stopped, looked at the pole left and right, looked over it left and right, looked under it left and right, and then, with the smallest amount of effort needed, jumped over. Nobody could believe the expression on his face as he looked back and forth along, over and under the pole.

The following week, we were going to try this exercise off-lead. I hoped, by then, he might have forgotten the warning he gave the Springer and that the Springer would not have forgotten that same warning. It was becoming clear that Mr Mac was a smart dog and he did think about things. Maybe too much at times, though. He could also be lazy; if there was a short cut, he would take it. He only applied enough effort to complete the task. His attitude is: why clear a jump by a foot when an inch is enough.

Mr Mac: *"That was fun. When are we going back?"*

22 May 2006

Every week I learned a little more about Mr Mac as his character slowly unfurled. This weekend he decided it was time to show me he could be the alpha male, if I would just stand aside and let him get on with it.

I had him on the grooming table in the garage with the big door open to let the extra light in. The door into the house was also open so I could hear what was going on inside. I was chatting away to him, telling him how good he was about getting the tugs pulled in his legs, when he started to growl low and menacingly. No snapping – just growling. I stopped, walked round to the front of him and looked him in the eye. "What's the matter with you?" I asked. Continuing to growl, he ignored me and looked over my shoulder.

I turned and walked towards the garage door. Just as I did, I heard the doorbell and realised that he had heard someone coming down the drive. Normally, he never bothers unless it is my friend Amy, because he knows we all go for a walk. Instead of going into the house to answer the door, I walked out through the garage door and surprised a man who was already walking towards the open garage door because no-one had answered the house door. He was even more surprised to get an eye-level view of an Airedale's large white teeth and an earful of Airedale growls and barks.

Mr Mac was restrained by the grooming table lead, but it was not tight and he could have slipped it as easily as he does his collar had he wanted; but, once again, he showed his skill in only using enough force to meet a situation. The man was looking for odd jobs and hand stripping an Airedale was not one of them. I doubt he'll return.

23 May 2006

On Sunday morning, Amy arrived at 8.00am and we headed straight out. She took Annie, while Mr Mac was with me. Once on the footpaths by the grain store, I lengthened his lead. Sometimes I let him off, but not every time or he began to expect it and became disobedient, deaf, or both. So there I was, being dragged along by Mr Mac with his nose to the ground, trying to read all the small print. I was half chatting, half watching where we were walking when I noticed what appeared to be a dead rat on the path about ten feet ahead. I started to shorten Mr Mac's lead, but he tried his level best to get over to the rat to investigate. I didn't want him touching it because we were near a grain store and they set poison traps to get rid of vermin. I certainly didn't want Mr Mac getting a mouthful of Warfarin-supplemented rat blood.

We eventually got past the rigid body with only one or two backward glances from Mr Mac. At this point, the concrete path stopped and was replaced by a dirt track with longer grass in the middle where the odd car or tractor hadn't killed it. I could now put Mr Mac back on his long lead so he trotted along about four feet away.

Amy started to say something but didn't finish because Mr Mac, without warning, leapt from the grass verge on my right, landing in one bound on the grass in front of me. His face was deep in the long grass and, when he lifted his head, he had a big rat in his mouth. Had Amy finished what she was about to say, she would have warned me that there was a rat in the grass just where I was about to step. The rat was alive and flicking its tail.

Picture the scene: big dog, big rat, little townie-bred blonde.

"Eeeek! Eeek! Drop it!" I squealed, while jumping up and down.

Mr Mac spat the rat out and it sort of bounced or maybe jumped towards the longer grass on the verge. Mr Mac was straining to get to the rat again, but I was straining with equal might to pull him in the opposite direction. For some reason, I didn't think the usual distraction of a fluffy toy or a biscuit would have been a suitable substitute for his prize. He was on the verge of winning the battle. I had started to slide on the gravel, but Amy grabbed my arm and his lead and we pulled him away. *"Great,"* he thought, *"we are going back to get the one I saw earlier"*; so he turned towards us and the lead slackened.

While we took a breath, Annie decided it was her turn. *"I want to play with the rat. I've never seen one before."* Fortunately, a short tug on her lead and she responded, returning to her place by Amy's side.

We ended up going the long way round along the edge of the fields to avoid any more wildlife – or wild-dead – encounters. When I got home, I washed Mr Mac's face and teeth and gave him his flea treatment, just to be on the safe side. I had watched a film about the black plague the previous night, so that didn't really help me feel assured when thinking about the local vermin my dogs had encountered.

His next few walks were punctuated with several head dives into the long grass. I hoped it was just on the off-chance of finding something rather than a misjudged catch. There were two inert bodies on that road; he knew it and looked for them, as we walked along that route. I do not think they held quite the same interest for him now that they did not give him the opportunity to show what a skilled hunter he was.

Jackie: "Gruesome!"
Annie: *"Get one for me now."*
Mr Mac: *"You, you dirty rat."*

12 June 2006

Monday was a lovely sunny day and I knew the agility class would take place outside. We arrived in good time to help set up the equipment jumps, weave, seesaw and tunnel. The only other dog there was a very bouncy Bearded Collie that loved hopping over the jumps and anything else that was there to be jumped on, over, under or through. Len had come along to watch and was very surprised at the progress I had made with Mr Mac.

Mr Mac was bounding over the jumps, through the weave and on to the seesaw, with the confidence of an agility veteran. The tunnel was now an issue for him and he wouldn't go through it. I tried to send him, but he stood his ground or ran round the outside. When the trainer held him at one end and I called him from the other end, he rushed through to get to me. Then we tried him off-lead again and he was good and did most of what was asked. It was almost as if he was showing everyone that he was as good as the Bearded Collie … well, almost.

At his obedience class on Wednesday, Len, again, came along to see his progress and, again, Mr Mac was so good no-one could fault him. I have to say lumps of cheese did help to keep his attention levels up. Eventually, he was working only for a chance to lick my now empty cheese-smelly hand. Yuk!!

I have noticed that when Mr Mac was good in class, he was ignorant in the garden and on walks, although he was treated the same at all times. I was nursing a very sore shoulder because Len was talking to a neighbour and I'd told Mr Mac to sit by my side. He'd done as instructed, but Len can talk for England, so Mr Mac got bored and stood up to look around. Just as he stood up, he saw a cat a second before I did and lunged forward.

"Mr Mac!" I yelled in surprise.

The cat, hearing this, changed direction and was

now running towards me. Mr Mac veered after it and, unfortunately, my legs were in the way. Just picture the Bugs Bunny scene: I had been turning to face the direction of the dog's line of vision when the cat changed direction and the dog crossed behind my legs and around to follow it. I quickly realised that the lead would wipe my legs out from under me, sending me crashing to the ground like a felled tree; so, to avoid this, I pirouetted on the spot very elegantly and hoped to rein the dog in when facing the direction of his travel. It was a painful way to learn that the lead does not stretch, but my arm and shoulder did. The scene was exacerbated by the audience laughing at the sight of me spinning like a top, but, luckily, stopping just in time so I didn't end up face down in the gutter.

You would think, from this experience, I would have learned not to trust a sleeping dog. Not me.

11 June 2006

On Sunday, after a long hot walk, I was sitting in the people-carrier facing out towards Len. Mr Mac was on his lead, lying on the ground at my feet. Len never spotted the off-lead Spaniel sneak round the back of the car, but Mr Mac did. He jumped up and bounded towards the dog in a friendly manner. Unfortunately, I'd been holding the lead in my right hand again and still had a sore shoulder. I left my seat in an almost horizontal line. How I landed on my feet must have been divine intervention. This was the final stretch; my arm could not take any more. I needed to stop him pulling.

The next stop was the Halti shop. Mr Mac was given a

nice black Halti. The label said, 'Control the head, control the dog' – that sounded pain-free for both of us. He hated it and spent half his walk trying to get it off. Because he was distracted he was not pulling, so my arm was returning to its original length.

15 June 2006

Mr Mac had his fourth agility lesson. He managed to complete three jumps off-lead, and negotiate the weave with some collar assistance. He still needed guidance with this one, as he had a tendency to take to a wide angle. However, he managed the seesaw without help. I sent him through the chute while the trainer held it open, through the tyre, over a jump, through the tunnel, and over another jump; but with two jumps to go he decided to run over to the fence to pee, which everyone found amusing and laughed.

Unfortunately, every time we did the course after that he would do well until about two jumps from the end. At that point, he would run over to the fence to mark his presence, pause for the laughter, and then complete the course

My biggest problem was maintaining his concentration. As soon as he thought he'd done what was required and he decided it wasn't required again, he clowned about. He'd run up to the jumps, stop and put his front feet on them, pause and then jump over. I tried not giving him the treat until he completed the circuit, but he was not food- or toy-orientated, so he could not be bribed. I also found that tiny treats were no good: because his mouth was big, he dropped them trying to take them gently. I decided to try bigger bits of sausage at his obedience class on Wednesday and hoped that might help things along nicely.

I didn't have time to cook sausage, so I cut cheese into bigger lumps. At 6.00pm, Mr Mac started running to the door and back to me. I thought he wanted out, so I opened the door and he ran to the car and waited for me to let him in.

"It's too early," I said, and called him back, but he was like a child on Christmas Eve. He was so excited; he knew he went to the class on a Monday and Wednesday. He never behaved like this on Tuesday.

I left early and gave him a fast walk along the small single track road near the training class. My idea was that the brisk walk would calm him down a bit and leave him with a completely empty bladder. I returned to the car park, where we waited and I chatted with other dog owners until the puppy class finished. The class started and for the first exercise we stood in a circle with all the dogs and owners facing the direction of travel. Well, all the dogs except Mr Mac, who would now sit when asked, but only if he was facing you. It was still a sit on command, so I wasn't complaining too much. He knew I had a lump of cheese in my hand, but I had been trying to make him do a lot more things before he got the treat. "You have to work first," I told him. He tilted his head to the side and back a few times, as if he was searching for the required response, and then he offered me his paw. I had to take it and give him his bit of cheese, because this was the first time he had offered his paw. We had been teaching him to give us a paw, not as a trick, but to assist us when putting his car harness on; so far, the training had been singularly unsuccessful.

For the rest of the class, every time he got the command 'sit', he offered me a paw. So he would learn that 'sit' did not always mean 'give me a paw', I renamed the command 'paw'.

When the other dogs were told 'down' or 'lie down', because Mr Mac had never mastered the 'down' command, I asked him to sit or give me a paw. I slowly progressed from holding his paw to trying to get him to the 'down' position. We managed it once, but I won't force the issue. I was sure that six months from now he would just do it and surprise everyone.

Mr Mac was so good I began to wonder if someone had swapped dogs while I was out. Maybe he had been trying to tell me all along those miniscule slivers of cheese or liver just didn't do it for him and he wanted the Big Mac with extra fries.

Annie: *"I like burger as well."*
Mr Mac: *"Super-size mine, please."*

27 June 2006

Len was to be interviewed for a documentary about care providers today and the camera crew turned up at noon. Mr Mac went out to greet them. *"Hi boys ... sniff your hand? ... oh well, if I must. I see you've brought all the gear. Let me check it over to make sure you haven't forgotten anything. Yep, it's in order, better follow me then. ... Out of my way – film star coming through!"*

The men were very nice and chatted to Len over coffee, explaining how the interview would go. All this time, Mr Mac was sitting beside the sound man and his big fluffy microphone. We moved from the kitchen to the lounge, where they would film Len, and Mr Mac bustled back and forth, inspecting everything. Once ready, we did a dummy run, where I had to ask questions off-camera so Len had someone to answer, rather than merely looking at the camera.

Mr Mac sat down beside Len, although normally, if I'm at home, he was always at my side. The men asked Len to move slightly because it was only going to be a headshot. As soon as he moved, Mr Mac stood up and put his feet on Len's knees, totally covering his face. I had to grab his collar and hold on to him till that bit of filming was done. They also wanted footage of Len's carer helping him open his mail, working at his computer, giving him his lunch and walking the dogs.

Eventually, I had to shut Mr Mac in the garage because he was so determined to be in the film. The last bit to be filmed was the 'taking the dogs for a walk' segment, and Len was filmed getting into his car with the carer. Then she came and got Annie and I took Mr Mac, who had leapt into his harness in record time. We clipped their harnesses or doggy seatbelts into place and then the cameraman jumped in to film Len driving down a country road. When we reached a little track, Len got out of the car. Because this manoeuvre can take a while, it was not filmed. The carer handed Annie's lead to Len so he could walk her. At last, it was Mr Mac's big moment. We were filmed walking towards the camera, Len with Annie on her lead at his left – he needed his right hand to control the chair – and Mr Mac on his lead on my left so he could walk beside Len's chair. There was none of the usual pulling or lunging into the long grass in search of wildlife; this was his moment of stardom and he was out to look his best.

Jackie: "I never wanted to be on camera, but Mr Mac insisted."

Annie: *"He's so pushy ... these Hollywood wannabe types."*

Mr Mac: *"I can search for wildlife any day. They wanted to see ME on TV, not my rear end."*

28 June 2006

We missed the class last week and, in our absence, two new dogs joined. One was a small, young German Shepherd and the other was an eight-month-old Ridgeback cross that was in your face − big and boisterous, but not mean. Mr Mac preferred a more refined doggy friend, preferably one he could boss about without reprisal. I arrived early at the class and took Mr Mac for a walk so he could pee on every blade of grass and, hopefully, be empty by the time the class started. In order to help set up the course, I had to put him back in the car. He was not happy about that and tried to pull me back towards the class *"It's too soon ... I haven't had my turn yet,"* he grumbled, and tried to avoid jumping into the vehicle. The poor boy looked most dejected when I left him in the car.

Once the course was set up, I collected Mr Mac from the car and joined the class. When it was his turn he had to sit off-lead at the start point; he was ready to go and couldn't wait to show off his skills to the new dogs. It was a complicated course with four jumps each at right angles to the other. We began, "Mr Mac! Over right, over right", etc. After that, it was straight into the weave, through the chute, two more jumps through the tunnel, over the seesaw, through the tyre and over a jump to finish. I was over the moon. He had an almost clear round with only the slightest bit of hesitation at the tyre. He'd only seen it once before. Nobody could believe how good he was. I should have recognised that look by now. It was the one that says, *"Now you've seen how good I can be, watch this space."*

All the other dogs took their turns, with the new ones taking longer as they were coached round the circuit. Then it was Mr Mac's turn again. I was expecting great things from him. I should have known better. I got him to sit at the start point. "Over!" I shouted. Nothing. "Over!" I said in a higher-pitched voice. He thought about it, then tried to impersonate a parrot by attempting to perch on each of the jump bars. The rest of the circuit was passable but, on his third attempt, he was still very much on the downward slope. He refused the weave and on the chute he chose to search and find a dead vole that all the other dogs had missed.

His last chance to redeem himself was on the jumps, which had been put higher to make him think about them a little more. "Right, Mr Mac. No sausage unless you work for it. OK! … Sit. Are you ready?" I gave him his start command: "Over." He stood up and looked at the first jump, grudgingly dropping his front legs over and kicking the bar away with his back legs. On the next jump, he sauntered up, lifted one paw and pushed the bar so it fell to the ground. At this point, he decided to look up sweetly as if butter wouldn't melt in his mouth, while he stepped over it. On the third jump he used his other paw and did the same, and on the fourth he walked straight into the bar so it fell to the ground.

I caught his collar and made him walk through the weave, which he did unwillingly while trying to prise the sausage from my fingers. He refused the chute altogether. Even when the trainer took his collar to encourage him, he put both front paws on the edge and refused to budge. I used some sausage to coerce him into completing the tunnel, which he did, and then he completed the seesaw and tyre.

He got lots of praise, which I didn't think had any impact on him. He seemed to thrive more on making everyone laugh. The more they laughed, me included, the more ways he found to get round the obstacle course using different techniques. You just had to love him. He could look you in the eye and appear to be the epitome of an angel and then he did something completely outrageous.

Mr Mac: *"Well, you did tell me it was a fun class rather than a serious competition."*

3 July 2006 − Week eight agility

I thought Mr Mac needed the exercise and the practice, so I bought a set of weave poles. They were quite inexpensive, just plastic tubes with a pointy end to stick in the grass and a rounded end so you didn't poke your eye out. I also managed to pick up two jumps made from the same stuff. I set them up in the garden and every time Mr Mac was in the garden I made him leap over the jumps and go through the weave at least once.

I showed Len Mr Mac's new skills and, of course, Len wanted to try it. Obviously, he did not take his chair over the jumps. He stopped by the first jump and made Mr Mac sit. Mr Mac had to face the handler when he sat down if he was to get his treat, so he was sitting side on to the jump, looking at Len. "Over, Mr Mac," Len instructed, and tried to wave the treat on the side of the jump he wanted Mr Mac to move to. Mr Mac, without hesitation, stood up and, like a spring lamb, bounced sideways over the jump set about 18 inches high.

Len moved on to the next jump and Mr Mac followed, again jumping sideways over the jump. He got his treat and Len was very happy that he'd done it for him, because Mr Mac didn't always jump over for me … and I only asked him to jump forward. Maybe my way was too boring for him.

Anyway, off we went to class. It was very hot and he'd already seen the treat pouch, so he knew it was time for school. He had a fair idea that last night's barbeque leftovers were going to be his treats: hamburger and sausages, yummy. He loved fast food.

He was first round the course, which was now quite complex. First was the chute, and he'd gone off that and refused to go in. When he eventually did go in, he came charging out the other side and bowled me over. After picking myself up and keeping him close, I got him over the next two jumps. It was far from the elegant manoeuvre I knew he was capable of, but he'd done what was asked of him.

When it came to the tyre, he dropped his front legs through the tyre and seemed to hesitate before completing the move. I stood in front of him with a piece of hamburger in my hand, shouting in a high-pitched, squeaky, fun voice, "C'mon, Mr Mac … what's this? … c'mon, son." The trainer was about to shove him through when we both realized that he was peeing on the tyre.

So I had a bit of a dilemma on my hands. I couldn't praise him for going through the tyre in case he thought I wanted him to pee on it every time and I couldn't chastise him for peeing or he wouldn't go near the tyre again. The only solution was to ignore him.

"Weave, Mr Mac, weeeeve." He did a very good weave, leapt over two jumps at right angles, traversed the seesaw and finished with some hurdles. He did very well, all things considered.

Next up was a little Lakeland-Jack Russell cross who'd been getting on very well with Mr Mac. We think he had become her role model. She refused the chute, and jumped on the cross bars of each of the jumps and then posed for a moment like a cat on a fence before jumping off. She ran into the tunnel and wouldn't come out and then ran through the tunnel several times just for fun. It would appear that Mr Mac had taught her everything he knew about agility. Just when I decided he could not surprise the class or me any more, he always thought up a new trick to make everyone laugh.

12 July 2006 – Belfast to England

The Airedale breeder phoned to tell us that she'd had to leave our new pup, Mahri, at the airport at 4.00pm; this was two hours before the flight would even leave. She wasn't happy about it, but these were the rules, apparently. We expected the plane to land at 7.00pm and we were told that the pup would be available at 7.30pm – perfect timing, so we could go for a meal before we collected the pup. We arrived at the cargo part of the airport at 7.35pm to find no pup!

"Oh," the man said, "it will take forty-five to sixty minutes to get her across from the airport." "Well … OK; we'll go to the airport [half a mile away] and collect her," we'd suggested.

"No, you can't do that. She's cargo. We'll have to book her in here," was the reply. So we waited, and every fifteen minutes I checked to see if she'd arrived. Eventually, at 8.15pm, we finally managed to find out that she was in the warehouse, but we still couldn't collect her because they had to do the paperwork. Why they couldn't have had the paperwork prepared I've no idea.

Finally, I took the now completed papers to door number three and asked for my pup. Following yet another wait, a man appeared with a large carry kennel. "Sign here," he said. I looked at the paperwork to see what I was signing. Next to the line where I was meant to sign, I was also supposed to tick a box to confirm my *goods* were 'received in good clean order'. Having looked in the crate as he approached, I already knew the pup had been sick, and pooped … and rolled and slept in it. Yuk! Looking at the box, I said to the man, "Do I answer 'no' to the 'clean and in good order' question?" He laughed and I signed, 'No − sick and smelly'.

It was 8.30pm now and this little dog was hyper with a capital 'H', not to mention smelly with a capital 'S'. We had a drive of several hours ahead of us. Luckily, I came prepared with rubber gloves, water, baby wipes, poly bags, newspaper, towels, and an old sweatshirt.

I opened the crate and out waddled a huge, furry ball of what can only be described as 'poo'. Love at first sight? It was most certainly not. I wiped her down, tied her to the tow bar on the car and cleaned the crate, adding some fresh newspaper. We put her back inside and gave her a drink, which she promptly tipped over on the dry newspaper. Figuring that our troubles were done and that we could look forward to driving home on some quiet roads, we put the crate in the car and set off.

As soon as the car moved, she started to scream – a high-pitched, ear-piercing, howling and yowling. She was safe and warm, and fairly dry. There was nothing else left to do but turn the radio up and try to ignore her. After thirty minutes, she actually went quiet, leaving me to wonder whether she was okay. I was terrified to even look in case she started again. I bit the bullet and I glanced round and saw the cutest thing I'd ever seen – well, at least for the next ten minutes. She was curled up in the corner, fast asleep, with her head in the empty water dish. For the duration of the journey, we peaked and troughed, with no middle ground in between, from total tranquillity to maximum noise and pandemonium. She awoke at intervals, screaming and howling for attention, then went back to sleep. Little did she realise that, in a short while, she was going to get much more attention than she'd ever bargained for.

On arrival at the house, I unloaded the crate and waited for Len to get out of the car. The plan was that he would distract Annie and Mr Mac while I quickly changed into my old clothes and got Mahri into the bath. Of course, it didn't go to plan. As soon as I opened the door, two Airedales came flying out, paying absolutely no attention to us. *"What's in the box? Let me see! Open it! I want to see inside now."* Annie backed away at this point when she remembered that Len was waiting to say hello. Mr Mac bounced up to the crate door. *"Ggrrrrr yap yap grrrr,"* said the crate. Mr Mac stopped suddenly, up on his toes with his ears flat to his head – "*something new ... whoa! – a growling box ...*" He backed up quickly. Deciding his safer bet was with Len, Mr Mac ran to his side. This was a big thing for Mr Mac, because he was not very keen on men and was still unsure of Len's wheelchair.

I quickly removed Mahri, aka 'the poo ball', and rushed through to the bathroom. Worried that she might be frightened by the shower, I was very careful with her, but nothing seemed to faze her. While I bathed her, Mr Mac came in for a sniff. At this point, Mahri thought it would be a good idea to climb out and play. I had quite a struggle to keep her in the tub while I rinsed her. The wet little pup was trying to shimmy up my arm like a boy up a coconut tree. I wrapped her in a big towel and sat her on Len's knee while I emptied the car and cleaned up.

Jealousy struck. Annie decided at this point that she was Len's baby and this pup needed to be made aware of her station in life. She walked right up to her and growled in her face, *"Grrrrr!"* In response, the cute little fluff-ball turned into a Tasmanian devil – growling, snarling and spitting. Len was struggling to hold on to her and she nearly bit his nose in the process. We were completely surprised, to say the least, but not as much as Annie. Our plan to get a pup and give Annie a new lease of life hadn't had the best start. So far, it had been more unsuccessful than it had been successful.

We put Mahri on the floor to let her meet her new brother and sister. Annie squeezed behind Len's chair and refused to come out. While Mr Mac sniffed and sat down next to me, Mahri ran an absolute riot. She was into everything. She was charging round the kitchen on her stumpy little legs, trying to reach the worktops to see if there was anything good to eat. When full-grown, Airedales do this: it's called counter-surfing. She was trying to counter-surf by climbing up the towels, which she eventually dragged to the floor. Next, she pulled the books from a book shelf; then, she yanked the wire for the answer machine, bringing it crashing to the floor, which scared poor Mr Mac, but not her. I sat on the floor to play with her and introduce her to some toys. *"Toys?"* She turned her nose up − *"I want to bite and chew. I'll start on your leg, then your arm, and then, hey, I can climb up and get your shoulder and nose."*

By now the scrambled egg I'd prepared for her supper had cooled and she soon tucked in, emptying the plate in seconds. Fed and watered, it was time to sleep; I had at least an hour before Mahri would be up and ready to create havoc in the normally quiet household.

14 July 2012

Friday morning, 5.30am, and she was still yowling! I was seriously beginning to question whether my will was stronger than hers. I gave in and got up. I put her lead on and took her out. She bounced about, trying to pull up the grass and bite the leaves off the plants. If it moved, it had to be chased; if it was still, it went in her mouth. I managed to stop her picking up a large snail − it was bad enough fishing stones out of her mouth, without snails too. She bit my thumb so hard it felt as if I'd shut it in a car door!

Back in the house, she got her breakfast: scrambled egg, cheese, baby rusk and milk – gourmet dining for a puppy. After she'd eaten, I lifted her out of the pen so she could sit by me and let her dinner settle; but she wasn't having any of it. She bounced over to Annie, who rolled her lips up just a little bit and snarled. Mahri backed up a couple of paces, then started barking and growling right back at her. Annie furiously lunged at the pup, faster than I'd seen her move since MacIain died. Annie nipped Mahri in the ear before we had time to grab her and the pup yelped and ran to hide under the kitchen chair for a moment. Then she rushed out to nip Annie in the leg while I was holding Annie and giving her a telling off for bad manners. Annie knew she was bad and put on such a sad face, but it didn't change the fact that, every time the pup went near her, she growled at her. Annie's sullen temperament failed to improve and she eventually snapped at Mr Mac, who I'm happy to say ignored her.

Mr Mac was the one we were worried about; because he came to us as an adult dog, we were not sure how he would react to this bouncing puppy. Some dogs can find them aggravating with merely a passing glance. I hovered at his side when Mahri was running around the kitchen. He surprised us and was really good. He would lie on the floor and play 'bitey face' with Mahri. I nervously watched while Mahri would pretend Mr Mac was a lion and she was the tamer, sticking her head in his mouth, or hanging from his throat, collar, cheek, and beard. She followed him everywhere.

I had thought that Mr Mac would become Mahri's role model, but then again, we originally thought Annie would be. It turned out that we were wrong on both counts. Well, not quite. Marhi was lead-trained with a great deal of ease because she followed where Mr Mac wandered, so forgot she even had a lead on. She was almost house-trained, again with ease, because she would copy Mr Mac, although she never lifted her leg. In return, Mahri had taught Mr

Mac how to play. I took some toys that he had completely ignored and threw them on the kitchen floor for Mahri, but Mr Mac picked them all up and put them back in the sitting room. Mahri was still on restricted access, so could not follow him into the room to retrieve any of the toys. I opened up a bag with a new ball, dumbbell, soft toy and rope pull. To maintain the *status quo*, I gave him the soft toy and Mahri the rope pull, with the others laid on the floor. Mahri ran up and down the kitchen with the rope pull and then dropped it at Mr Mac's feet; he then picked it up, trotted up and down and finally dropped it at Mahri's feet. This game provided light entertainment for some time before progressing into a comical but most unfair game of tug. Mr Mac stood still and Mahri tried with every ounce of strength she had to pull him around.

After a while, Mahri gave a little whine and ran to the back door and jumped up, trying to reach the handle. That was her signal for me. I put her lead on and took her out. Yep, she wanted out, and, at this rate, she looked like she was going to be smart enough to open the door and let herself out. She certainly wouldn't be the first dog I owned that forced me to reverse all the door handles. Our first Airedale, Carrie, used to open all the doors too.

All this activity and it wasn't even 9.00am. Just thinking about getting through the whole day made me sigh. My friend, Amy, arrived and we took Annie and Mr Mac for their long walk. It was a lovely day and we enjoyed the peace and tranquillity. Puppies are sweet, but it's nice to get a rest. When we got back, Mahri was fast asleep. Not that I did, but the thought of squealing in her ear, "I'm still awake! Play with me!" crossed my mind. For my own sanity, I let her sleep.

After her lunch it was time for more walks; Len had Mahri on the lead. She wasn't a bit bothered by his wheelchair as he walked her round the garden. Mr Mac now had the freedom of the back garden and he'd run full pelt to the bottom tree line, wait a second or two and then sprint back, bowling Mahri right off her feet. He loved to play-bow and tuck-butt run, his tail going round in circles like a propeller. The tuck-butt run's a very typical running style of the Airedale, with the hind legs passing the front legs in a sprint. He'd come charging up, screech to a halt, rip up some grass, throw it in the air and roll over on his back, before leaping up again. He was so happy he had a playmate to whom he could show off. He'd never behaved like this since we got him. His new-found playful streak meant we had to watch him in case over-enthusiasm led to him being a little too rough. Marhi was a bit young to cope with him but, in a few months' time, we knew she'd be giving him a run for his money. With all the walks and games, little Mahri was puffed out by teatime and slept till 11.30pm. Then she was wide awake just in time to yowl all night and keep me awake.

15 July 2006

On Saturday morning at 5.30am I went into the kitchen once I could no longer pretend I wasn't hearing Mahri yowling. There she was in the middle of the floor! How she got out of the three-foot high pen, I had no idea. When she stood on her hind legs, her front paws and chin could only just rest on the top. After playing detective, I found out how the little minx escaped − she literally walked up the side of the pen like a tiny mountain climber, one foot in each square, till she could drop over the top.

The rest of the week was much the same. She was getting bolder with Mr Mac as each day passed. He told her off one day because she jumped up and bit his nose! OUCH!! I know how that feels. Annie was almost able to tolerate her presence in the same room, provided they were at opposite ends. Mahri sometimes tried to get Annie into trouble by running up to her and barking and growling, staying just out of Annie's reach, unless she stood up. Mahri had learned that Annie couldn't get up very fast.

Mahri had also worked out that if she couldn't get the toy you were holding, then the next best thing to do was to go for your arm or hand. You would soon drop whatever it was you held when she sank her razor-sharp teeth into it. I growled at her, yowled at her, and shouted at her. Her response? She'd come right back, barking and growling at me. If Mahri thought she was going to grow up to be a wild child, she was wrong. She was going to have to learn some manners … and fast.

The Airedales had to add their comments:

Annie: *"Grrrrr ... get lost brat!"*
Mr Mac: *"She bit me!"*

26th July 2006

Now we are four, or to be accurate three and a half. We made the one-hour drive to the kennels last night to pick up an eight-week-old Welsh Terrier, Elle. We saw the litter at five weeks old and picked the one we thought we wanted, but the breeder said we'd best not make up our mind till eight weeks. In twenty-four years and six Airedales, we have never picked a pup. With the first Airedale, the breeder kept one of two bitches and we got the other one. With the next three, they were picked and shipped over to us. Mr Mac, on the other hand, was more of a rescue dog than a pup. And Mahri! Well, our first sight of her was as a 'poo' ball at Birmingham airport.

When we got to the breeder's house, he'd bathed the two girls and they were in a pen waiting. One seemed the tiniest bit browner, rather than beige, and had a finer face; the other had a wider face or shorter nose and was a bit less interested in her surroundings. I said I liked the darker one and the breeder handed Len the other one. She went to sleep in his arms. We swapped after that and it was my turn to hold the sleeping one. The darker pup sniffed Len, chewed his fingers, sat in his arms and watched everything going on round about her. I could see that Len's mind was made up: she would be Elle. This was the same one we'd chosen three weeks earlier, so there must have been something special about her. The breeder told us that, if he'd been asked to choose one for himself, he would have chosen the same one as us, but for different reasons – short back, good tail set, nice face, etc – but, as we had no plans to show her, our criteria were based on healthy, happy and friendly.

I got to hold her while Len drove home. We had Mahri's travel kennel with us, but Elle was about the size of a two-pound bag of sugar, so we were concerned that it might have felt like being in a huge black hole for her. She sat up, looking around for a while, and then drifted off to sleep, and that was her till we got home.

It was very hot, so we'd left Annie and Mr Mac in the day kennel. Mahri was in a big crate in the house since she couldn't be trusted to stay in the pen. I gave Len the pup and took Mahri out for a walk, but she knew there was something new in the house and wanted back in.

Mahri didn't like the pup. I was convinced that two little pups would get on, but she barked and growled, *"Bark, barge, bark, grrrr! I'll huff and I'll gruff and I'll push the pen down! You'll see!"*

The pup whimpered a bit, but we knew she was safe. I was hovering ready to grab Mahri or the pen when, from literally nowhere, this tiny wee scrap of a pup started to bark back, and growl and show lots of little teeth. Mahri was shocked and ran for cover behind Len's chair and sneaked along the side, barking back. It became a competition to see who could bark at the other the loudest. I lifted the pup out on to the floor, thinking they'd get on all right now. Nope! Mahri chased Elle and tried to nip her again. The pup sat by my feet and fended off Mahri. I hoped they'd be getting along a bit better in a few weeks; although best of friends might have been slightly optimistic at this point.

I let Annie and Mr Mac, the two 'big pups', into the kitchen. Mr Mac had to have a drink first and proceeded to soak the poor wee mite with his dripping chin. Annie was much more non-committal. Similarly to the way he played with Mahri, Mr Mac set about trying to play with this little pup, but she was still a bit young and would not be ready for this little, or should I say big, treat.

Elle would get on great with him, I could just tell, and Annie wasn't growling at her, so that was a big plus. Our original plan was to let both pups sleep in the pen, but then we thought we'd let Mahri sleep in her crate in the pen with the pup. Common sense certainly nudged us in the right direction and we decided that would be a bad idea, as she would be liable to try and dig her way out. Eventually, we decided to let the pup sleep in the travel crate next to Len's bed and put Mahri in her crate in the utility room.

Fortunately, they were all completely puffed out with all the excitement and went straight to sleep, so no yowling. At 12.30am, it had been one long day and I was already thinking about getting up in five hours to do it all again ... well, not collect a third pup. I may be mad, or even a few sandwiches short of a picnic, but I wasn't quite insane yet. At least I thought not, but I was too tired to work it out anyway. Must sleep now, was the last thought that entered my head on that particular day ... zzzzzzzzzz.

Annie: *"First I was alone and now there are 3 of them ... I'd have her committed."*
Mr Mac: *"More playmates, yeah!!!"*
Mahri: *"They're all mine; toys, beds, food, humans – ALL MINE! DO YOU HEAR!?!"*
Elle: *"I'm very small; can we share a little bit?"*

28 July 2006

Mr Mac and I went to the agility class last night. I was running a bit late because I'd spent too much time playing with the pups. On arrival, I took Mr Mac up the road for a quick walk so he could pee on as many weeds as possible before the class started. When we returned, a new dog had arrived: an adult male Border Collie. This dog was one day out of rescue and should have gone to obedience classes

Let me come too

first. It immediately clashed with the young Ridgeback
Cross with a great snarling and growling. Mr Mac, who
was at a safe distance with me, growled and stamped his
front feet and tossed his head from side to side.

"Silence in class, you unruly mob!" he seemed to say,
"Do I have to come over there and sort the two of you out?"
Fortunately, the trainer rushed over, separated the dogs and
admonished the owners for their inattention.

Mr Mac was ready to go round the course, which was
just a simple one to get their muscles warmed up and their
brains in gear. The heat over the last ten days had turned the
grass golden and crunchy and the weeds were a foot high
and jaggy. We started well; Mr Mac cleared the first two
jumps, then on to the next obstacle, which was the seesaw.
He started over it nice and steady, then he paused on the
yellow touch band and then refused to move; in front of

him was a large clump of jaggy weeds. He backed up on his tip-toes – it had to be seen to be believed – to the middle and balanced somewhat precariously while he formulated his plan of escape. The next part of the course was the chute, and he was not its biggest fan. You could see the wheels turning in his head as he tried to decide between the weeds or the chute. He was not one to be rushed, though, and wouldn't be coaxed or pulled off the seesaw before he'd made his mind up. As soon as he was ready, in one bound he jumped from the pivot of the seesaw to the chute, where he sprinted through and finished the last two jumps.

While we waited for our next turn, I chatted to a little frail old lady sitting on a deckchair. She often came with her daughter and two Lakeland/Jack Russell crosses. Her two dogs got on very well with Mr Mac, even though one was an entire or un-neutered male. Over to my right, the two owners who were supposed to be keeping their dogs apart had another lapse in concentration and, with a great thump and gnashing of teeth, the two dogs clashed again. Mr Mac, who was on my right side on his lead, let out a low rumbling growl, crossed in front of me and over to my left and stood in front of the old lady and the little bitch she was holding while her daughter took the dog over the course. Roo, the bitch, had taken cover and was hiding under her chair. You could tell by Mr Mac's stance that he was the rearguard. If the dogs got by me, he was protecting the lady and her dog … or, on second thoughts, was he just hiding behind me? *Hmmmm*.

A second course had been set up for the people and their dogs who were waiting for their next turn on the main course. This course was not supervised by the trainers, so the dogs had to be kept on their leads. There was a short weave, the tyre and a little jump. Mr Mac saw this as his personal circus ring and assigned himself the job of entertaining the others in line. Unfortunately, I was the stooge to his clown act.

"Weave, Mr Mac!" He went through the first three or four posts really well until he encountered another jaggy weed. He froze and glared at me. You could see him thinking, *"Oh no, I don't think so ... I haven't forgotten the last set of weeds."*

He eventually jumped over the weed and had to be bribed with extra sausage to continue over the jump and on to the next obstacle. "Tyre, Mr Mac. Tyre!" He stepped through one leg at a time and then looked at me as if he'd done so well. After he rested, I tried the reverse of the course. "Tyre, Mr Mac!"

I hadn't noticed the big jaggy weed in front of the tyre and neither had he until now. He stared at it, knowing if he jumped through the tyre he would land on it. Eventually, he stepped through, managing to avoid the weed, and then it was on to the jump and through the weave.

It wasn't a bad attempt, except that he now knew he had the full attention of the audience. I had to push him through the weave in one direction, grab his head and pull him back to me. It was like pushing a donkey up a hill. At one point his body was between three poles. If he could have done this quickly it would have looked so good. Then there was the jump. Any dog can just jump, but Mr Mac thought it would be cool to lie down and roll under the bar, then jump back over it sideways. Because that earned him a round of applause, he thought it might be clever to try jumping through the tyre sideways, almost forgetting about *that* weed for a moment.

Mahri at 9 weeks

He turned and nodded to the onlookers. I could swear he winked at them; and then he trotted off towards the little old lady and sat down beside her. I followed him, holding on to the other end of the lead, feeling like a magician's assistant. I was really only there to stop him tripping over the lead and looking silly.

Mr Mac: *"That's all for now, folks!"*

30 July 2006

We eventually settled into a nice routine at home and the pups had stopped yowling for attention. Why yowl for my attention when they could have a yapping competition?

Mahri would try to out-yap Elle, whose descant yapping was unabating. Nobody told me that Welsh Terriers came without a volume control.

Both pups had doubled in size and confidence. I could almost walk round the back garden with them both on the lead. Mahri, apart from the odd accident, which was usually due to my lack of attention, was clean in the house. Elle was starting to understand she had to go outside. We still had a bit of work to do with her yet, but then she was only nine weeks old. We would let Mr Mac and Mahri have a rough and tumble together and, when she was a bit puffed out, we'd shut him out of the room so Mahri and Elle could play. I was the nominated referee for when playtime turned into a wrestling match. If Mahri was lying down and the pair were playing 'bitey face', Elle would climb on Mahri's back and try to chew her neck. For the most part, Mahri ignored this; a flea could probably bite harder. Eventually, Mahri would get fed up and slap Elle with a giant paw, sending her sliding across the floor. Sure enough, Elle would be back again, leaping through the air like a flying squirrel to land on Mahri before they began rolling around as one collective fluff-ball. I'd hover to make sure neither hurt the other. As soon as Elle started to squeal, I'd grab Mahri by her collar and pull her away. One day, Elle was still squealing, and, when I looked, her back foot was in her own mouth. She obviously thought she was biting Mahri.

At one point, I gave them a fluffy three-legged octopus toy to play with. Mahri was running round with one of the toy's legs in her mouth and underneath her tummy was Elle with another of the toy's legs in her mouth. From where I was sitting on the floor, it looked like an eight-legged dog running around, since she fitted perfectly in the space, just like a Russian doll set.

Elle used to run as fast as she could, up and down the kitchen, with her little legs going ninety to the dozen. Mahri would take two bounds and catch her by the tail and drag her about. It was like a scene from a Tom and Jerry cartoon. We laughed, but we were very careful to make sure Elle didn't get hurt. One day, thinking Elle would be exhausted with all her running around, I'd put her back in her pen; but she wasn't ready to give up playing. The two puppies played 'bitey face' (or feet or anything else that they could reach) through the wire. When I told Mahri to give Elle a rest, she continued with her attempt to remove Elle from the wire pen by using her ear as a handle. Eventually, they gave in and went to sleep.

I had been working on 'sit', 'down' and 'stay' with Mahri and having some success; plus, of course, the universal command 'No'. This means 'don't', 'stop', 'cease', 'desist', in any language except in Airedale. 'No, don't bite!' meant losing a lump of skin from my hand. 'No, don't jump!' meant another slicing gash to my finger right next to my nail – OUCH!! 'No, don't pull!' meant sink your teeth into the nearest ankle she could find. Mine! Ouch, ouch, ouch, or words to that effect. 'No' also didn't apply to eating grass, leaves, earth, gravel, tissues and plastic. The list was endless. Unless it was food – good, high-quality nutritious food in her dish – then 'yes' suddenly meant 'no'. Sigh!!

And to top it all, Mr Mac, who was supposed to be an adult in dog years, had forgotten all his training and reverted to puppy games. He gave me such an enthusiastic welcome this week – much like Fred Flintstone and Dino.

His flying welcome home leap had drop-kicked me in the chest and as I bent forward, winded by the impact, my arm brought his head to an abrupt stop. Damage to dog: none … zilch … but I would soon be sporting a huge bruise on my arm. I was in so much pain I was sure it was broken. There are such a lot of good things to be said for owning a more senior Airedale like our Annie, the grand old duchess. I really should listen to my own advice! I looked forward to getting back to work for a rest.

The dogs shared their thoughts with me:

Annie: *"Take me with you, please."*
Mr Mac: *"Is it time for school yet?"*
Mahri: *"I'll huff and puff and push the pen down."*
Elle: *"I'll squeal and you'll get a row."*

2 August 2006

The master plan was to have two little pups that would play together, snuggle up at night and keep each other company; but, as that great Scottish bard, Rabbie Burns, wrote: "The best laid plans o' mice and men aft gang astray".

Mahri, at ten weeks, was a hulking great lump, weighing in at 16 pounds. Elle, at eight weeks, was a diminutive two pounds, and only six inches high and six inches long. They tolerated each other, but only till Mahri pounced on one of Elle's appendages and tried to drag her or get her to play chase. At that point, Elle would turn into a miniature Jaws; her lips curled up, exposing the tiniest of teeth, snapping and snarling. Mahri always retreated to her bed and left Elle to calm down.

I woke early the next morning before any of the dogs, so it was with devilish mirth that I entered the kitchen to rouse the pups by talking loudly and taking them out to watch the sun rise. Because they were still half asleep, I managed to get a couple of photos of each of them beside my new garden swing, a most convenient hitching post. They were certainly awake by the time we returned to the house. Mahri was permitted the run of the kitchen while I prepared their breakfast. Elle was confined to her pen for my safety as well as hers because she had developed a bad habit of nipping at ankles and tripping one up.

Mahri had initiated a full-scale wrestling match with Mr Mac, and Elle, green with envy, was squealing because she wanted to be out to play as well. She tried to climb up the side of the pen, just like Mahri did. I dangled my arm in the pen to distract her and it did for a moment. She stopped squealing, but then she started once again. I was still petting her, so was at a loss for what could be wrong. Then I noticed Mahri had sneaked up and was biting Elle's foot, the one that was protruding through one of the pen's wire squares. I chased Mahri away, but she showed no remorse whatsoever.

By this time, breakfast was a welcome distraction. I gave Elle hers in the pen, and Mahri hers just beside the pen, so the pups could eat together – an improvement on trying to eat each other. Annie and Mr Mac got fed in the garage, where their bowls were elevated to prevent things like gastric bloat. It was also easier for Annie to eat if she didn't have to bend down. For some reason, Annie decided to be awkward and would not go into the garage. Then Mr Mac joined in and hung back with Annie. Mahri thought it would be much better in the garage and made a bid for freedom under both dogs' legs. She was free all right! First, she grabbed the hand brush and dustpan and made off with them. In her haste, she knocked over the long-handled broom, which clattered to the floor. Poor Mr Mac nearly had a heart attack; for some odd reason, poly bags and brooms scare him. Annie had gone back to her bed. Mahri didn't even blink when the broom landed beside her. As quick as a flash, she'd grabbed the broom handle and tried to run off with it, fighting me for possession. The cheeky thing nearly won as well! Eventually, I got Annie and Mr Mac into the garage to eat their breakfast, but then I had the same carry-on to get them back out of the garage. I spent another ten minutes chasing Mahri round, emptying her mouth of anything she could grab as she ran up and down. I was convinced that one day I would be prising the car from her jaws.

Food all finished and cleared away, I took Mahri out for a walk, leaving Mr Mac and Annie in the sitting room for a bit of peace and quiet. When I got back, Elle had pooped in the pen. I dropped a paper towel over it so she didn't tread in it and donned my rubber gloves. Suddenly, I heard a clunking noise. I turned round and Mahri had jumped up, stolen one of my wellies and made off round the kitchen. After retrieving the wellie, I returned to deal with Elle, who was now trying to kill the paper towel. Quickly, I scooped up the offending article and deposited it in a poly bag. I stretched over to get more of the paper towel, but it had rolled off the shelf. Mahri was trying to shred the whole roll into a million pieces. I rescued the roll and started the cleaning; but now Mahri had made off with the poly carrier bag. I reclaimed the bag and hung it up inside the pen. While I tried to wash the floor with antibacterial wipes, it was Elle's turn to cause mayhem as she attempted to climb up and get the poly bag. I tried to grab her and wondered what my jumper had snagged on when I didn't move as freely as I expected to. When I looked down, Mahri had crept between my legs and had a firm hold of my jumper. At this point, what should have been a one minute job to scoop some poop had taken me 20 minutes.

Oh joy! The carer had arrived. She took Elle to Len, and Mahri went into her crate. I skipped up to the shower in preparation for a nice peaceful day at work. Whoever said 'it was just as easy to clean up after two pups as it was one' lied like a cheap watch bought on a sunny European beach.

The dogs were always willing to share their thoughts on the situation:

Annie: *"I've no sympathy for you; it's self-inflicted."*
Mr Mac: *"I could eat Elle. That'll stop her pooping on the floor."*
Mahri: *"I'm first to eat her; then I'll eat you too."*

6 August 2006

I'd taken Elle to puppy classes over the last couple of weeks because she was verging on turning a bit wild; but this week I had to adjust my priorities slightly and reinforce Mahri's training due to her recent forgetfulness. I'd been shouting for Mahri to 'come', but she kindly responded by going. If I asked her to come 'here', she went elsewhere; when I asked her to 'sit', she ran around; if I told her 'down', she jumped up. However, as soon as I shouted 'Mahri, dinner!', it was like a scene from the Road Runner and the Coyote as she left skid marks on the floor, coming to a seated halt by her plate, looking innocent and angelic.

I walked into the hall where the puppy classes were and was swiftly reminded of the contrast from the previous two weeks. In the preceding fortnight, I had a ten-pound Welsh puppy on the end of a red lead. This particular day, I walked … well, I should say was dragged in, by a thirty-pound Airedale puppy on the end of a tartan lead! Several people gasped, mouths wide open, before one said, "'My, hasn't she grown?'" The rest all nodded in agreement. It did make me smile, and I almost didn't bother explaining to them that it was a different dog. If the trainer hadn't spoilt my fun, it would have made the next week all the more interesting to see if they thought the dog had shrunk when I took Elle back.

9 August 2006

Mr Mac was the model of perfection this last week. He's played nicely with the pups, walked politely on the lead – he only dragged me once on a long country walk when he thought his harem was threatened by a wee dog trying to be a big bully – and, at agility, Mr Mac was a star.

He went through the tyre without hesitation, over the jumps and, although collar-led, he looked really good through the weave and on the seesaw. To complicate the course, we had a couple of right turns and jumps to negotiate, which he did very well.

After that, all the jumps were put in a circle and we had to stand in the centre and send our dog out of the circle, over one jump and bring him in over the next. There were seven jumps in total and, much to my surprise and astonishment, Mr Mac did them. The circle was widened to create a gap between each jump and we had to send the dog out over the jump and back in through the gap again, which he also did.

I was very pleased with him and he got special treats for being so good. Three days of excellence must be more than any Airedale can stand, because he went for the Jekyll and Hyde personality trait yesterday: bullying the pups, bullying Annie and peeing on everyone except me. Len was not amused. Mr Mac peed all over a small tree, then ran back and forth, rubbing his back on the branches, before he ultimately broke a branch off.

As he was getting too rough with Mahri, despite the fact that she kept going back for more, I said I would shut him in the house, but Len said to leave him. Big mistake. At that point, he saw a cat outside the garden and took off. I shouted so loudly, the pups got a real fright. I picked Mahri up, now nearly twenty-four pounds, ran half way up the drive, dropped her in the puppy pen and then ran after Mr Mac, just in time to see a car slowing down to miss him.

I tried sweetly calling him to me, offering a tissue – always a favourite trick when you have no treats in your pocket. I tried turning my back and walking away, but this didn't work either and he trotted further up the road. As a last resort, I tried shouting in an authoritative manner and also screaming in high-pitched panic, but he stayed just out of my reach. Another car came round the bend and forced him to change direction. Fortunately, it was towards me and, as he turned, I grabbed him by his collar. Earlier in the week, I'd wondered whether his collar might be getting tight and whether I should loosen it. Luckily, I'd forgotten to do anything. The collar did not appear tight at all as it almost slipped over his head. Airedales and probably other dogs have the ability to make collars and harnesses look too tight one minute and step out of them the next.

So there I was, a whole five feet tall in my trainers, carrying a sixty-six pound dog in a headlock, dragging him back to the house. He knew he was going to the kennel by himself and was putting up a mighty struggle. I was so mad he'd nearly got himself knocked down, not once but twice, that I found the strength to drag him unceremoniously down the road, shout at him and shake him by the scruff of his neck all at the same time. "Mr Mac, you ... you maniac!! Do you think I shout for the good of my health? What part of 'come here' confused you? Have you forgotten all your training? You are going straight to the kennel by yourself and no dinner either. Any more nonsense and you will go back to Ireland with your family jewels in a bag!" A passing neighbour just smiled quietly and disappeared from the street. "It's that mad Scots woman again," you could almost hear her mutter.

Once he was safely shut in the kennel, I stopped to breathe. Len told me I was silly for dragging him, as he could have bitten me. I think Mr Mac knew I was so mad he didn't dare risk biting me, as I'd already managed to rip off two nails, which were becoming increasingly painful, not to mention my swollen hand, which was turning black. You'd think, with the bruises I was sporting, I had just gone a round or two with Mike Tyson, but it was only Mr Mac pulling against the collar. Fortunately, I'd bought him a very substantial leather collar with a big metal buckle, so he didn't snap it, like previous ones.

Mr Mac was grounded. No off-lead walks and if he didn't do as I asked the first time, there was a kennel waiting for him to sit in and think about it. I tried putting him in Mahri's crate, which was our first Airedale's crate and had housed all of them so far at shows and when camping, but he was too big for it and he couldn't stand up, lie down or sit because he was too tall and too long in the body.

Annie: *"He's a brat. Send him back."*
Mahri: *"Wow, I think she can run faster than me."*
Elle: *"Eeek! What was that noise? It's scary."*
Mr Mac: *"Oops ... should have listened. Please don't send me back."*

21 August 2006

Mahri was fifteen weeks, so it was time to introduce her to the world outside. I took her for her first walk along the tracks near our house. She loved it, chasing smells and birds and anything else that caught her eye. I decided that she was ready for school and booked her into the next puppy class at the local training centre.

We arrived at 6.00pm and as we entered the hall the first dog we saw was another Airedale puppy. This was most unusual because outside of the show ring you rarely saw an Airedale. In most of the places we've lived we were always referred to as the Airedale people and whenever we met older people in the street they would always tell us how their parents had owned one before the war or how they remembered learning to walk with a toy dog on wheels that looked just like our dogs. Look, Mahri, another Airedale! I asked the owner how old the pup was and found out that she too was fifteen weeks. She made Mahri look quite minuscule. At home, Mahri always came across as a hulking great brute of a pup. The other pup was called Skye; I'd originally picked that name for Mahri, but Len had disagreed. Skye bounded across the room and shoved and pushed and growled and barked. In general, she bullied Mahri, who suddenly seemed to be very much a baby. Once the class settled down, Mahri did very well and walked almost to heel and sat on command. This was a refreshing difference to Mr Mac, although he had improved enormously. Mahri could also be coaxed into lying down, although, because she had not quite come to terms with the command, lying down was more of an involuntary manoeuvre, undertaken when her legs were worn out from chasing Mr Mac around the house.

After some heel work, the pups were allowed off-lead two or three at a time to socialise. The tiny puppies, like the Yorkies and Border Terriers, were first, followed by the young, larger pups such as Mahri, with older small pups: a Shitzu, a Rottie and Skye the Airedale. They kept them close in size to prevent them being intimidated. Mahri, maybe slightly overwhelmed, chose to investigate the room and avoid contact with the other pups. She was quite happy trotting around, sniffing here and there. All too soon, she had to be back on-lead. Mahri, when called, would come sometimes at home, but not always, so I fully expected her to ignore me and go for a wander instead of returning to my side. She actually came bounding straight up to me and nearly managed to execute a finish, as well, by running round behind me and sitting down at my left. The class was soon over and I took a tired but happy puppy back home.

28 August 2006

Mahri had her second obedience lesson and did very well, although when allowed off-lead she preferred to explore everything in the room rather than play with the other dogs. I think this was because, to her, having a real dog to play with was no novelty when she already had three at home.

I had to buy Mahri a harness; Elle had been sporting one for some time now because she pulled so much on the lead. On one of our walks, Mahri had been particularly stubborn and she'd made herself sick by pulling so much trying to chase leaves across a field. For the next few months, she was sporting a nice blue harness to protect her throat. .

Mahri was now allowed into the sitting room for an hour in the evenings and would charge past the dining table, round the couch, and under the coffee table, with Mr Mac in hot pursuit. She would trip Mr Mac, or nip his feet. He loved it. They'd play tug with the toys and the rug, which generally led to a shout from me or Len to cease forthwith. This game was followed by lots of 'bitey face'. When Mahri was exhausted, we'd put her to bed and let Elle out. Elle loved this time and would chase Mr Mac, while he would run round the furniture and do hand-brake turns in Annie's basket, or on the rug. The pure joy in his face is a picture I will always have in my memory – all because he had a playmate that could run faster than he could! It was lovely to see him racing at full pelt with this tiny pup chasing him, barking as she ran. Sometimes, as he dashed the full length of the room, Elle would run so fast trying to catch him, she would disappear right under his legs. She'd tire first and he'd end up chasing her before, eventually, they'd both collapse on the rug, panting away, but quite happy, beside each other. Oddly enough, this was how I'd pictured the two pups would be. To be truthful, sometimes I actually felt like I was living in a house full of World Wrestling Federation members, the way they bounced off each other and rolled around on the floor.

The dogs shared their thoughts with me:

Annie: *"Just shut that door and leave me in the hall in peace."*
Mr Mac: *"Catch me if you can."*
Mahri: *"I'll get the toy away from you."*
Elle: *"Run, run, yip, grrr, yip, grrr, yip, run like the wind! You still won't catch me."*

3rd October 2006

Mr Mac is in the dog house; or is it me? Saturday was a rare calm end-of-summer day with warm, clear blue skies. As it was probably one of the last we were going to see for a while, we decided to take the gang for a walk at a local nature reserve.

I got the trailer out and loaded it with Len's off-road wheelchair, all the picnic stuff and things we needed for Len and the dogs. After getting washed and changed, I got all the dogs strapped into their car safety harnesses and off we trooped.

We arrived at the car park, and the place where we usually parked was still empty; this was good, because it was the best space for loading or unloading wheelchairs. I got the dogs out and tied them to the bumper while we transferred Len to his off-road wheelchair. Then we put the everyday wheelchair in the car, locked everything up and set off. This whole process, including a 17-mile drive, took about two hours. Len had Elle on her extending lead. Brian – Len's carer, a really nice sixty-two-year-old lovey-sort-of-a-person – had Annie who, because of her advancing years, was such a quiet girl now that she was never a problem to anyone. Annie had a dual-length lead which, if you opened it out, doubled in length for country walks. For some reason, Brian opened the lead to full size, then wrapped it round and round his hand until the poor girl was almost strung up. I politely reminded him that he should not get into the habit of doing this because, if it was Mr Mac and he pounced on something such as a poly bag, he would pull him over at best and break his arm at worst. I, being the youngest and fittest of the group, had Mr Mac and Mahri.

We strolled along, enjoying the sun on our backs and looking at the scenery. The path was only wide enough for Len and Brian, so I walked along the sloping grassy bank several yards ahead of them.

Two middle-aged women were walking towards us, obviously returning from a walk with two very fat Cairn-type Terriers. One woman, on seeing us, bent down quickly and lifted her dog, as if we posed a threat. She looked at me, "Airedales; you don't see many of them around," she commented rather brusquely.

"No," I countered, and made Mr Mac and Mahri sit to show how good they were. Just then she noticed Len with Elle. "A puppy," she shrieked, and ran towards Len, flapping her free arm (the other was still holding her dog).

Mahri was bouncing up and down; she thought the woman might give her a cuddle as well. After all, she was only four months old and still a puppy like Elle. Suddenly, without warning, Mr Mac lunged in Len's direction. I pulled hard on Mr Mac's lead, glad I'd listened to my own advice about not wrapping the lead round my hand. He lunged again and again. Then Mahri joined in. Calling his name and pulling as hard as I could had no effect whatsoever. He totally ignored me. The last tug was just *too* much and I flipped up in the air and landed on my back. With legs still in the air, I was dragged unceremoniously down the slope. I might add that not once did I let go of the leads. Mr Mac continued trying to drag me towards Len and the women, while Mahri wanted to run in the opposite direction. I did not have the strength to pull both dogs back to my side while sliding head first down the slope. I had to distract Mr Mac so I could stand up, as my legs were the only appendages that were not fettered in any way. I thought I would use my foot to nudge Mr Mac to make him look at me. My right arm was already stretched to the full extent, holding on to a lead which was also taut with Mr Mac on the end of it. I tapped him with my toe on his rear end. "Mr Mac," I hissed through gritted teeth, and at last he looked at me and the tension on the lead slackened. Just as I was about to stand up, the stupid woman started screeching again. "Ohhhh, look, she's kicking her dog. Look, do something," she started squealing, and flapping her arms about again.

She'd have been singing a different tune if I'd let Mr Mac go and he put her flat on her back. Mr Mac really didn't like this woman's screeching and lunged in her direction again but, by now, I was back on my feet and managed to grab his collar and pull him round to face me. I shouted at him to bring him back in line; he hated being shouted at. That was the second worst punishment for him. The worst is to be left in the kennel on his own to think about his misdemeanours.

I yelled at him, my arms gesticulating wildly. "What are you playing at? When I say here, I mean HERE, not there, HERE. Do you understand that?"

Of course, all this set the woman off again. In her eyes, I had beaten my dog to within an inch of his life. Len, instead of telling the woman to walk away so the dog would calm down, told her, "We've had Airedales for over 20 years and we know what we're doing." Of course, she wasn't going to believe this because a) she had just seen me being dragged along on my back by two dogs playing tug-of-war with me in the middle; and b) she was too full of her own importance to see that she had caused the situation. She eventually went on her way and Mr Mac calmed down.

Len then thought that this was an ideal opportunity to have, how shall I put it, "words with me" for such a public display of not being in control of my dog.

Mr Mac and Mahri returned to normal and trotted along beside me as if nothing had happened, while I began to feel the bruises surfacing on my ribs, knees, legs, and arms. I also won the first prize for best nettle rash of the day, courtesy of Mr Mac, so all in all I was doing really well! Did anybody ask how I was? Nope. They all just stood and stared.

I still don't know what set Mr Mac against the woman. Perhaps he thought she was going to attack Len or Elle. On Mr Mac's next outing, he would be wearing his halti, which he hated almost as much as being shouted at, but at least he wouldn't pull me off my feet. And Mahri, whose lead I'd also held, had enjoyed the game of pouncing on me and chasing Mr Mac, so she would wear one as well. I was certainly not going to be dragged about with them barking at some silly women making strange noises again. When we got home, Len told me off for being over-protective of Mr Mac and molly-coddling him and always taking his side.

Jackie: *"Some days you just can't do right for doing wrong."*

19 October 2006

On Friday night, in anticipation of a holiday, I'd taken my three hairy little monsters to the Welsh Terrier breeder who'd promised to care for them as if they were his own, including bathing and grooming them ready for our return on the Wednesday night. Off we went to Scotland for a few days to visit with my wee sister and get a fix of haggis and hills. We needed to make this journey every now and then because we lived in one of the flattest areas in England and Len missed the hills and mountains.

We had a good drive back down the road from Scotland. It was still light when we arrived at the house where the dogs had been kennelled. I saw Mr Mac first, bouncing up and down, trying to see over a kennel door. He looked so handsome – just like the show dog he was. Len spotted Mahri first and I asked him to point out where. He gestured to the Airedale bouncing beside Mr Mac. She was no longer a fluffy young pup, tripping over her feet. Instead, she was a tall, well-proportioned Airedale with a nice, long face. "Where's my puppy gone?" I asked. Then she came bounding across the garden and with one jump was on Len's lap. We thought she would topple the wheelchair. Next was Elle, skipping and bouncing on to Len's knee,

Cool Haircut

which fortunately Mahri had vacated. She too looked so grown up with her new adult haircut. The three of them ran round the garden, in and out of the man's house, around the grooming room and under the parrot cages. They watched the goats and chickens in a fenced-off part of the garden and had obviously had a great time. If it was up to them, I think they would have chosen to stay there. Eventually, they were rounded up and put in the car to go home. It would be well past their bedtime by the time we got there.

6 November 2006

Mr Mac had been going to agility class for six months now and, last week, he had the best week ever. He had gone from class clown to gold star pupil over the last few weeks. The course had been made a little more difficult and a new piece of equipment had been introduced each week.

We had a huge eight-month-old black Labrador join the class, and if anyone has read the book *Marley and Me* by John Grogan, they will be able to picture the dog. The owner had read the book and reckoned she had the 'son of Marley'. Well, he was now the class clown. He'd broken the high-walk and several jumps with his enthusiasm and he was not allowed on the A-frame. Furthermore, he demolished the weave poles and dragged the chute around while he was in it.

I'd been telling Len how well Mr Mac was doing in class but, judging from the grin on Len 's face, he didn't believe me. He hadn't seen Mr Mac perform in the class in four months and, when I tried to make Mr Mac work on my little jumps and weaves in the garden, he'd refused. He only worked in class. Anyway, Len decided to come to the class to see for himself. I knew this was an opportunity for Mr Mac to impress Len, but was convinced he would let himself and me down. At first, Mr Mac played up. Typical, I thought. *"He knows Len's watching, so he's being awkward."* Then I thought that maybe it was because of me. I know that when I'm being watched, it makes me self-conscious. After a couple of poor rounds and general misbehaving, Mr Mac settled down and produced a clear round. Len was suitably impressed and applauded Mr Mac, who trotted right up to him, sat down and offered a paw.

Mr Mac: *"Give me five ... I am the main man round these parts."*

I could see Mr Mac was really pleased with himself; he was positively grinning. Len just couldn't believe it. The last time he saw him, he wasn't allowed off-lead because he wouldn't do as he was told and could be a bit pushy with other dogs. Now he sat watching me, waiting for my next request. I use this verb advisedly, as I could not command or order him to do anything. He sometimes did things for me because I asked him to and sometimes he wouldn't do

Too bad about the fence

as I asked because it was simply not on his agenda or he was too busy chasing a squirrel. Sometimes he just thought it was a bad call and he was saving me from my own ineptitude. Even after 11 months, I still could not get him to lie down on request. He would stand or sit beside me and when I went to bed, he would lie down outside my room door. When I was sitting watching TV on an evening, he would lie down in the hall so he could watch all the doors. He was still an enigma and probably always will be, but I loved him to bits.

10 November 2006

Winter was fast approaching. The mornings and evenings were cold and dark, so dog walks were short and only with one at a time. Mr Mac, who could run faster and further than my torch could reach, would disappear into the darkness, and I couldn't tell if he'd sneaked under or over the fence. I could hear his dog tags, but that was not always helpful, as he might easily be in the farmer's field or in a neighbour's garden. I simply could not hold two pups and a torch and retain any degree of dignity. The pups always pulled in opposite directions and I'd end up shining the torch in my own eyes, blinding myself, and tripping over leads when they changed direction. I wondered if the inventor of the straitjacket got his idea from walking two young dogs?

Last night, while walking Mahri down to the bottom of the paddock, I heard a strange yet familiar sound. At first I couldn't place it, but then I realised it was a helicopter – the police helicopter. We lived not far from a prison and there had been one or two escapes. The last one was about six years ago and they found the man hiding in the ditch at the bottom of our paddock. Irrational fears were scary enough … but rational fears were worse! By the time I was almost at the tree line, Mahri had stopped and growled deep in her throat, followed by a little bark, as if she was losing her bravado. Another growl and she was starting to back up; the helicopter was now above the farmer's field. Mahri's nerves caved in at this point and she did an about-turn and dragged me back towards the house – big lights and safety. I must confess I didn't need much dragging because I was as spooked as she was.

The helicopter veered off and headed back to its base. Maybe they had just paused to admire my little ugly duckling of an Airedale. There'd been no reports of any prison breaks, but erring on the side of caution is not to be mocked when there's a prison so close.

12 November 2006

'Mahri limpy legs' – aka the thief

Mahri had developed an intermittent limp. The vet thought she might have grown too quickly and recommended short walks and lots of rest. To rest an Airedale pup is a bit of a misnomer, so Mahri had to stay in her crate-bed with the door shut to stop her racing around like a lunatic. Whenever the opportunity arose, I would let Mahri out of her crate to wander around the kitchen with me so she didn't feel quite so punished. I'd have to shut Mr Mac out of the kitchen or the two of them would race around like little thugs, head butting and body slamming each other.

Last night, both pups were quietly dozing. Len was feeling unwell and had gone to bed early, so I'd said I would get his medicine ready and wake him at 11.30. I prepared all the pills and left them in his bedside drawer, took the sachet of Movicol (a laxative) into the kitchen and put it on the breakfast bar; then I let both pups out of their crates to wander around the kitchen with me while I cleared up. As I was filling the dishwasher with my back to the breakfast bar, I thought I heard a noise and looked up to see what it was. I saw Mahri run to the utility room with Elle in hot pursuit. In the time it took me to stand up and shut the door, they had already repeated this behaviour several times and were now in a stand-off with each other, one in Annie's basket and the other waiting to jump in. One had obviously found a tasty treat and the other was bent on stealing it.

I walked towards them to see what the valuable prize was. Mahri shot past me and stood under the breakfast bar. She dropped the contents of her mouth, challenging me to get to it before she did. Eek!!! It looked like the Movicol wrapper! I lunged at her and grabbed her muzzle, wrestling her jaw open – she wasn't about to give up this prize easily – and pulled out a foil sachet with lots of Airedale teeth-shaped puncture holes. Luckily, it appeared to have retained most of its contents. I glanced at her face and laughed at her beard, which was covered in a fine dusting of white powder – she looked like she'd snorted a line or two. I grabbed a paper towel, dunked it in the soapy water I had in the sink and washed her beard, tongue, teeth and gums. I really didn't know what I thought this would achieve, though. Next I checked Annie's fleece bed and it had lots of little patches of white powder on. I shook it on to the floor, swept up, mopped (just in case) and put the fleece in the wash. By now, it was well past my bed time, so I took my little ugly duckling out for a last toilet break before putting her to bed. She smiled so sweetly at me, but all I could think was, '"She'll be getting me up in an hour or so"'.

I was lucky. It was 4.30am before I heard the first plaintiff cries. *"YOWL. I want out!"* I jumped up and into my tracksuit in one continuous movement. I knew I had to get her out or spend the next hour scrubbing the utility room. I made it. Poor baby! She had obviously ingested enough Movicol to speed up the passage of her dinner through her digestive system. She stood looking at me with her huge, sad eyes. *"What have you done to me?"*

"No, Mahri! You did this to yourself," I told her.

She got me up again at 6.30am, so she was encouraged

to skip breakfast in the hope that doing so would settle her tummy. Thank goodness she was too greedy to share the Movicol with Elle!

22 November 2006

Usually, after dinner, we played a game of chase round the table – I'm too big and old to follow, so the dogs always cheated and ran under the table. I'd played this game with all my Airedales. Sometimes I'd crouch down and hide behind the couch and then jump out, barking at the dogs. They would leap in the air and rush off round the table into the kitchen and back, looking for me to jump out again; but I'd moved to just inside the door. Over the years, four Airedales have loved this game, but then came Mr Mac.

I'd been playing chase with Mr Mac after the pups had gone to bed for the night. Mr Mac was having fun running back and forth, staying just out of my reach. Then I hid behind the couch and jumped out at the poor boy. After he'd scraped himself off the ceiling, he was quite aggressive towards me. It was my own fault. Only an idiot would jump out and say 'boo' to a two-and-a-half-year-old Airedale of unknown background ... and I was that idiot.

He was very wary of me for several days. I still played chase round the table, but would never sneak up on Mr Mac the way I did with the pups. They loved it and saw it as an excuse to go rushing off round the house.

Eleven months have now passed since Mr Mac came to stay and, while I was sitting on the floor with Mahri, he came and lay down beside me and allowed me to rest my hand on his back and neck. This was a huge step forward, as you couldn't make him lie down and, if he did, he had to have clear space all round him. He had lain down beside me once or twice in that time, but if I reached out and touched him, he stood up and walked away.

28 November 2006

Mr Mac didn't go to his agility class last week because I did not get home in time to take him. This week he was rushing round at my feet, determined that I would get out the door and get him there on time. He didn't even want to go for his walk before we went in, which surprised me, as he usually liked to walk up the country lane to pee on everything.

When we got into the hall, there were three new dogs: Bonny, a six-month-old Jack Russell cross from the Wednesday puppy class; a rescue Border Collie; and a young German Shepherd. Roo, the Lakeland cross that just loved Mr Mac, squealed with delight as she did every week when we walked in. She dragged and hauled and pulled till she got up close to greet him with a nose rub. Then Maisy, the Yorky cross who was only nine months old, had to join in. She was also a member of Mr Mac's apparently growing fan club.

Bonny had met Mahri and Elle, but not Mr Mac. She was obviously impressed with his chiselled good looks and aloof demeanour, so she was squealing to get to him. He just stood looking down at the three little dogs, sort of whinnying, and then he touched each one with his paw. I bet they didn't wash for a week! Mr Mac stood surrounded by his fan club, posing fit to win Crufts and letting everyone see what a great show dog he'd been.

The class started and all the little dogs went round first, then the medium dogs and Mr Mac last because the jumps had to be set higher for him than for the rest of the class. If they were too low, he stepped over them with little enthusiasm. I said to Roo's mum, "Mr Mac won't work tonight … too many new faces and he's getting bored waiting for his turn." We laughed and wondered what antics he would get up to.

At last, it was Mr Mac's turn. "Are you ready, Mr Mac? Ready?" He was through the tunnel in a flash, then just as quickly through the turns and over the jumps; next the seesaw and the weave were met without any hesitation and he'd finished the course in one clear round and it was fast as well. He even did the weave on command and did it without having to be dragged by the collar. Everyone applauded and you could see the pride in a job well done written all over Mr Mac's face. As he trotted back to our seat, you could almost hear him say, *"Well, class, that's how it should be done … lots of fun and lots of enthusiasm."* Mr Mac had another clear round. Then the course was reversed and it was much harder to work on the right, as there was now two about-turns. But he was round it like a whippet and just clipped the last pole.

Mr Mac: *"Honestly, I didn't touch the last pole. It was the down-draft as I flew over it."*

While they were moving some of the equipment, Mr Mac was sitting next to me. Maisy was jumping up at him, which upset Roo because Maisy was being a tart. Bonny joined in and Roo was really mad at these young upstarts trying to muscle in on *her* man. She certainly let it be known. There was such a snapping and squealing, Mr Mac got up and walked round to my other side so nobody could get a piece of him. He sat making grumbling noises till they calmed down a bit. "Mumble grumble … *I can stay at home and listen to yowling, snapping pups* … mumble."

He got up, walked over to Roo and, lowering his head, pushed her into the corner and with his back to her he sat down in front of her. Silence reigned once more.

30 November 2006

I took my cute little Airedale puppy, Mahri, to the puppy class last night, for puppies up to nine months; she was going to be seven months the very next day. Time to stop dreaming and tell the truth.

Okay, let's see. I took seven-month-old Mahri to the puppy class last night. She hadn't been for four weeks because her leg was recovering from the limp that appeared off and on for several weeks. I lifted the wriggling, writhing 38-pound hairball from my car so she wouldn't jar her legs jumping out. I should have recognised that, from then on, she would be hyper.

I was dragged through the car park and into the hall, arm outstretched, barely managing to remain upright – the epitome of a person with an untrained wild dog. A veritable hoodlum! Once in the class, Mahri was like a mini-twister, dragging me from dog to dog. With most of them only being about ten pounds, her exuberance terrified them into snapping at her before she flattened them with a paw or two.

At home, she would sit, lie down or even wait and stay; but not tonight. She lunged at anything and everything and the only command she actually listened to was 'Mahri, come!' When she did, she got to the sausage so fast that she took a little piece of my finger as well. *Had she turned in to a vampire dog?* She'd already had quite a bit of my blood in the five months we'd had her. I honestly didn't know whether I was ever going to be allowed to take her back to the class.

Mahri: *"Who's this? What's that? Gimme, gimme, gimme! Bite? Who? Moi? I'm a cutie."*

3 December 2006

I had spent three weeks trying hard to keep Mahri quiet with short walks round the garden on the lead and keeping her on the lead by my side in the house so she couldn't rough-house with Mr Mac and Elle.

This last week, I've let her have a bit more freedom. Each day her limp appeared to be getting better. I began to wonder if it might have been a phantom injury, because she had been spending most of her time on her back legs – either jumping up to clear the worktops in the kitchen or dragging me about on her lead.

Last night, after her walk, I let the three pups – Mr Mac being the third – run round the kitchen and utility room. Mahri turned into the karate kid, running back and forth at full pelt, drop-kicking Mr Mac on the way, and then bouncing on the wall before turning to run back.

I had footprints three feet high up the wall. Elle thought this was fun, so was hot on her heels. Mr Mac stood in the middle like an umpire at a tennis match as they ran back and forth. To no avail, I yelled, banged tin plates, and blew the time-out whistle. The response – total disregard.

Eventually, Mr Mac had had enough. *"Grrrbark ... grrrowf ... grrrthwack."* The noise of his jaws air-snapping was like shutting a big book. The two hooligans stopped and looked at him, and then, simultaneously, ran at him and grabbed his ears.

He was mad; such insolence. He growled, shook his head and stamped his feet. The pups let go and he shoved each one with his nose all the way into the corner, daring them to talk back. I sent the scoundrels to bed for ignoring me and Mr Mac sat in the middle of the room feeling a bit sorry for himself because they'd ganged up on him. He got some extra treats to take his mind off his chewed ears. As a result of the high jinks, Mahri was limping again, so it was back to lead walks and rest for another week.

4 December 2006

Have you ever used chopsticks? Are you good with them? Were they two feet long? I took Elle and Mahri for their early morning walk on Saturday. With the howling wind and horizontal rain, it was just *perfect* for a *'sniff of every blade of grass'* type of walk. We almost got to the bottom of the big paddock before Mahri deigned to go to the toilet. I used to ask her if she needed a six-figure grid reference to find the right spot.

Although Elle was the one shouting to go outside, she really just wanted to chase anything that moved and, in the wind, the targets were plentiful – leaves, flower-pots, discarded poly bags. Elle stopped for a moment and picked something up. She trotted along, sniffing grass, and ruminating on this something.

"What has she got now?" I asked no-one but the wind. Mahri was headed for home, so my left arm was fully stretched in that direction; but Elle, who was now backing away from me because she knew I wanted her prize, forced my right arm to extend in the very opposite direction. Just to make the walk more interesting, the wind was beating me about the ears and my hair was whipping my eyes like a sail flapping in a storm.

I eventually managed to draw both arms together so I could bend down and grab Elle's head to open her mouth and see what required so much chewing. I peered down her throat and in the gloomy light I could just about make out something that looked like a crab. Well, we don't get crabs in the middle of the country and we are too far from the coast for one to have migrated, so I figured it must be a piece of grass root and left her to eat it. I didn't really have a spare hand to remove it anyway.

I let her go and she spat the item out. Then Mahri grabbed it. "Drop it!" I yelled at her and she did. I peered at the grass root to see why it was so interesting. "Arghhhhh!" It was a pigeon's foot! "Yeeeuk!" And to think, I nearly pulled *that* out of her mouth.

I got the pups, who were still tussling over the tasty morsel, under control and back in the house. Then I went out with my shovel to clean the garden and dispose of the foot; but do you think I could find it? Nope. I walked up and down in the wind and rain, but it had vanished, disappeared into thin air … for now at least.

Mahri came out with me for an extra walk while I collected the marker poles. They were actually my weave poles for my Mr Mac and were about two feet high, white, and half an inch thick with a nail in the bottom to spike into the ground.

I spiked them in the ground whenever the dogs left a little pile so Len wouldn't roll over it or somebody else step in it. And it made it much easier to walk round and clean up the garden.

I'd collected two sticks when Mahri pounced on something in the grass. "Drop it!" Arggggh! ... It was that pigeon foot again and I didn't have a shovel or poly bag on me this time. I pondered how I would get rid of the offending article.

Eureka! It came to me in a flash! I used the two poles like gigantic chopsticks, something that was a lot more difficult than it sounds because of the difference in thickness between the pole and nail. And before you ask, why couldn't I just spike the leg? ... No, I couldn't. Have you ever tried to skewer a pigeon foot?

I eventually got the leg across the garden, under the trees and into the dyke. In hindsight, it would have been quicker to mark it with a pole and fetch the shovel, but as the saying goes, 'hindsight is a wonderful thing'.

For several days Elle continued to follow the trail right to the trees, still searching for her little prize.

5 December 2006

On Saturdays, the dogs were always given a special treat. They ran around the kitchen while I made my toast for breakfast and then would sit very nicely by my feet, waiting for their piece of toast. I used this time as a training session; 'sit', 'lie down', 'give a paw', 'stay'. Generally, they didn't try to kill each other for at least as long as the toast lasted.

This Saturday was no different; they'd been walked, pooped and peed and had had their toast and I was cleaning round the kitchen when a really bad smell wafted past my nose. Yeeuk! I looked around and couldn't see anything. I assumed one of them had wind, although the smell was so bad that Len would have suggested that something had crawled in their rear end and died. He has such a nice way with words.

I continued my work, when the smell wafted by my nostrils again. Only this time, when I looked round, I saw where it came from. "Who did that?" I shouted and pointed. Either they all looked guilty or they were on the verge of passing out from the fumes. I donned my faithful rubber gloves and my CSI hat and set to work.

As I cleaned, I deduced that Elle was the perpetrator of the crime. I had no idea why she should need to go again so soon, but then I heard that familiar squirting sound. "Elle! Noooo!!!"

Mr Mac was shut in the hall, Mahri was sent to her crate and Elle also was sent to her crate, where she yowled pitifully. I figured she couldn't possibly want to go again, so she was just crying for attention. I cleaned, disinfected and sterilized the room, but the smell would not go … hmm. I went to get Elle out for a walk and guess what … more of the offensive, runny matter … argh!

No wonder she was yowling. *What to do with her now?* … Aha! I tied her to the tow hook on Len's car in the garage. Just as everything was nice and clean again, I went out to check on Elle. "Aggghhh!!! You little brat!" She'd chewed clean through the electric cable for Len's trailer connector, so we would not be able to use the trailer any more, as it would be without indicators or lights.

I didn't even know if it had affected any other electrics on the car and, worse still, I knew I had to try and explain to Len how and why this had happened. "Len, we've had a disaster," I said. "*Elle's eaten your car.*" Silence.

Len responded, "You've been told a million times not to exaggerate. Which bit has she actually chewed?"

I gave him the abridged version of the smell, the rubber gloves and the crate and waited for his reply. "Oh well … greater losses at sea. I'll take it to the tow-bar people on Monday," he said very calmly.

"I've put duct tape on it," I said. As if, like a magic plaster, it would make it better.

I tried to make Elle drink a spoonful of kaolin to settle her tummy, but nope, she wouldn't put her face near the bowl; so I opened her mouth and poured it in. *"Mmm, that was nice,"* she decided, and fought me for the dish to lick it clean.

By night fall, she was back to normal and did not appear to have suffered any ill effects from her Mercedes lunch. I suppose she thought Len's car was fast food or a drive-through diner.

I tried to work out whether it was the pigeon foot or perhaps the toast. I didn't know, but at 2.00am on Sunday, Mahri was yelling to go out … squirtee! Yep, that's right … and again at 5.00am and 6.00am. But you can be sure SHE was NOT tied to anybody's car. Luckily, she recovered quickly too.

We took the car to get repaired. The man in the garage just shook his head and made that funny sucking-in noise, the one they made when the bill was going to be expensive. Len had to go back later to see if it could be repaired. Elle had got herself crossed off Santa's list. Annie and Mr Mac, who never touched the pigeon foot, were both fine, so the final conclusion was that the foot was to blame.

Elle: *"Well, you do say I'm a live wire."*

8 December 2006

I tried to take a festive photo of my little furry friends wearing Chez Andrea Christmas bandanas. Andrea is one of my cyber-friends in Wisconsin. She makes seasonal bandanas and runs photo competitions for Airedale and Cairn Rescue in America. She is also the glue that holds us all together because she organises and runs our website. Annie was laid back as usual and she didn't budge from her basket until I was ready to take the photo. Mr Mac sat patiently posing, while Mahri became a Mexican jumping bean. Elle turned into a whirling Dervish, and was trying to catch the bandana ties, which were longer on her because of her tiny neck. Mahri thought she could help Elle and proceeded to chew and swallow the bandana, which unfortunately was still round Elle's neck. The photo-shoot was cancelled before Elle disappeared down Mahri's throat. Oh well, best laid plans and all that …

10 December 2006

Last night, Len was sitting at the computer. All the dogs had been out for a walk. It was grey, cold, and blowing a gale, so nobody was keen to stop out any longer than necessary. I let all the dogs have the run of the living and dining room – all thirty-nine feet – as well as the kitchen.

They screamed up and down and round the table like a swarm of bees, and just as noisy too.

I decided to trim their claws. I caught Elle after a bit of a skirmish and got her claws all trimmed. When I called Mahri, she came at once and sat and waited for her treat. Snatch. "Oy!! Mind the fingers." No sooner had I picked up one of Mahri's feet and the clippers when mild-mannered Mahri morphed into a wild cat. In fact, she resisted with the force of two tigers, biting, clawing and scratching. It took me at least two hours to get her to sit calmly and get one claw cut each time.

Meanwhile, I had not been supervising Elle as closely as I perhaps should have been for a six-month-old Welsh Terrier pup, and neither had Len. But with pups and children you sort of develop a sixth sense and could usually tell by the noise or lack of noise that they were up to no good.

Eventually, all the claws were trimmed: it was 10.00pm. I called the three pups to me for a special liver treat. Elle wandered into the kitchen. *"Hi, you wanted me?"* The look was Innocence personified.

I was trying to make her sit when an odour reached my nostrils. "What is that smell? Elle, you little brat! If you've pooped on the carpet you're going to the dog's home!" I shouted at her, and I shoved past Len, who was half-blocking the door into the kitchen. As I was squeezing my ample posterior through the tight space, Mahri ran through my legs.

"I'm free!" she squealed with delight, as she made two or three circuits of the sitting room and rounded the table. *"Freeeeeee!"* Zooming back into the kitchen and bouncing around.

I collected the cleaning implements and went back to the sitting room, leaving Len to keep the dogs in the kitchen, except for Elle, who was sent to bed in disgrace. Mahri jumped on Len's knee and bounced round the worktops like a tiger with a spring in her tail.

Meanwhile, back in the living room, I muttered to myself. Not only had that little brat pooped on the carpet, she'd stepped in it and left little pawprints here, there and everywhere.

I went back to the kitchen and Len kindly pointed out some pawprints on the kitchen floor, which I cleaned. Then he suggested I check Elle's feet, which I did, and, surprisingly, they were clean.

Better check Mahri's feet. Oh no!! She had a lump in the hair on her front foot and on one pad. That was why the pawprints were so small and I'd thought it was Elle.

Len couldn't stand anything like this. "You have to get me out of these clothes," he panicked. "And clean the worktops and the floor and the walls!" He wittered on and on, making me feel a bit snappy. I took Mahri outside, washed her feet and then put her to bed.

"It's all your fault," I remonstrated, as I slammed the door shut on her crate. "If you'd sat quietly and got your claws done, this would not have happened." The next thing I knew, Len told me off for being unreasonable and pointed out that, if I'd been paying the proper attention, it would not have happened. As usual, he was right.

I got Len into bed, gathered up his clothes and threw them in the washer. At this point I still had to sterilize the kitchen, go over the carpet, sterilize Len's chair and throw my clothes in the wash and head for the shower. When I checked on Len, I enquired where his mobile phone was.

Len couldn't remember for sure, but he thought it might have been in his pocket. Oops!!! I walked slowly through to the washing machine … the inevitability dawning; and yep, sure enough, there it was … plainly visible through the glass in the middle of a 40-degree wash cycle.

This was one phone that wasn't going to be working again – 'water ingress' was what we would tell the insurance company. Strangely enough, Len was less upset about his phone being ruined than the pawprints on his trousers.

She'd destroyed his car electrics last week and his phone this week, so I'm blaming Elle for this incident as well. After all, it wasn't me that forgot to check his pockets. I dreaded to think what it would be the following week.

"I think I'd like your Christmas decorations outside in the fields, if you don't mind, Mahri," I remarked.

> Deck the halls with bits of poop
> Cos I've got it on my foot;
> Run around and have some fun,
> Spreading stuff from Elle's b*m!
> *[Inspired by manic Mahri.]*

That little incident reminded me of a similar one several years earlier. We, that is, *Len*, decided the garage was in need of tidying. Now, for most people this might have been a quick sweep round and put things up on shelves or out of the way. When Len decided to do anything like this, every cupboard and shelf had to be emptied into a pile in the middle of the floor. From there, it was sorted into smaller piles such as rubbish, tools, painting stuff and Jackie's stuff, which was often the rubbish pile as far as Len was concerned. Once everything had been tidied away, and we started to sweep the floor, we noticed the blue pawprints. We guessed that it was MacIain, because he always shuffled his feet. We eventually captured him, washed his feet in lots of water and put him in the day kennel while we looked for whatever he'd stood in.

We found a small plastic tube decorated with some Airedale teeth marks. Oh dear, this was the blue tint Len, who was a painter and decorator by trade, had used to create his own coloured paint, rather than buying pre-tinted paints. The punctured tube was duly relegated to the bin and we never gave it another thought.

All was clean again and safe, so the dogs were allowed out of the day kennel to wander round with us or follow trails in the garden. I had gone back to the garage to get some dog treats and I noticed some more blue pawprints had materialized. Where were they coming from? After cleaning all the dogs' feet and the floor several times, we realized that some tint was still on MacIain's lips and gums, so every time we washed his feet, he wandered off and licked them, depositing more tint on his wet feet. *Ergo*, the cycle was repeated. For those that know nothing about tint, one small tube can tint 60 litres of white paint, sky blue.

We got hold of MacIain, who was not keen on having his feet washed again, never mind his mouth and teeth. That should have fixed the problem, we thought. We laughed about it for a bit and, just as we were thinking everything was free from tint, Annie came trotting over for a cuddle from Len. He put his hand down to give her neck a good old scratch. He looked at his hand, which had turned that all too familiar royal blue colour. Eeek! It transpired that MacIain had been playing 'bitey face/neck' with Annie and transferred some tint from his chin to her neck, which Len had now spread around. So it was straight into the bath for her, followed by MacIain for good measure. Once again, I went round with soapy water cleaning kennels and anywhere else I thought they might have been. I'm so glad they hadn't got into the house. Our toffee peach carpets and sage green suite would not have suited blue pawprints on them.

18 December 2006

Little Mahri 'Limpy-legs' still had an intermittent limp, so we'd decided to take her to the vet's the following day for x-rays on her right shoulder. We were sure it was a strain, but it hadn't got any better and, when it did, it tended to just be for the one day, and then it returned to its former state of injury. I still didn't know how she could have injured it, as she spent all her time on her back legs, either counter-surfing, dragging me, trying to climb on Len's knee or wrestling with Mr Mac like a set of boxing kangaroos.

Mahri was about forty pounds of pure mischief now; twenty-two inches neck to tail, and twenty-two inches neck to ground. The vet thought the problem was growing pains. She might have grown too quickly and once she stopped her growing spurt, the limp would disappear. I'd seen her father, two brothers and sister. Apart from her slightly longer face and slimmer body, most likely due to the breeder's own admission of over-feeding, there was little difference to be seen. Mr Mac was three inches longer and taller and twice I'd grabbed his collar and put him in Mahri's crate, thinking I'd grabbed Mahri to stop her escaping.

Mind you, she had taught him to check out the worktops for any goodies, but he was so fussy. He always told her there was none, so she would jump up to check it out herself, only to see paper towels, newspapers, wash cloths and washing-up liquid – a veritable feast in Mahri's eyes.

In an attempt to discourage her from counter-surfing without sending her to bed every time, I filled one of those treat balls with some kibble. She rolled the ball and ran round, snatching up the bits like a duck. Next, she picked the ball up and shook it … nothing. So, she put it down, rolled it again and got some kibble. She was trying to eat the spilled kibble and guard the ball so Elle couldn't have it or any of the kibble. After several tries at this, she managed to pick the ball up and shake it so the contents spilled out. Then, the little monkey worked out how to widen the hole so more food came out. Consumed with greed, she took the ball into her crate and scoffed what was left of the kibble before proceeding to chew the hole wider just in case there were some bigger bits still trapped in the ball … and they say dogs can't reason!

19 December 2006

Mr Mac went to his agility class last night. It was the last one till mid-January and it was so foggy and cold I considered not going. When I got home, though, Mr Mac was so excited at the prospect of going to his agility class I couldn't let him down.

It was, after all, his night out, so I forced myself to get changed and go. The road to the training class was a tiny wee back road with passing places and fields on either side. The fog was so thick I could just about see the road in front of the car. Foggy weather is normally the ideal climate for non-attendance, so I was a bit sceptical as to whether anybody would turn up.

Encapsulated in thought and busy looking at the road, I hadn't realized that I'd driven into a parking place, and I nearly drove into the field behind the space, which was three feet lower than the road. I stood on the brakes just in time and came to an abrupt stop.

We arrived at the class and I put Mr Mac's best bib and tucker on – aka Chez Andrea's Christmas bandana – and we went in to the class. He trotted along proud as punch, knowing he was the 007 of Airedales and that women and dogs would be swooning at his feet.

We'd organised a little collection, so before the class began we presented the trainer and her assistant with some flowers and a gift. They couldn't believe how nice the gesture was and said that no-one had ever thought of thanking them for the time and understanding that they had given to each of us and our furry companions.

As it was party night, they suggested that we do something different. They suggested five jumps in a row. "What was different?" I questioned. They clarified that the owners were doing the jumping and the dogs were to run along on the outside under control.

Mr Mac had problems with the first jump, but once he got the idea he completed the line. After turning around, the dogs jumped as normal and the owners ran. The next event entailed a sausage being placed between each jump, where the dog must ignore the food and complete all the jumps. Mr Mac excelled himself. He didn't even glance in the direction of the sausage. Of course, for every positive effect there had to be a negative and Mr Mac could always be trusted to provide his take on the course. On the third round, Mr Mac did the first jump, doubled back and jumped it again. He chose to do this with the second and third jumps, going back over the previous ones and then over all five in a row. He cleared them all and got a round of applause because he had still ignored the sausages. We swaggered back to our seat on the edge of the arena and watched the other dogs stealing the sausages and running off searching for more … generally being out of control.

The trainer explained that the point of the exercises was not just to have fun but to demonstrate control of the dog. After that demonstration, all the dogs were allowed to run free. I chose to keep Mr Mac on the lead, as there was a young German Shepherd bitch that, for unknown reasons, he always growled at. There was also a huge one-year-old black Labrador that he constantly growled and muttered under his breath at, so better to be safe, as they say.

He sat for a while, but as the noise levels started to rise eventually, he could stand it no more and stood up and barked, not a ferocious bark, but more of a big deep, *"aarrooof aarroof!"*

I thought about letting him go and play, but common sense prevailed. He'd had a good night and I wasn't about to take a chance on spoiling it.

Mr Mac: *"Aaarroof … quiet down, you lot. I can stay at home all day if I want this kind of behaviour."*

20 December 2006

It had been mild and wet for several days, but then the temperature dropped to minus one Celsius, and this caused lots of fog and frost. The weather still hadn't improved on this particular morning and it was just starting to get light when I took the dogs out.

The first blue and lilac streaks appeared in the winter sky, and everything in the garden was covered in a three-day build-up of frost. It looked as if it had snowed; the trees had a beautiful lace-work of frozen cobwebs as if they had been decorated for Christmas.

The pups had never seen snow or this much frost before. Elle trotted about, picking each leg up really high as the frost touched her feet. Elle liked to have a mad zoom about in circles, which usually ended with her lying down in the grass; but today, she leapt up in the air and zoomed off in circles again as soon as the frost touched her tummy.

She tried lying down in several different places but, each time, the cold to her belly was too much of a shock. Elle liked things to be in order. We often thought that she suffered from obsessive compulsive behaviour. Grass certainly shouldn't be freezing one's belly. It hadn't felt like this since she moved here, so why should it start now? She pounced on the offending bit of grass, barking and growling at it, *"grrr ... yip ... grrr ... yap!"* She stomped and ripped at it with her tiny paws. *"Freeze my belly. I'll show you. Yap! Yap! Yap!"*

Mahri had stood transfixed by the goings on; she liked to wake up slowly. She'd watched Elle, her head tilting from one side to the other. *"Yawn ... what's up, Elle? Is it a mouse? Is it a rat? Another pigeon foot???"* Suddenly, she was wide awake. *"Let me help you,"* she sniggered, and pounced on Elle, shoving her aside. *"If it's food, it's mine ... all mine! And I'm not sharing cos I'm bigger than you."*

I shouted them in from the cold with the magic word, "Breakfast!"

Mahri: *"Oops, did I hear the B word? C'mon, Elle ... let's go in and eat real food that we don't have to catch. Then we can play the safari game; I'll be the lion. You can be the prey and I'll catch you and eat you ... snigger snigger!"*

Mr Mac had been charging up and down the garden, following all the smells trapped in the frost. I loved to see him running at full stretch; there was sheer delight etched on his face as he took big, powerful strides, thundering past us. He'd always had to be at the front, and, on this particular morning, Annie, our grand old duchess, had even managed to grace us with her presence.

She wandered round the garden and walked beside us as we headed back to the house. She even had a little play with Elle and was barking at her because she was lying on her nice thick fleece bed. *"Get off my bed! Bark! Bark!"* she seemed to say.

Elle responded by sticking her bum in the air and bouncing round in circles.

Annie "Do I have to move you off my bed? Bark! Bark! ... I really will! ... Bark! Bark! ... oh, got to go. Breakfast is served."

Silence at last.

I glanced at the clock and it was after 7.00am. I should have already been dressed for work. I was going to be late! I'd spent too long playing with the pups. It was more of an occupational hazard, though. Some days, you just have to do it. My work would always be waiting for me when I got there.

It was as if someone was smiling down on me when I

drove to work. The traffic was quiet and I hit all the green lights, arriving at work with five minutes to spare … and I was still smiling … and no, I had not been speeding!

24 January 2007

I'm normally up by 6.00am and out with the dogs, but today I was so warm and comfy, I stayed in bed a bit longer, listening to the woman on the radio wittering on. By the time she announced that it was 6.30am, I was already late. The wild bunch unusually was more placid and cosy than bouncing and demanding, so they got the blame for letting me languish in bed.

Brian, Len's carer, arrived. "Morning, Brian," I called over the dawn chorus greeting from the wild bunch. "What's it like out there?" I asked.

Brian, as I've explained before, was 62 and a bit of a lovey. He was very caring and helpful, but could also be a bit slow, which was irritating at times.

"Oh," he said. "Well, there's a hold-up on the Bypass. There are road works."

"I know. They've been there for three months," I said rather sharply. If I had not cut him short, his story could have gone off at a tangent and we would have ended up back in 1965 or some other point in history and I would have been late for work.

At this point, I opened the door to go out with the dogs. "Wow! Brian, you never mentioned the place was covered in snow."

"Didn't I?" he said, as I was dragged out the door by Mahri.

We had about an inch of snow; everything was smooth, white and so far untouched. It looked very pretty.

"Where did this come from?" Mahri enquired, whilst staring at me with her big eyes. *"And who left it here? I'd better eat it all before they get back."* Mahri proceeded to hoover up the snow in the same manner in which she approached her dinner. After the enormity of the task had dawned upon her, she settled for running all over the snow, making as many pawprints as possible and snuffling and nosing the snow to see what was under it. Her next strategy was to lie down on it and get Elle to help, although I don't know what this was meant to achieve. Both pups casually lay in the snow cooling off their bellies, while I, on the other hand, had cooled off a bit too quickly; the cold was seeping through my wellies and freezing my feet.

"C'mon, Mahri. Hurry up and be clever. Then you can have some nice breakfast!" As soon as the magic word was uttered, Mahri immediately headed for the house and the breakfast bar.

Elle, though, still wanted to play. Her tiny legs and feet were making a funny kicking movement in the snow. This was causing little lumps of snow to be thrown ahead of her and they turned into little snowballs. She pounced on them to catch them and looked surprised when they disappeared from sight.

I took them all back into the house and fed them. Elle's a slow eater, so I took Mahri back outside, but, this time, the novelty of the snow appeared to have worn off. She was more likely distracted with the thought that Elle might leave her some breakfast. After she'd quickly done the necessary, she rushed back to the house to check out Elle's dish.

Elle had finished eating, so I swapped leads and took her out. She only wanted to play in the snow – chasing here and there, digging up yesterday's discarded twig or anything else of interest to a Welsh Terrier.

Just as I was admiring the beauty of the rising sun, in its delicate pink and lilacs, I remembered I'd left the foil cover that I'd taken off Elle's food container on the worktop. Mahri was loose in the kitchen and that could only mean one thing – she would be after a free treat. The foil wrapper on the dish was quite thick and about the size of an oval dinner plate. I'd sort of scrunched it and laid it down. "Quick, Elle! We need to get back to the kitchen." When I rushed into the house, Mahri was already looking guilty.

I checked the worktop in the utility room where I prepare their food and no wrapper. Mahri still looked guilty and was sitting in Annie's basket. I opened her mouth. Nothing. "Should I shine a torch down there … hmmm!" I felt her throat in case the foil was stuck in there, but she wasn't coughing, so that was a good sign. Next, I searched the dog beds, pulling out all the fleeces. I searched all around the kitchen and utility room. By now, a major panic had set in and I was even double checking the work surfaces. Why? I couldn't tell you. Did I think she'd pick it up and hide it up there for fun?

I found a piece of chewed toy and went to put it in the bin and there, glinting back at me, was the foil. Without thinking, I'd screwed it up and binned it so Mahri wouldn't eat it. I've got so used to moving anything that's not screwed down out of Mahri's reach, which is surprisingly mammoth considering she's not fully grown, I don't even realize I'm doing it any more.

Talking about Mahri and her kleptomaniac genome

reminded me of some other acts of theft by my dogs, past and present.

One of my fondest memories of MacIain was when he stole a half pound of cheese. I was sure I'd left it on the chopping board when I was called to assist my husband, but on my return I couldn't see it anywhere. Then I realized that MacIain was drooling. Airedales are not generally slobbery dogs, unlike a St Bernard, for instance, so I tried to make him drop whatever he had in his mouth by command. When that failed, I attempted to open his mouth to see what it was he had. I wondered why he was putting up so much resistance to me opening his mouth. After all, this was my dog – the one who would do anything for me. I had to hold his beard with one hand and pull his upper jaw open. Only then did I find the lump of cheese with his top and bottom teeth firmly stuck in it so he couldn't drop it. Every time I let go of either the upper or lower part of his jaws in order to grab the cheese with my spare hand, his mouth would close. This was clearly a two-person job and, eventually, Len had to hold MacIain's mouth open while I prised the cheese out. MacIain never stole anything from the worktop after that little episode. For a dog not to be able to open its mouth must be quite scary.

MacIain would steal any sort of soft toy as well as cheese. Once he stole from a shop we passed. Here in UK, dogs were not allowed in shops except seeing-eye-dogs, or guide dogs for the blind, as they're sometimes called. As a child we always referred to them as blind dogs, although I never really understood why you'd call a dog that's used for helping somebody else find their way around blind. Anyway, in small towns, especially by the coast, a lot of the shops displayed goods outside their doors in baskets and you would have to walk close by them or walk on the road in order to get past.

MacIain thought these were his personal toy boxes and quite often embarrassed us by quietly lifting a small ball or fluffy toy on the way by. He'd always choose one he could hide in his mouth. Then he'd get bored carrying it and drop it. How could we identify the shop it came from and offer to pay for the goods? We couldn't. We just had to hope there were no witnesses to his crimes.

Mahri and Ellie were into stealing everything. If it went in their mouth, it was gone. Mahri, in particular, seemed to be able to hide things in her mouth. You'd hear her crunching on something, but, when you opened her mouth, there was nothing to be seen. Let her go and she resumed chewing. Hold her mouth open again, and shake her a little and out would drop a stone the size of a walnut. Where she had it hidden was anybody's guess.

McGregor never really stole things, but we always had to warn lady visitors not to leave an open bag on the floor as he would creep up sometimes, unseen and unheard, and empty the contents of their bags, laying the items one by one in a straight line on the floor. He didn't chew any of the items and, when he was done, he would lie down and watch them waiting for our response to his artwork.

It did cause a few embarrassing moments for the occasional visitor – especially the one on a diet extolling her virtuous resistance to temptation, and there in the line-up was a half-eaten bar of chocolate.

The only thing Carrie ever stole was Len's blanket. He used to take her on exercises (army games) with him and he woke one night freezing and saw Carrie had pulled his blanket over and then rolled it round her so she was nice and warm. Mr Mac stole dish towels and, on occasion, the odd glove or scarf hung on the radiator to warm.

30 January 2007

Puppies, don't you just want one? You do! Then read on.

Just to remind you of how mad you would be to contemplate the full-time care and the huge responsibility of owning a puppy, here's what my poor starving eight-month-old Airedale, Mahri, ate after breakfast today: four walnuts in their shells, one grape, two twigs, one lump of horse droppings, one worm, and two lumps of grass. She still managed to think about consuming a passing truck.

When we returned from our walk, she ate three blue washing sponges, two blue dusters, one black sock, half of a treat-filled ball, and I do mean the ball, since the contents were long gone, one collar which Elle was wearing at the time, one letter – fortunately it wasn't important – and her toothbrush.

Now you may think this poor deprived pup had been abandoned to entertain herself in an empty house for three days. Well, you'd be wrong and, for a large majority of the time, I was in the room with her. Granted, I might on the odd occasion be guilty of not being entirely focused on her 100% of the time. After all, I do need to make a coffee or prepare her next meal. Following a chase around the room, table and various other pieces of furniture, I usually managed to retrieve and count the bits of whatever it was she had attempted to eat to see how much she'd actually swallowed.

The problem was that, while I gathered up the bits, she

was off destroying another cloth or toy. The only genuine deterrent that slowed her down for a while was Elle, who was more than a tad upset when Mahri, who had already eaten through her collar, didn't stop at that. Elle herself was in danger of disappearing into Mahri's cavernous Airedale jaws. After a bit of an altercation, they both got sent to bed to cool their heels.

While Mahri went to bed without a murmur, Elle was not as quiet and grumbled, muttered, snapped and growled with every step. She just had to have the last word. Only I hadn't realized it wasn't going to be the last and it was more like, *Just wait till I get out ... you're g'ttin' it! Grrrr"*.

After 30 minutes, when I let them both out to play, Elle went straight for Mahri's collar, or was it her throat? *"Told you I'd get you! Grrr ... you thought I'd forget, grrrr, but I didn't ... grrr, yap, grrr!"*

At this point, I'd had my fill of them both and sent them back to bed again. Roll on Monday. Work and sanity.

Elle: *"If it moves, chase it."*
Mahri: *"If it moves, chase it, catch it, eat it! If it doesn't move, just eat it right away."*

13 February 2007

Last night, Elle had another little altercation with Mahri. Now Mahri is a big, lovable lump and, most times, when Elle has been at her throat snarling and growling, Mahri's just given a shake and trotted off; but last night Elle pushed

I'm trying to fix it

her luck and for no apparent reason launched an attack straight at Mahri's throat.

Sally, one of Len's carers, had both dogs on leads at the time and was waiting for me to park my car. I had to jump out and help separate them. We got them calmed down and back in the house; but 30 minutes later Elle picked another fight with Mahri. I reached for Elle's tail and missed, so grabbed Mahri's tail. "Leave it!" I yelled. That is my universal request for all or any of the dogs to stop what they are doing immediately and adopt the prone or semi-prone position. Mahri wouldn't 'leave it'. She had decided that the little upstart needed to be taught a lesson. It was only a few seconds, but it felt like minutes – I had my arms round Mahri and was prising her jaws open to make her let go. I couldn't believe Mahri had managed to grab Elle by her head when only a few seconds earlier Elle had been swinging from her throat. Elle, who had been snarling and growling, was now squealing. As soon as I got them calmed down, I put them in their crates. Elle stayed in hers all night to calm down, but poor Mahri, who'd really done nothing wrong, bless her, was allowed out once my blood pressure had returned to normal.

Later that evening, I walked the two of them in the garden on leads. They were as nice as nice can be, but as soon as they were off-lead in the kitchen, Elle started again. I got Mahri into her crate and sat Elle down to calm her, then took her through to Len. We both agreed that we couldn't allow them to go on arguing like this and it appeared that we had only two choices: one, keep them crated and only allow them out one at a time. The other choice would be to take Elle back to the breeder, as she was the one picking all the fights and being aggressive, not just with Mahri, but with me on several occasions and with Mr Mac as well.

I gave Elle some Aconite, a homeopathic remedy for fear, amongst other things. I thought I would try it to see if it would help calm her down. Aggression is usually a response to fear. I didn't want to take her back to the breeder. I felt as if I'd failed her in some way, but it would be nothing short of cruel to have her caged like a budgie all day.

I took her to the puppy class that night and hoped the trainer would shed some light on the situation. I'd heard fellow dog owners say that having a dog on a lead usually caused aggression problems; but she was doing the opposite. We thought it might be because she was bored. She wouldn't do anything you asked of her. She wouldn't even play fetch; she'd just go looking for a fight.

117

Mahri, on the other hand, would play games with you or amuse herself with her toys. Elle's favourite game was pretending to be a condor or moray eel, as she'd hide in a make-believe cave under the chair and leap out to kill anything that passed; or, to be more precise, anything that looked, smelled and acted like Mahri. The only thing I could think of was that it was Mahri coming into season that was setting her off.

25 February 2007

Mahri had grown up fast. She was playful, cheeky, a bit vociferous at times and very loving. We put Mr Mac in the kennels for a couple of days to cool his amorous advances towards Elle, so the pups had been a bit quiet, but Mahri couldn't stay quiet for long.

On Friday, I was admonishing Elle for being too rough with Mahri and pushing her around. I had even seen Elle shove Mahri over and jump on her chest. In a mock worry, I liked to tell myself that Mahri went over voluntarily as part of the game, but sometimes I wasn't so sure.

Anyway, I was down on my knees – no, I was not pleading with her to behave – giving Elle a stern scolding, when Mahri decided to break the land speed record for crossing the sitting room. Whack!!! Our heads collided with a resounding bang. I don't know which bit of her head hit mine, but I do know the pain was more than Airedale-sized, and my posh and very expensive new varifocal spectacles were now a twisted piece of metal dangling precariously from my nose and ear. Yes, just one ear. I was speechless. The pain was so great that I could not have blasphemed even if I wanted to, as I waited for my nose to drop off or my eye to fall out. Len asked if I was okay. I could tell he wanted to howl with laughter. Sally also asked, "You OK?" Again, I could detect the mirth in her voice.

Mahri stood completely still after the collision, probably in shock that I'd thwarted her record-breaking run. Elle sat completely still, staring at me. I removed my glasses and held them up to peruse the damage and see if they were beyond economic repair. "Look," I whimpered, "my glasses are all twisted." These were the gateway words everyone was waiting for so they could fall about laughing.

The dogs leapt on me to lick me better and, as my senses slowly returned to normal, I was able to stand up and survey the full extent of the damage. Mahri had managed to hit me right in the centre of my eyebrow, bending one leg of my specs upwards, and pushing them across my face into the side of my nose, twisting them so one lens touched my face and the other was in the opposite direction. It certainly felt like it, but my nose did not appear to be broken, and my eye appeared to be in the right place; although the way my eyebrow was swelling, I soon wasn't going to be seeing it. I took some Arnica pills and applied Arnica cream to the eyebrow area; even that was painful. I was a great believer in the healing ability of some homeopathic remedies. I used Arnica whenever one of my body parts had come to an abrupt halt with an inanimate object or collided with Mahri when she was trying to get somewhere ahead of me.

Have you ever noticed how, when you hurt a bit of your body, it becomes a magnet and attracts further damage from other things as well? For the next few days, if there was anything flapping about that could come into contact with my bruises, it would − dogs, dog leads, kitchen doors. Everything, it seemed, contrived to prolong the injury to my eyebrow.

I managed to have my specs straightened so I could get to work and, thanks to the Arnica, my eye did not appear to be too black, although it was still very sore. I suspected there was more bruising waiting to surface.

26 February 2007

It was decided that Mr Mac should pay a visit to the vet and return minus a little bit or bits of his anatomy. I was mindful of my earlier threats that, if he didn't behave, he would be returning to Ireland with hand luggage, so I made a big fuss of him when I left him at the surgery and told him that Len would pick him up later that day. I didn't want him to think I was leaving him there or sending him back from whence he came.

Len was asked to collect him because his car is a people carrier and it has the lift in it. It's also half the height of my car and Mr Mac doesn't like me to lift him. I didn't want him jumping in or out of my car with his new stitches.

Len nearly forgot to go to the vet's clinic, so had not returned by the time I got home from work. This was the second time I'd felt panicky as, earlier on in the day, a lady called me at the office and I hadn't recognized her name. She started her call by saying she was calling from …? But I'd already stopped listening at that point, convinced it was the vet and there was a problem with Mr Mac. They went to such pains to tell you the things that could go wrong that you were on tenterhooks all day.

I called the vet and was relieved to be told that Len had just left with Mr Mac, who was fine. I took the pups out for a walk while I waited for Len. At last, I heard the car drive into the garage and, at the same time, the pups both rushed to the door, Elle squealing and chirping. She sounded more like a budgie than a dog at times. Mahri, who had a huge deep bark, was bouncing about.

I removed my glasses. I hadn't forgotten the damage Mahri could do while in bounce mode. I got hold of her by her collar and put her in her crate until Mr Mac got in. I didn't want Mahri jumping all over him in his delicate state. I eventually managed to catch Elle, who wriggled so much I nearly dropped her and then I opened the door into the garage. She didn't want to greet Len, which was what I thought all the fuss was about; she wanted to greet Mr Mac, who was still looking a bit dazed.

I gave poor Mr Mac some Arnica, put Mahri in Elle's crate, put him in Mahri's crate, then let Mahri out to play. Moving the dogs in and out of crates was like some kind of giant Chinese chequers game. Mr Mac lay down quietly and slept for an hour and then I let him out for his tea. Mahri always calmed down when there was food on the go, so she left him in peace. He'd been a bit snappy with her recently, but that might have been because Elle had been in season.

I took them all out for a walk after their dinner. Poor Mr Mac, he definitely had a funny walk. I felt really sorry for him. He slept most of the night until Elle decided to take a shortcut and walk over him rather than round him. This wasn't the best of moves and he was very unhappy with her, which took us all by surprise. He reminded me of a lion that a cub had just climbed all over.

Mahri, the intelligent one, thought *"better safe than sorry"*, so did a belly crawl under the coffee table in order to give him a wide berth, then scampered off in the direction of the kitchen. He had a quiet night and didn't seem to bother about his stitches; but he would, of course, when the healing started and they began to itch, so I had the big lampshade collar on hand in case it was needed.

1 March 2007

Mr Mac had been fine for a couple of days without the lovely lampshade collar on, but, then, I'd been at home keeping an eye on him. He has several dog tags that jingle so I can tell where he is and what he's up to; this allowed me to hear if he was licking or nibbling the stitches. Before I left for work on Tuesday, I left strict instructions that if Mr Mac was spotted nibbling at his stitches, someone must put his lampshade on.

Len had to go out and never thought to put the collar on before he left. He was longer than expected, but when he got home all was fine and they took all the dogs out for a walk. Len switched on his computer while Brian made him a cup of tea and, in the time it took to boil some water, Mr Mac had either burst a stitch or chewed one.

Brian came out of the kitchen, saw Mr Mac covered in blood and called for Len. Now, Brian is the person looking after Len, but it was Len who had to take control of the situation. Len called the vet to say they were on their way. Brian got the car lift down so Len could get in the car and then put a big blanket in for Mr Mac. Getting Mr Mac in to the car was no small feat. Mr Mac would not be pulled, pushed or lifted by me, so Brian had no chance, especially with his 'lovey nature'. I don't know how, but he eventually got him in and rushed off to the vet, four miles up the road. Len had called the vet's to let them know he was on his way as it was nearly closing time. He told them he thought it was an arterial bleed, so they called their head vet back to the surgery.

When Len got there, Brian rushed in with Mr Mac, then went back to ensure Len got out of the car without plunging off the lift before it was lowered to the ground. The vet explained that Mr Mac would need to have an emergency operation and he had to sign the papers so they could go ahead. I think it was more of an agreement to pay rather than an agreement to let them operate.

When I got home from work, Mr Mac was not at the door to greet me, but Len was. I looked round expecting Mr Mac to wander through. "Where is Mr Mac?" I asked. Len started to tell me the story and I started to grin, convinced it was one of his little jokes. "You can wipe the grin off your face," he said. "I'm not joking."

It was at that point I noticed Brian on his knees cleaning the hall carpet and realized that Len was not joking, and, judging from the volume of blood on the carpet, had been somewhat parsimonious with the truth. I quickly changed and helped Brian clean up; it would give me something to do while I worried about my special boy. We had to clean the car, the garage floor and the kitchen walls. Poor Brian; he said he'd never seen anything like it. It was like a scene from the *Texas Chainsaw Massacre*.

The vet phoned at 7.00pm to say Mr Mac was fine and

that they wanted to keep him in hospital for a couple of days because he had suffered a major bleed.

Thank goodness Len was home or I might have come home to an empty dog.

3 March 2007

Mr Mac was released on Friday. His walk was still a bit stiff-legged and he was a bit quiet, but he was happy to be beside me again and leaned on me at every opportunity. He was on painkillers, antibiotics and something to keep him a little bit sleepy. After two incisions, the skin was a bit tight, so the vets didn't want him bouncing about.

The buster collar, or his lampshade, as I called it, had to stay on for ten days, no matter what. Mr Mac always was a bit skittish and he was ten times worse with the collar on. He bounced off every doorpost, pinned Mahri to the wall a couple of times, pinned me to the wall several times, dug up some mud and split the collar. It was a nice new see-through one when he came home but, after a day or so, it was sporting some go-faster stripes made from silver duct tape.

I had to take Len's car to the garage on Saturday, so Mr Mac got to go with me and sit in the garage office for two hours being petted and spoiled by the office girls while I waited for the car to be fixed.

This meant Elle and Mahri could run around like wild things while we were out. Mahri had always run up and down the length of the kitchen, as well as running up the wall in order to about turn and either jump on Mr Mac or drop-kick him on the way past. She loved his new collar because she could slide off it on the way by and he couldn't get to her. She was such a hooligan.

On Sunday, I took the pups for a long walk to tire them so Mr Mac could be left in peace, but the pups' recovery rate was so fast. After a swift forty winks, they're up and ready to go again. The best way I ever found to keep them quiet for ten minutes was to put the toaster on. It worked every time. They would sit waiting for the toast to pop up, and then they would wait for it to cool so they could have their treat. I've noticed on the odd occasion that, if I sat the toaster on the worktop, with nothing in it, just in full view, the result could sometimes be immediate obedience.

Now all I needed to do was figure out a way to take it on our walks!

5 March 2007

Mahri was proving to be just as big a clown as Mr Mac when it came to agility training. Mahri's obsession with food was much more helpful, though. On her first week, she only did some weave and low jumps; but this week she was introduced to the rigid tunnel.

I showed her the entrance. "Tunnel, Mahri! Tunnel!" She went in and I ran to the other end to call her. *"Oops, I thought you were coming in here too,"* she thought, as she did a quick about-turn and came back out.

The trainer tried to hold Mahri and send her through when I called, but Mahri was struggling so much the trainer thought it best to let her go. I led Mahri to the opposite end of the tunnel and showed her the treat I'd dropped just inside. Gulp! The treat was gone, so it was back to the start end of the tunnel. While she sniffed around inside, looking for a treat again, I ran to the other end and beckoned, "C'mon, Mahri!" Through the tunnel she trotted and got her treat when she came out at the other end.

The next obstacle was the tyre. Mahri dug her heels in and refused to move. *"No way. Put my head through there; are you nuts? Think again, my friend!"*

The trainer once again came to my assistance and held the lead while I walked round to the opposite side of the tyre and held out a treat. It was Frikadeller. This is a sort of German pork burger, one of Mahri's favourites. *"Hmm!! Why didn't you say? I can reach through and get the treat ... oh, and I suppose I could just step through to make it even easier to reach."*

The jumps had been kept low because Mahri was not fully grown and we didn't want to damage her joints. Mahri was just like Mr Mac when he started agility – she didn't even break her stride to walk over the bars. This meant we had to raise them a little bit so she at least stepped over them.

With the weave, she was not too bad, aside from trying to gnaw my fingers going after the entire treat before getting to the end of the obstacle. It had taken Mr Mac several weeks to deal with the seesaw and I expected Mahri to take just as long. She would gladly walk up to the middle of it and then jump off, usually because there was only my fingers left and she was gnawing on them. Sometimes, from the higher viewpoint, she could see things that might be more fun, like a forgotten tennis ball, which she probably thought she could grab before anyone noticed.

She'd already forgotten I was on the other end of the lead and pulled my dodgy shoulder several times; memories of early days with Mr Mac came flooding back. She'd get used to the see-saw in time. When we reached the chute, I'd expected her to resist, but she went straight in to look for a treat and trotted through at what would be described as a deliberate pace rather than a panicky run. I was quite proud of my little fuzzy-faced girl. But, as they say, pride comes before a fall, and Mahri was always the one to bring you back down to earth with a bump. After emerging triumphant from the chute, she felt obliged to walk along on top of it and then back through the chute, just to prove she could do it by herself.

The only downside of the class was that we appeared to be ostracised once again. Several of the dogs did not like Mahri, which surprised me. Even a Lakeland cross that got on well with Mr Mac was very aggressive towards her. Although Mahri would take a lot of stick from Elle, she made it clear that she would not suffer it from any other dog, so we had to sit out of reach on the opposite side of the room.

Strangely, the big black Labrador, Hugo (aka Marley), who is only 18 months old but big, bouncy and in your face, actually got on well with Mahri, but he had the right idea: sniff first, then decide. Koffi, the Lakeland cross, whose peace-keeping effort ended with his name, came at Mahri's face, snapping and snarling.

On the plus side, I used this distance to enforce some other training which would help her with her agility. I made her lie down and placed a treat on the floor just out of reach so she could look but not touch till I gave her the command. Surprisingly, she was very focused, but then it did involve food. Sometimes, I made her sit for the same exercise, just to mix things up a bit. This helped with her training for getting in and out the car, as she had a tendency to over-excitedly jump before I even had the door open properly.

Mahri: *"Are we going again next week? That was fun ... so many treats as well."*

9 March 2007

It was the annual Crufts Dog Show this weekend. We liked to go on Terrier day and meet our friends, Roy and Marion, who were the breeders of all the Airedales we've owned. Just for a change, the Airedale judging was on at 1.00pm. It was normally at 9.00am and we would miss it because the earliest we could get there was around 11.00am. It's a two-hour drive and it takes two hours to get Len up and ready to go out.

We got to see Mahri's brother take best puppy in the breed ring and her sister was placed fourth in puppy bitch. Her brother was stunning; Marion took him into the ring last and as soon as she entered you heard the spectators gasp. He had a dark walnut brown and shiny black coat. Mahri and her sister were much more grizzled in comparison. You could just tell who was going to win and everyone cheered when he did, so he was obviously a very popular choice.

Of course, there's nothing like seeing dozens of well-groomed Airedales to make you want to get home and make your own prize Airedale look every bit as stunning. So, on Sunday I took Annie's undercoat out and clipped her. She was nearly eleven years old and was too old to be bothered with hand stripping. Next, Elle and Mahri got their undercoats taken out and I stripped out a bit of their top coats. I spent six hours on the three dogs and my battery was running on empty; Mr Mac would have to wait till the following weekend.

I paraded the dogs in front of Len. Annie was slightly patchy, but looked very good, and Len said he wouldn't be ashamed to walk down the road with her. That was a real compliment coming from Len, because he used to do all the dog stripping and clipping. He thought Mahri's coat was coming along very well, even though I'd managed to make a dent in her head. It must have been a clump of puppy fluff that came out, leaving a patch that looked as if I'd gone too deep with clippers – only I hadn't used clippers.

I'd managed to fluff up Elle's face so it started to look like a 'Westie's' face on a tiny little body; it still needed a lot more work. The trouble was that Elle wriggled so much it made things very difficult. She would stand quietly on the grooming table so I could do her body, back legs, and cut all her claws. However, as soon as I started combing her face and front legs, she would turn her head, pull her foot away and try to turn round, most probably out of boredom.

Mahri was very good when it was her turn to be groomed. She was always happy to sit on the table while I did her face and chest, and even stood for me while I combed her legs and trimmed her claws. The only time she would turn her head away was when I started to clean her ears. She was not very keen on that.

14 March 2007

I took 'Miss Goody Two Shoes' aka 'Evil Elle' to the puppy class last night. She should have been awarded an Oscar for her performance; she certainly had everyone fooled, including me.

When I got home from work, Elle had been on the lead by Len's side all day, while Mahri was free to run around. Apparently, Elle had been good until the moment I walked in and Mahri jumped all over me to say welcome home. I should mention at this point that Elle was on a twelve-foot extending lead. Elle utilized the full lead extension capacity and charged at Mahri. Len reckoned that, because there had been no trouble all day, *I* must have been the root cause and hence suggested that perhaps Elle should stay and *I* should be put up for re-homing. He was joking (I think!).

I quickly got changed and sliced up the sausage I'd had to buy from the canteen at work as we'd used all the ones we'd prepared the day before. The look of disbelief on the canteen lady's face was very much a picture when I asked for a single sausage and no bun because it was for my dog training class. Everyone thought I was trying to cheat on my diet.

Elle squealed all the way out to the car and scrambled to get in before I even had a chance to lift her. Then ... oh, yes, you guessed it ... she squealed all the way to the class and only stopped when I opened the training hall door. The class had started, so I joined the circle of pups walking to heel.

Round she went, trot, trot, trot. Sit, stay, down, trot, about turn, trot. I was turning blue holding my breath waiting for her to show her true colours. Next we had to change dogs and make a strange dog sit. The lady that got Elle said, "Oooh, she's so good." I opened my eyes wide in amazement. This lady had a perfect little Shitzu; as regal as the queen, the little dog never did anything wrong and she thought Elle was good? Hmm! Next we had to drop the dog leads. Elle stood looking around at all the scary pups, most of them about her size. She put on such a good act of being shy and timid as she ran and hid behind a couple of people's legs and peeked round to see if another dog was going to come near her. When the playtime was over, I only called her once and she ran right up to me and sat down. I nearly fainted with shock.

The class finished and the trainer congratulated everyone. He turned to speak to me. "I thought you said you had a problem with Elle?" That was the cue for Elle to revert to her normal self. She snapped and growled at several of the pups; the ones she'd been hiding from ten minutes earlier. The little witch!

I chatted with the trainer and he confirmed our thoughts that two bitches of close age spelled trouble. His thoughts were to get the least dominant one spayed, which would most likely be Mahri, but not the other, and this would sort out the pecking order as Elle never has a problem with Annie, who was spayed a lot of years ago.

We were going to have to wait until Mahri had had a full season, plus three months on top, as this was the best time for the operation. Mahri was perhaps going through the early phase coming into season, and maybe not. It was hard to know for sure. She was definitely giving off some smell which was driving Elle a little bit crazy, so, until the next stage could be resolved, Elle was resigned to being on a lead in the house and would be following me around like my own shadow. Mahri could roam free unless nobody was in the room to supervise and then it was the crate hotel for them both.

Len had approached a charity that helped train dogs for the disabled. They'd train your dog with you. He was keen on the idea of training Mahri because she was such a friendly dog, but that meant I was left to try and do something with Elle. A small dog agility course to use up some of her energy was definitely in order to quell the aggression we assumed was brought on by boredom.

20 March 2007

We kept Elle on her lead all last week; no games of tug or chase. She had to walk everywhere Len or I went and sit or lie down at our feet. She was only allowed a toy when we said she could have it and, because the lead could be extended, we could let her wander off and call her back with an encouraging tug on the lead. Mahri, who never held a grudge, was free to play with Mr Mac and all was calm.

Over the weekend we let Elle off the lead for short intervals and each time she was well-behaved. On the Sunday night, because Elle had shown no signs of aggression for several days, she was allowed to join in with Mr Mac and Mahri playing chase. I kept a close eye on her as she ran back and forth, hanging on to Mr Mac's back leg and growling for all she was worth. Mr Mac eventually tired of her attentions and grabbed her by the back of the neck and laid her head on the floor. This happened in a nano-second.

She was quiet and he was very softly growling. He kept her like that for half a minute and then released her without any reaction. She simply trotted off and picked up a toy to play with. Mahri was laid down at the far end of the room, just watching.

Once Elle had wandered off, Mahri decided to have her mad half-hour zoom, back and forth from the sitting room through the dining room, to the hall, followed by a handbrake turn in the kitchen and then back again, leaping over Elle and bouncing off Mr Mac; her tail was like a little fat rudder whipping from side to side, back and forth. Zoom! Zoom!

Mr Mac, who was now dizzy from all this motion, grabbed her on the way past, just like he did with Elle, and she lay down immediately. Well, her head and shoulders did, but her bum was kept in the air. Mr Mac just growled softly, but sweet nothings they were not. She eventually lay completely down. Mr Mac, who was from this day forward to be known as Mr Caesar Milan Mac, let go and walked over and sat at my feet. He looked at me and smiled his typical Airedale smile. *"Now you've seen the right way to control the brats!"*

Every night, Elle would lie in Annie's bed till 9.00pm and then she would silently creep into the room to sit at my feet, looking at Len first, then me. If I ignored her, she'd put her front feet on the couch and nod her head at the big cushion. As soon as the cushion was put on Len's knee, I would lift Elle on to his knee and she'd settle down to watch the TV for the night. She looked so cute lying on the cushion with her front legs crossed – a regular little diva. The only thing that she was short of was a tiara.

My Airedales loved lying around the floor like discarded

clothes. They appeared to be asleep, but were really guarding the throne. One little yelp from Elle and they were on their feet at her side – well, Annie takes a little longer, bless her – *"You rang, Madame? Oh, you don't like this programme ... Okay then, we'll bark at it till they change channels. ... Is there anything else your highness requires?"*

Last night, we were enjoying a UK police drama, but Elle was not. She stood up on Len's knee, turned her back on the TV and flopped on to the cushion with a big sigh to snooze until something more interesting was on offer. She was definitely more a fan of *CSI Miami* or *Bones*. I'm starting to wonder if she was a pathologist in her past life.

22 March 2007

Elle, Mahri and Mr Mac spent the whole day with Len being as good as gold; then Mahri, for no apparent reason, decided to rip the paper off the wall in the hall. And was it a discreet corner? No, not when Mahri's concerned ... it had to be a foot-square lump right opposite the door, so it was the first thing you'd see on entering the hall.

Len chased her into her bed, but it was too late; she'd already swallowed the paper. She felt the wrath of Len's best sergeant-major voice. It was a verbal gale about how fed up he was with her destroying the house. Mahri just sat staring up at him with big eyes: *"OK, I won't do it again ... till next time at least."*

Len pulled back on his wheelchair's joystick and crashed straight into the fridge. Then he pushed forward and crashed into her crate, getting himself stuck in the process. The stubborn so-and-so was determined to get out of the space without my assistance, even though it was clear he didn't have enough turning space. Crash! The fridge door got it again. Meanwhile, he muttered about the dog destroying the house and how she could stay in her bed for the rest of the night.

"Yes," I said. "Look at the state of the place … just go straight to your bed and stay there cos I'm fed up with YOU destroying the house."

He saw the funny side of things. "It's all her fault the fridge is damaged," he said. The fridge looked like it had been banger-racing. *Hmmm, maybe that could be a new hobby for Len.*

I took Elle off to the puppy class and once again she was perfection personified. She was allowed off-lead with a Norfolk Terrier, a Cavalier Spaniel and a Labrador cross that were all about nine months old. The first thing Elle did was run up to all the spectators – mums, spouses, etc – and jump up at their knees to say hello. After she'd been round everyone, including the trainer, she trotted round the room taking in the smells. I called on her: "Elle, come!" – *trot, trot, trot* – and she came right up to me, got her treat and sat there.

I left her to play a little longer so she learned that coming when called did not always mean the end of play time. I called her three times and over she came. When it was time to go home, I cuddled her, praised her, and gave her lots of treats. What more could a little dog want?

After we got home, she played with Mr Mac while I told Len how good she was and then we let Mahri out to play. No problems so far. *Good.* It was going to be a peaceful night.

After dinner, Elle came and lay behind my feet, just

touching Mahri, who was lying at the other side of my feet, and there they stayed till 9.00pm when, like clockwork, Elle indicated that it was time for her to be on Len's knee.

Rather smugly, I thought that we might have turned a corner, but that was a bad thought – a bad, bad thought, a situation-provoking thought – because at 6.00am the following day, in the snow and hail, I was rolling around in the paddock trying to hang on to Elle and calm her down, keep an eye on Mahri, whose lead I'd let go, and shouting at Mr Mac, while hoping that nothing was broken and my heart would manage to keep beating … at least long enough for me to get them all indoors.

It had all started well enough. Their leads were on for the walk down the paddock; but then, on the way back to the house, Elle grabbed her own lead and started to growl at it and shake it; she did this sometimes. On this occasion, it was Mahri who upset the apple cart – *"Oooh…this looks like fun"*, she appeared to say – and she grabbed Elle's lead and shook it vigorously, rattling Elle from side to side.

"Enough!" I shouted at Mahri. "Leave!"

Mahri's response was to shake the leash harder; Elle growled louder and shook her end harder, with Mahri doing the same thing at her end. Holding both leads with one hand, I reached down to open Mahri's mouth to make her let go of the lead; but, at that moment, Elle decided she wasn't playing nicely any more and launched herself at Mahri's throat. Unfortunately, because I was holding Mahri's mouth open to make her let go of the lead, Elle managed to stick her head in it. Oops! This made Elle really mad.

While I was trying to separate the two dogs and keep all my fingers and any other appendages from total destruction,

Mr Mac – aka the cavalry – arrived. He chased Mahri round my legs; Mahri was also chasing or being chased by Elle, snapping and snarling. I had let Mahri's lead go in order to pick Elle up, but, with the restriction gone, Mahri was off, BOING! BOING! Across the paddock she bounced, leaving me being spun like a spinning top from the unravelling lead. I, on the other hand, was sent crashing to the ground. The first thing I did was glance round to see if anyone had witnessed my predicament. It was embarrassing enough without thinking that somebody else had caught sight of the event.

I sat quietly on the wet grass, talking to Elle, pretending that it was part of the plan; then I picked us both up and hobbled towards the house. Mr Mac rounded Mahri up and brought her in with him. Of course, by this time, her lead was now tangled round her legs. I must have been concussed or something because … *stupid me*! … I bent down with Elle still in my arms to remove the lead from Mahri's legs so she wouldn't break a leg, but this was the cue for Elle and Mahri to kick-off again. … Argh!

All this had happened before I'd even had a coffee. Luckily, there was no damage done to the pups or me, although I could confess to feeling a bit stiff. Once the food was on the floor, the fracas was forgotten. Elle went off for a snooze on Len's bed, Mahri sat begging Brian to drop some of Len's breakfast and I went to work.

"You're in charge, Mr Mac," I shouted, as I shut the door. Because I'm sure I've been relegated to bottom of the pack. Caesar Milan would have a field day here.

26 March 2007

I arrived home from work last night to find Len's carer Brian wandering somewhat aimlessly up and down the road. I was immediately suspicious. I opened the car window. "Have you lost Mr Mac?" I asked, with a fast-disappearing sense of humour, "or Mahri?"

"Well," he said, and started to give me one of his long-winded explanations. The summarized version was that he couldn't find Mr Mac and he'd now lost Len as well. I turned the car about and headed in the direction of the grain store.

We often walked along a footpath that ran alongside the silos. There was a field between our garden and this path and, although we had a high hedge, Mr Mac could see the path from the garden. I saw a young girl who looked around fifteen or sixteen. "Excuse me. Have you seen a black and tan hairy dog wandering around?"

"Does it look like a husky?" she replied.

"Well … no, more like a teddy bear." Mental note, must keep photo of the dogs in glove compartment.

"Well, if it looks like a husky, I've seen one over by some porta-cabins."

These cabins are about two miles in the opposite direction and, fortunately, further away from the busy by-pass. Off I went, just in case this girl had seen Mr Mac. I drove around, asking people in their gardens, passing horse riders and cyclists, but no-one had seen him.

I returned to the house and interrogated Len. "Why did you have him out of the house without his lead? You know what he's like!"

And as for Brian, he will tell you the dog was there

two seconds ago, but time meant nothing to Brian. Twenty minutes could have elapsed since the last time he noticed if there was a dog at his side. I called the police station to report Mr Mac AWOL. There were no reports of a dog running around or one that had been picked up by a dog warden, so I changed out of my work clothes and into my tracksuit and wellies. I jumped into my car and drove back down the road towards the grain store. I stopped to ask another person, but he was a migrant worker and he didn't speak any English. I drove up and down some of the little access roads to other warehouses in the area, which also allowed me a view over the fields. No dog could be seen and I returned to the house. A truck was now blocking our drive, so I parked by the kerbside opposite the drive. I crossed the road to tell Len that I was going to take a walk down a drove road to see if Mr Mac was loitering on that path or in the nearby fields.

Just as I turned to walk down the road, I heard the familiar jingle of dog tags. The first thing I did was check the lead in my hand. I was holding the metal clips, so the noise didn't come from me. I turned and looked back. Len and Brian were standing at the gate with Mr Mac sitting beside them as if he'd been there all the time and we had just failed to notice him. I called him and he bounded over to greet me.

Len and Brian hadn't even noticed his return. My first instinct was to yell at him for making me worry, but he had come back, so I put him in the day kennel for an hour while I called the police to report his safe return. I also had to let all my neighbours know that Mr Mac was off the missing dog list.

Needless to say, there was no agility class for Mr Mac

that night. When I did let him into the house, Elle gave him such a telling off I didn't need to say a word to him. He stayed very close to me for the rest of the evening.

I've no idea where he was and can only assume he had got into someone's garden and found it more interesting than ours. When I searched for a missing dog, I generally called his name and hoped for a response. When Brian searched, well – picture a sixty-two-year-old rather camp gentleman rushing hither and thither, flapping his arms and wringing his hands, saying, "Oh dear, I seem to have lost Mr Mac."

Mind you, it didn't help that Len told him that, as he'd lost my dog, he would have to tell me and I was probably going to rip his lungs out.

I was pretty sure that I'd given the right instructions when I left the house. I'm not sure how else the order of the day could have been made clearer. "Mr Mac does not get out of the house without a lead, and that means him on one end and someone on the other."

28 March 2007

With all the concern over Mr Mac and his little walkabout, we hadn't noticed that Mahri wasn't quite herself. Well, we did, but thought it was a reaction to our rushing around searching for Mr Mac. I had been a little bit concerned the day before when Mahri had gone from manic to lethargic in just seven hours. When this happens, you can only watch and wait to see what might develop. It is no good rushing off to the vets when the only symptom is, " She's been a bit quiet".

Mahri appeared frightened of her food and, although she was eating, she had lost her enthusiasm. Usually, she inhaled ingested whatever was put in front of her in a matter of seconds and water would have been consumed in great snatches as she raced past the bowl. At other times she would have had her face in the bowl up to her ears, with water being flung about all over the place. Now she was sipping tentatively, as if expecting a monster to emerge from the depths and eat her. She only wanted to sit or lie down and sleep.

Len offered her a treat. In her healthy state he'd have lost a hand, if not his arm, in her eagerness to snatch it; but, instead, she stretched forward and took it so nicely that we nearly fainted in disbelief. Then, Sally, Len's carer, arrived and Mahri never even got out of bed to say hello. That was very unusual, because Mahri loved Sally and always gave her a big bouncy welcome. All these little incidents by themselves were nothing to worry about, but the combination caused me a great deal of concern. I booked into the next available appointment at the vet clinic.

I actually thought the vet might think me a little silly for saying my dog wasn't herself and had no other notable symptoms, but he didn't, and we found out she had kennel cough, even though the cough had not really developed yet.

She had to be kept quiet and was given an injection, along with some pills. The vet said he'd call me the next day to see if she had improved and would then see her again in eight days. I also treated her with Drosera, a homeopathic remedy for kennel cough, just to make sure she was well on her way to recovery.

The Wild Bunch was not quite so wild this week

because Mahri, the ring leader, was confined to the house and garden.

25 April 2007

Len decided we needed a break, and the dogs could do with a rest from us. They would appreciate us more on our return, he argued. He decided on a little cottage by the Thames near Oxford. We could walk to the village pub for our evening meals, and sit and watch the world go by. We had a lovely holiday wandering round a warm and sunny Oxford. We walked along the banks of the Thames, and visited quaint little villages for cream teas, apple pies and blueberry muffins. As with all holidays, we ate too much and did too little, so I was ready to get back to the hustle and bustle of the Wild Bunch.

The dogs were in kennels while we were away and I had really missed the little monkeys. In our absence, they were hand-stripped and bathed; they looked so smart upon our return. Even my little ugly duckling, Mahri, looked beautiful; she really had turned into a swan. Mr Mac always looked so handsome with his short back and sides and 'Evil Elle' looked less like a Tasmanian devil and more like a Welsh Terrier, albeit a diminutive one.

Elle was nearly eleven months old. I thought she would have been fully grown by this time, but she seemed so tiny compared to the ones we met when out and about. She loved Len. He was the only one she hadn't savaged and she would take on any and everything that tried to come between her and her chosen one. Every night at 9.00pm she would look at me, then the cushion, and nod in Len's direction; she made it crystal clear that she wanted to be on his knee for a snooze or to watch the television, her other favourite pastime.

Len was out last night. At 9.10pm, I made a cup of tea and began to wonder where Elle was, because I couldn't see her. She wasn't on any of the dog beds or under the tables. I told myself to forget it. She couldn't be lost if she was in the house and I went to sit down in front of the TV. Lo and behold, there she was, clinging precariously to the cushion she normally sat on when on Len's knee! Only because it was leaning against the back of the couch and she knew the furniture was out of bounds, but the cushion wasn't; she was lying almost vertically, trying to snooze on her cushion and not put her feet on the couch. She reminded me of a koala bear. Taking pity on her, I put the cushion on my knee so she could watch the TV in comfort. Elle, the diva that

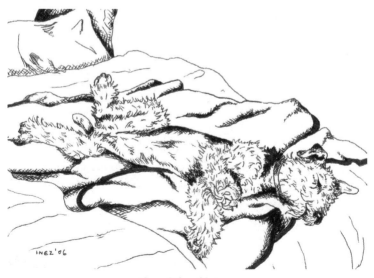

Ah, a life of leisure

143

she was, just crossed her front paws and settled down to watch the detective programme.

Mahri was one year old on the first of May. She looked so grown up now and, because she was reasonably obedient, we decided to let her off-lead in the big paddock with Mr Mac, hoping that, if we called one, both would come. It was really great to watch the pair of them running like the wind.

Mahri was really fast and because of her shorter back could turn on a sixpence; she was much faster and more agile than Mr Mac. She whipped her tail about and, when she ran at full speed, she carried it with a funny bend in the middle, as if it was broken.

Next, we decided to be really brave and let Elle loose. The three of them ran round in circles, jumping and rolling on the newly-cut grass. They were only allowed ten to fifteen minutes of this new game; as soon as one started to lose interest, we called them all back and put them on their leads, just in case they thought the field next door was a more interesting playground.

Mahri's interest in counter-surfing had been diminishing, probably because every time we caught her with her feet on one of the counters or worktops or caught her with the evidence that she'd been up, it was straight to her crate. No other words and no more chances for the night. Then we'd give the others a biscuit, so she realized that she'd get more biscuits by not looking for them on the worktops.

The Wild Bunch now had the run of the house, with the exception of the bedrooms, for most of the day and night. Mahri by choice went to bed around 10.00pm; she would get up, go to the kitchen, re-arrange the fleeces in Annie's bed and make herself comfy. When I took Elle through to

144

put her in her crate for the night, Mahri was usually lying on her back, legs in the air, half-in and half-out of the basket. She covered her eyes so I couldn't see her and send her to her crate. One night, she looked so cute I left her there and shut the kitchen door. In the morning she was still in the basket and nothing was touched, so from that day onwards she was allowed to sleep in the basket and had the run of the kitchen and laundry room. It was good to be back to normal again. I'd almost forgotten what it was like to be able to trust a dog not to eat the house while I slept!

26 April 2007

A couple of nights ago, I took Mr Mac off-lead and Mahri on-lead out for their pre-bedtime walk. Mr Mac always went a bit wild and grabbed Mahri's back leg and generally annoyed her because he knew she couldn't get to him while on the lead.

I'd chased him a couple of times and told him to go back to the house for being too rough. He kicked his heels in the air and trotted off to inspect the *Leylandii* hedge. I thought I heard a little yelp and looked round to see where the noise came from. Mr Mac was running round the garden, snapping at thin air, and he ran back to the hedge and gave another yelp.

I walked towards him to see what the problem was and he met me half-way with a big hedgehog in his mouth. It must have been the size of a football. He put it down in front of me and was about to paw it. "Aaahhhh … leave it! It's a nice hedgehog," I advised him. Then I grabbed his collar and wrestled him away, while trying to reel Mahri in on her extending lead like a fish caught on a line, and who, by now, was jumping up and down on her back legs, howling because she wanted to play with the hedgehog.

I eventually had both dogs by their collars, one either side of me, walking up the garden on their hind legs like dancing bears. I got them into the house and checked Mr Mac, who was frothing and spitting and gulping down lots of water. I assumed he'd been jagged by one or more of the hedgehog's spines. I gave him some Arnica to help with the pain, but he still slavered for a long time.

I went back out to make sure the hedgehog was okay; it was still curled up in a tight ball. There was one small round, wet patch on its back. I assumed this was where Mr Mac had slobbered on it. When I went back out an hour later to check, it was gone.

Now, you'd think that between an Airedale and me, one of us would have the sense not to repeat the exercise. Well, it appears not.

Yesterday was clearly Elle's night for the brain, because I did the same thing again. Fortunately, it was not so dark. I had Elle and Mahri on the leads while Mr Mac was inspecting the perimeter fence. I saw him poke his head through the fence and shouted at him. His only response was to push further into the hedge. I kept shouting and walking towards him, but he kept wriggling and pushing under the fence. Eventually, all you could see was his tail wagging back and forth.

As I got close to him, out he popped with the big hedgehog in his mouth and was positively grinning from ear to ear. I could tell that from the look in his eyes, not by his mouth, as it was full of hedgehog. He presented me with the gift, his tail wagging sixty to the dozen.

"Well, you said it was a nice hedgehog and then threw it back in the hedge ... there's gratitude."

Once again, I was embroiled in a wrestling match, trying to drag two recalcitrant Airedales and a Welsh Terrier back to the house, hoping the hedgehog was undamaged and would make a fast exit when the coast was clear.

While the dogs busied themselves with chews, I went out to check the poor wee beastie. As before, he was still curled up, but with not a mark on him. And Mr Mac was fine; he had obviously learned very quickly how to pick up a hedgehog without getting stabbed. Bad lesson! I didn't want him scaring them away because they ate the slugs in my garden, which saved my plants from certain death. And hedgehogs are quite cute, so I liked having him around.

22 May 2007

My little furry friends had been so good these last few weeks that I was almost convinced someone had switched them when they were in the kennels. Finally, the novelty of being back home wore off and their true Terrier nature could no longer be suppressed.

On Friday night, Elle and Mahri were running around playing chase with a toy, round and round the table. Elle's little high-pitched bark nearly shattered the glass, not to mention damaged our eardrums, and Mahri's thunderous boom of a bark almost caused the old air raid sirens to be set off.

Then, silence. Hmmm ... they've puffed themselves out at last, I thought, as I enjoyed my cup of tea in peace and quiet. When I got up to put my cup back in the kitchen, I had to walk past the dining room table. I casually looked under it to see if they were asleep. … Eeeek! I saw the reason they had been so quiet. They'd metamorphosed into beavers and the two of them were chewing through the leg of one of my dining room chairs!

"Bed!!! DO NOT PASS GO. DO NOT COLLECT £200.00. AND NO GET OUT OF JAIL CARD!!"

Mahri got up and went to bed without a backward glance. Elle went to Len, thinking he would protect her from the wicked witch who was trying to spoil her fun. When I eventually caught her, she went to bed as well.

It seemed really strange without the pups running around for the rest of the night. With the next day being a Saturday, I was looking forward to my long lie-in. Usually, 7.00am is a late start for me; but, because the pups had been sent to bed early, they were wide awake at 5.00am. That was me up and out walking the pups before leaving them to play around in the kitchen while I tided up. There was little point trying to catch a bit more sleep now, as I was wide awake.

Brian arrived at 7.45am to look after Len. He came in, said hello to all the dogs and chatted to me for a while. I don't know what came over him, but he picked up a bit of cardboard, opened the back door and turned to me, saying, "I'll just put this in the bin."

"Noooo! Shut the door!" I shouted at Brian. "Elle, come here," I screamed, whilst trying to perform a flying rugby tackle in an attempt to catch Elle.

I was too slow to catch her and I think I also terrified Brian into the bargain. Elle stood in the drive with a bemused look on her face. At this point, Brian should have shut the door, but, instead, he opened it wider. He stood at the door like a butler welcoming high-ranking guests. "In you come, Elle," he said, as he theatrically swept his arm through the open door to encourage Elle's return to the warmth of the kitchen. Elle completely ignored him, but Mahri took this as an invitation to join Elle in the garden and she performed a flying leap past him, closely followed by Mr Mac, who clearly thought this was a new game of chase.

I sprang past Brian, calling, "Mr Mac! Come here, Mr Mac! C'mon, Mahri!" I hoped that if I got one into the house, the other two would follow.

Brian then made his third big mistake that morning; he decided to walk up the drive to the gate. "Noooo! Don't walk to the gate!" I yelled at him.

It was already too late; the three dogs had beaten him to the gate, which Brian had left open after his arrival; in hindsight, *that* was probably the first mistake. The three dogs ran out the gate and up the street, with me in hot pursuit.

Brian, trying to make amends, came to the gate and shouted at Mr Mac, who did an about-turn and returned to the garden, followed by Elle; but Mahri thought it was much more fun to race round several cars that had fortunately stopped. Then she took off down the street, running into a neighbour's garden, where I was able to corner her and grab her collar before she got back out on to the road again. Just as I turned to head for home, Elle appeared. She must have evaded Brian and darted across the road again.

Somehow, I managed to get the two struggling pups back to the house, where Mr Mac was sitting by the door waiting for me. They were sent to their crates to contemplate the dangers of the open road, or more likely why Mr Mac got a treat and they did not.

The rest of the day passed without incident until 6.00pm. I had them all milling about in the kitchen waiting for their dinner when Brian gave me a repeat performance of his morning's stupidity. Fortunately, I managed to grab Elle, but I still had to chase Mahri round another neighbour's garden before running her into a corner so I could capture her.

On the Sunday, to avoid further episodes of the dogs running free and to burn off some of their energy, I took Mr Mac and Elle for a long walk. For an hour or more, we trekked up and down country paths, and, because of the rain we'd had for the last couple of weeks, it was all a bit messier than I'd thought it was going to be.

Some of the paths were very overgrown with weeds and others filled with huge muddy puddles. I ended up carrying Elle over the puddles because some were so big I could have passed my swimming test in them. When I got back I hosed the mud off my wellies and Mr Mac's feet, and then took Mahri out for a similar walk. Only this time I returned by the road to avoid the mud.

Were they tired? Not one bit … not even a smidgin of visible fatigue. They still had enough energy to eat the kennel door while I cut the grass, and then run around the garden chasing birds. When I called time up and everyone indoors, they pretended they were deaf and carried on running round the garden. I eventually coaxed them into the house with biscuits. The next time they were out in the garden they weren't allowed to run free until they remembered what 'come here' means. I didn't even mind if it wasn't an immediate response, just as long as they responded without going via the by-pass and the next town.

29 May 2007

We had a long bank holiday weekend and I had planned a nice barbeque; but, because an Atlantic storm blew in, the only aroma we were treated to was damp dog, damper dog and sopping wet dog. The little hooligans were bored, so when I took them out for their necessary toilet breaks, which couldn't wait until the rain stopped, they soon got up to mischief.

Mr Mac grabbed Mahri by the back leg and rolled her over in the sodden grass. As a result, she got more than just a little bit wet. She actually looked as if she had just stepped out of the bath. Mr Mac, of course, did his best to get as little rain on him as possible. Elle … she could have easily drowned in the wet grass just running around trying to keep up with the Airedales.

My brother called round to visit me and Elle got so excited because there was a new face in the house she was bouncing from the floor to shoulder height. I picked her up so she would calm down and not cause any injury to herself. I should have remembered picking her up *never* works. Whack! She threw her head back abruptly, crashing it against my top lip, which in turn came to an abrupt stop on my front teeth. While I waited for the excruciating pain to subside, my lip did the exact opposite and began swelling enormously. I could taste blood – mine, unfortunately – and didn't particularly want to entertain the idea of looking in the mirror at this point. Nevertheless, I checked anyway and took some Arnica. Who needs Botox when you have Elle around?

I had a nice fat lip; it was cut on the inside, which posed a couple of dietary problems, and I had some difficulty eating and drinking. Luckily, three or four doses of Arnica later, the swelling had gone down, leaving only the cut to heal. It was three days before the wound was almost healed and I could enjoy sustenance once more.

Not content with her attempt at a face-lift, Elle next decided to redesign my knuckles. I was sitting on the floor playing tug with a dog who'd already worn out two Airedales. She jumped back and forth, growling and shaking her head, tugging on her end of the rag. I was not about to let go of the other. *Yep, I'm a meanie.* She pulled as hard as she could to the right, really testing my grip on the rag; but, as soon as she felt the full resistance, she let go and, yes, you've probably guessed it … whoosh! Smash! The sudden release of tension from a seven-kilo dog sent my arm flying left and I rattled my knuckles off the wall, just as if I'd punched it.

"Oweeeee! That's it … I'm not playing that game any more!" I shrieked.

Sure enough, I was suckered back into playing, though, and how did she thank me? She sank her teeth into my other hand. She tried to pretend she was aiming for one of the orange toy octopus legs that I was dangling for her to catch. I know she missed it on purpose … the witch.

"Here Len, I give in. Play with your dog before she kills me outright. Her battery just won't run down."

She climbed up on his knee, curled up in a little ball and went to sleep for the rest of the night … typical!!! Leaving me a physical wreck.

I decided that we should have a collar tag printed for Elle that said: 'GOVERNMENT HEALTH WARNING – THIS DOG COULD SERIOUSLY DAMAGE YOUR HEALTH'.

31 May 2007

I took the dogs out for their last walk of the night about midnight. The rain had stopped and the storm clouds had moved on. All was quiet and clear. I nearly said clean, but when has mud ever been clean? Anyway, I put the pups on their leads and opened the door.

Mr Mac was on the starting blocks, up on his hind legs, running on the spot like something from a Tom and Jerry cartoon or the Road Runner. As soon as he could squeeze out the gap, he was off. He usually ran a complete circuit of the garden then came back, but last night he didn't. I hadn't put my wellies on, so didn't want to wade through the sodden grass. I shouted, called, and clapped my hands; nothing. Then I heard him whimpering. I spotted him in the moonlight, standing halfway down the garden, his head drooping. My heart flew into panic mode.

I knew if there was something wrong I could not handle him and the pups, so ran back indoors with them, jumped into wellies and grabbed a torch; but the pups wouldn't let me get to the door unless I took them with me. I snatched Elle and bundled her into her crate and then Mahri into hers, ran back to the door and, when I opened it, there was Mr Mac, with a rolled-up hedgehog at his feet, blood dripping from his mouth.

"Arghhhhh … that better be your blood, Mr Mac," I muttered. "I can cope with you and fix you, but a chewed hedgehog … how would I fix it?"

I pulled him into the house, and, using some paper towels, wiped his chin. He was drooling a lot, but then I saw the spine from the hedgehog sticking in his lip. I pulled it out, and checked all round his teeth, gums and lips. Everything seemed fine and the blood had stopped.

I went out to inspect the hedgehog and it was still rolled up in a little ball. I didn't want to touch it in case I caused it more stress. I looked it over as best I could and it appeared fine. There were only drips of blood where Mr Mac had been standing, so I thought it best to leave him for a while. I switched off all the outside lights to give the hedgehog a chance to feel safe and, when I went back out later, he was nowhere to be seen.

Mr Mac thought I was his hero for saving him, or perhaps he believed I was an ungrateful brat for not accepting a gift that he'd valiantly captured from the wild suburban jungle.

25 June 2007

On weekdays I got up at 6.00am to walk the dogs, feed them and get me ready for work, but on weekends I had the luxury of a lie-in till 7.00am. Mr Mac and Annie had the run of the house, but each preferred to sleep in their own bed at night. My radio alarm bursting into life was Mr Mac's cue to come and nudge me out of bed.

Elle, on the other hand, was still confined to her crate at night because she simply couldn't resist the flavour of plastic. Her favourite was the bendy stuff that covered electric cables – remember the towbar saga earlier on this year? Mahri was shut in the kitchen, but was permitted to sleep in Annie's big, comfy basket or her open crate; it was her choice.

The past two or three days I had been abruptly roused from my slumber at 6.00am by a dog landing on my bed, having performed a flying leap from the door with a landing perfectly engineered so the exact point of contact produced the swiftest of wake-up calls. On waking, I was expected to be ready to appreciate the bouncing circles and play bows, not to mention having to fend off the head butts and tail whips into the bargain. I knew it had to be Mahri, as Mr Mac's approach was much more subtle – but how did she get out?

I knew I'd shut the door. I made a mental note to keep an eye on the door, but still could not decide if Mr Mac opened the door, which would be easier, as he would just have to press the lever-style handle and push, or if it was Mahri who opened the door. This would be much more difficult, as she would have to pull the door towards her while pressing down on the handle. Could it be that they were working together and it was a combination of her operating the handle and Mr Mac pushing the door?

I was sure it was the latter, but I was wrong. Later on that morning, the three hooligans were shut in the kitchen while I went to speak to Len, who was still in bed. I'd got as far as his room door when I heard a noise, looked round and a pack of dogs led by Mahri was heading in my direction. They executed a right turn in a formation that would have done the Red Arrow display team proud. Mahri broke away from the group and jumped on to Len's bed. Unfortunately, she leaped on to the bed at his head end and about the only part of him that feels pain. I tried to push her off, but she wanted to stay and so promptly sat on Len's head. "Get her off!" Len pitifully cried.

While I was trying to push Mahri off the bed, Elle jumped on at the foot of the bed. *"Did I hear a bugle calling the cavalry?"* Elle appeared to be asking, as she squared up to Mahri. You could almost see the speech bubbles appearing

Play Bow

above her head. *"It's my Len! It's my bed! Gerrofff, before I rip your lungs out,"* she squealed at Mahri. Mahri decided she was not going without a fight and bounced towards Elle. Phew! At least Len couldn't feel her bouncing on him now and I could try to get them both off the bed. Mr Mac decided to play at being Jaws and circled round the foot of the bed, waiting to consume the first to be jettisoned, either by me or each other.

Then, all of a sudden, I had a 'eureka' moment. Len had a wire-free doorbell by his bed so he could summon help if there was no-one in the room. I pressed the bell and ran to the kitchen to see who was at the door, with the three dogs following close on my heels; or, should I say, ahead of my toes in their rush to get to the door before me. Back in the kitchen, I shut the door to – fingers crossed – contain the hooligans.

I should mention in their defence that it had been raining for 40 days and nights, or at least it felt like it. So I couldn't really blame them for being a bit hyper.

Roll on the summer!

16 July 2007

We have had Mr Mac for just over 18 months. He was two-and-a-half years old when we got him − a retired show dog, because he got grumpy in the show ring. It took him quite a while to settle with us and it was six months before he would sit on command or even acknowledge we'd called on him. He would rather starve than be coerced into anything he hadn't planned to do.

After we'd had him for a year, his breeder, who was also his previous owner, came to visit. I was a bit worried about how Mr Mac would be, but he was fine and stayed very close to me, hardly acknowledging the guests. I was pleased, but I think they had mixed feelings. I would imagine that, if I was in their shoes, I'd be happy he was close to me and had the good home he'd been promised, but sad he no longer had any interest in them.

Things had been going smoothly, well, 'Airedale smoothly', until two weeks ago. My big sister came to stay for four days. It was supposed to be four and ended up as ten while she was trying to buy a new home in our part of the country. After the first four days, I noticed Mr Mac was a little on the grumpy side and not doing as he was told. These were mainly little things, like staying just out of reach when I tried to put his lead on or not coming into the house when called. I thought he was just playing up as

157

my attention was a little bit more divided; or maybe it had something to do with Elle or Mahri.

I'd also noticed that Elle was always in his face, telling him off for something. He took hold of her ear, dragged her across the room and slew her into a corner. Back she came in an instant, threatening to rip off any appendages that were in her reach; so both were often sent to bed to cool off.

A few days later, when my friend and I took them for a walk, Mr Mac was on the aggressive side to all and sundry, even gruffing[1] at people with dogs on the opposite side of the road. It wasn't like the puppy barks that Mahri used to try and gain some attention when she saw somebody. We thought he might be reacting to the higher levels of tension in the house because of my sister's extended stay. And she was stressed by the house search and purchase. On the Friday, I drove my sister to the coast to stay at her holiday home for a couple of weeks and, when I got back and let Mr Mac out of the day kennel, he raced up and down the paddock. I thought he was about to clear the gate and run off; but no, he bounded back to me, absolute joy in his face. He leapt up and down, bouncing about, and, when we went into the house, he sat very close to me for a long time.

I came to the conclusion that he was worried that these strange people had come to take him away and, if he behaved badly, they wouldn't want him. He knew the breeders didn't want him back because they'd already given him to us. I hoped now he had come to believe he was our dog forever.

---

1   A combination of a growl and a bark.

17 July 2007 – Waking-up tactics

Carrie, our first Airedale, used to come into our room and blow in my face. She would never wake Len up; he was her favourite. I was her servant. Mcgregor and MacIain would come into the room when the alarm went off and place two paws on the bed or on me. MacIain would also sneeze in my face if I tried to ignore him. Annie never bothered. It was MacIain's job to get me up in the morning and my job to get everyone else up and fed.

Mr Mac entered my room by banging the door open with his head, so that it flew open and heralded his entrance, with his tail slapping the door like a big drum. He didn't have to wake me as I was already on my feet by the time he reached the bed – with one exception.

Last week I was on the roll-away bed in the computer room. I'd let my sister and husband have my bed for the week. At 5.00am: Bang! The door slammed against the wall. Boom! Boom! Mr Mac's tail whacked the door as he strolled in. Half asleep, I leapt up, thinking, "Where am I? Who am I? What am I?" It was only four hours since I'd assumed the prone position. While leaning over to check the time on my mobile phone, my elbow slipped and I hit my ear on the side of the bed. I was now in a great deal of pain and very wide awake, but Mr Mac decided to curl up on my bed, where he immediately fell asleep … for about as long as it took me to decide I was no longer able to curb the desire to cry, throw up or thump him, or any combination of the three. Then he was chased back to his own bed.

Next, it was Mahri's turn to push the door open, but only enough to get into the room so I didn't hear her. Then, in one bound, she was on the bed, leaping and jumping for joy as she discovered me and this new game of hide and seek – her view – or fend off cold nose and scratchy claws – my view.

23 July 2007

Mahri had to go for her annual boosters and check-over. It was a year since the little 'poo ball' touched down in England and brought chaos to our calm household. Well, maybe just more chaos to the household better describes her arrival.

She'd been to puppy classes and was always having her training reinforced at home. She could sit, stay, come when asked, give a paw, lie down and show her belly. I could check her teeth, ears, feet, and cut claws. Her only failing seemed to be her tendency to bounce up in strangers' faces to offer kisses. She couldn't understand why everyone wouldn't want to love her like we did.

When the time came to go to the vet, Mahri was so good. She waited to be told to jump into and out of the car, and even sat while I opened the vet's door and again when I closed it. I got her on to the scales easily enough – weighing in at 19 kilograms, she greeted everyone that came to say hello.

Then we headed into the vet's room. It's a small room with a breakfast-bar-size consulting table for small dogs, a fold-up metal seat and a computer. I sat down to wait for the vet to enter from a door that was opposite the one from the door through which I had entered. Mahri sniffed around, belly crawling to extend her sniff area as far as possible. I pulled her back and insisted she sat at my side, but she was so curious she had to keep sniffing everything within her each. I heard a rustle in the hallway a fraction of a second after Mahri had heard it. Without any warning, Mahri lunged at the door, dragging me almost horizontally off the seat and bouncing me on the floor. At that precise moment, the vet walked in. "This will be Mahri then?" he asked. Was he expecting someone else? I'd booked her in for the check-up and it was definitely the right time, day and place. "Yes," I said, picking myself and the chair up.

He offered her a titbit before I had the chance to make her sit and take it nicely ... OOPS! That was her other failing I forgot to mention. ALL food belonged to Mahri, to be consumed with gusto as quickly as possible in order to free up her eating mechanism for any further offerings.

I could see the mask of fear slowly forming on the vet's face. He'd always seen Annie and MacIain, who never seemed to do a thing wrong at the vet's, and now he was dealing with a maniacal jumping-jack in a very confined space.

"Just hold her head, please," he instructed, as he tried to listen to her heart.

"Oy! You hiding food on my belly? I want it! Let me have it!"

She wiggled and squirmed and then he wanted to examine her hips ... more wiggling. Her ears and eyes got a cursory glance and he never even checked her teeth. I asked him to have a look at her nipples, as they seemed a bit large and swollen.

"Lie down, Mahri." She lay down. "Show me your belly." She rolled over. But as soon as the vet touched her, she stood up. She decided to repeat this game a couple of times and I had to hold her so he could take a look.

"That's fine," he said. "Here are her worm pills and flea drops. See you next year," he communicated, as he was ushering me out of the room. At least I had time to work on her obedience training before the next visit.

Mahri: *"He could have warmed his hands."*

17 August 2007

We had a thirteen-foot gate across our drive. It was in rag order and was left open more often than not; so, for the safety of our fur-kids, and to preserve our sanity, we decided to have it replaced with a nice four-foot-wide pedestrian entry-gate, and a nine-foot-wide, five-bar gate. The workman arrived at the appointed time and spent eight hours digging out the old posts, cementing the new ones in place and fitting our nice new gates.

The dogs had been languishing in the day kennel while the work was in progress. I brought the dogs into the house at 7.00pm and fed them, so they could have an evening romp in the now dog-secure garden. The gate-man was just putting the finishing touches to the gates and clearing up. I heard Len bang the back door and yelled for him to wait while I lunged and grabbed Elle so she couldn't sneak past him and out the door. Then, to my surprise, Mahri ran at Len. I thought she was going to jump on his knee; but no, her back feet gently brushed his knee and the wall as she manoeuvred like a stunt car driving up the side of a tunnel … whoosh … straight over his shoulder, past his ear.

"Freeeeedom!"

Len was blocking the exit and became all dithery,

preventing me from pursuing Mahri with maximum speed. By the time he had backed out of the way, Mahri was sitting at the steering wheel in the gate-man's truck. "Look!" he said. "She's so funny!" *"Yeah, she's downright hilarious,"* I muttered …

I thrust Elle into Len's arms and went to get Mahri, thinking the gate-man would hold on to her; but no, he stood there like a gentleman holding the door open for her. As soon as she saw me approaching, she once again morphed into a James Bond stunt man, leaping past the two of us and out on to the road, by-passing the new gates that were supposed to keep her in, because 'Mr Gateman' had left them open. I was in hot pursuit – well, as hot as flip-flops on pea gravel allowed one to be without breaking something. Back and forth, Mahri zig-zagged across the road. Then I saw it … the cat! I was about to go home and call the police to tell them that my dog had run off and I couldn't catch her because she was chasing a cat, when I realized the cat was still sitting on the fence; it refused to move. Mahri stared at it, and the cat stared back. *"Run,"* she said. *"Can't be bothered,"* it said. *"Run,"* she said a bit louder, in case it misunderstood her first request. It yawned and stared back, slowly flicking it's tail in the most insolent manner.

While this was all going on, I'd slowly walked up the gravel path and managed to grab her. I think she thought I was coming to help, judging by the surprised look I got when she was marched back up the road in double time.

"You," I yelled, "are a bad girl! … That was not inspired free-style agility, it was a bad career move, and the only promotion," I reminded her, "would be to become bird food or slippers." When Mahri mis-behaved, I would often suggest to her that she could be re-homed or we could have her made into a pair of slippers or worse. I'm sure she took a great deal of notice of my idle threats.

Just as I was nearly back at the house, Len and Mr Gateman were out in the road. Elle had got a little over-excited, wriggled free from Len and escaped. Called back into action again, I darted off, leaving Mr Gateman in charge of Mahri. He took a firm hold of Mahri's two collars, while I approached Elle, who was in a neighbour's garden.

Now these neighbours are not particularly fond of us. In fact, the words 'strong' and 'dislike' are usually muttered in the same sentence if we are asked what they think of us.

"Sugar!!!" I uttered, or at least some words to that affect. I boldly walked towards Elle and she ran up the side of their house. Good! Their house was squeezed into a small plot and the fence was so close to the wall of the house, I doubt whether any dog bigger than Elle could have squeezed up there. I gingerly squeezed sideways along the space while Elle backed further away. Then it dawned on me that I could never have reached her as I couldn't bend down in the space. A new plan was needed!

I sidled out and stepped back from the space just enough so that Elle couldn't see me and prayed that the owners would not arrive home to find me leaning on the wall near their sitting room window.

Sure enough, back down the passageway trotted Elle and, like a hawk, I swooped on her from above. "And *your* new career choice would be … road-kill, that's what! Do you hear me?" Both dogs were taken into the house and crated. Mahri knew why and went quietly, but Elle was a different story.

"It's not fair ... I didn't run away Len let me go," she screamed and screamed some more.

I was glad Mr Gateman got to suffer the noise, so that he could also bear witness to the fact that we were not beating this dog severely around the ears or otherwise maltreating her, despite the fact that she could certainly drive somebody to do so.

In the end, I gave in and took her outside to the day kennel before she shattered all our eardrums. Len paid the man and gave him a nice tip because he'd been a lot longer than he'd probably planned.

Well, if we hadn't had to spend an hour chasing two dogs, he would have been finished earlier. I know what my tip would be. SHUT THE GATE!

Mr Mac had surprised us all and stayed in the house the entire time; he must have been turning over a new leaf.

23 August 2007 − The 'extend-o-paw' (USA pat pending by Intrepid Airedale Molly Karrier)

One of my cyber friends in America has an Airedale who goes by the name of Molly. Well, that was her official name, but, as she got up to as much mischief as Mahri, I'm sure she had some other titles as well. After one of Molly's kitchen raids, her owner decided that Molly must have some sort of extendable paw. That described Mahri exactly. She could go from a little dog curled at your feet to a six-foot-tall dog that could reach across the table to steal paper napkins or anything made of non-edible components. What the paw couldn't reach, she could vacuum up with her huge Airedale nose. Yet, strangely enough, I could leave bread on the worktop and she would sit waiting for me to give it to her. Leave the bread on a napkin and the bread would be untouched, but the napkin devoured.

Mahri was doing well with her anti-steal training. She knew not to steal and, if she did, the consequence was to go directly to bed. One day, I came back into the kitchen a little quicker than expected, and caught her pulling a piece of paper towel from the roll. She dropped on to all fours, ears down and went straight to bed, giving me a hang-dog look. "Yes, I should think so. You're a bad girl!" I admonished her. "You know better." Then, just as I was about to walk away, she decided she couldn't wait any longer and dropped the paper towel she had concealed in her mouth!

I couldn't believe it; she'd actually been stealing the towel, one sheet at a time, like a child raiding the cookie jar.

8 September 2007

I saw some new leads advertised on a UK website from which I often buy dog supplies. The leads were made from that stretchy latex stuff that physiotherapists or people in aerobics classes like to use to assist in their training workouts.

The lead was rated according to the dog's weight and would stretch to double its size. The idea was that, as the lead stretched, the dog would feel the resistance and would stop pulling without your shoulder joint being removed in the process. They sounded marvellous, so I bought two three-foot leads, one for up to eleven kilograms for Elle and the other up to twenty-three kilograms for Mahri.

The parcel arrived early on the Saturday morning. I was

very keen to try the leads out and volunteered Elle to go first. I quite liked the weight of the lead. At first it seemed a bit strong for her, but she got used to it and it seemed a worthy purchase. Len tried them; first just the new lead on Elle, then, after persuading him of its good qualities, I attached the lead to the extending lead he normally uses for Elle. The extending lead allowed her space to run without the opportunity to escape. Elle ran at full speed and came to an abrupt halt. Hmm! It wasn't supposed to happen like that. What happened to the increased resistance bringing the dog to a gentle halt?

Next, I tried the heavier lead on fifteen-month-old Mahri, a nineteen kilogram Airedale. The lead said it was good up to twenty-three kilograms, so I was confident that we were well within the prescribed weight limits. Mahri trotted beside me round the garden and the lead never stretched once. She was quite happy to go to the end of the lead, feel the lead take up the slack and pause to wait for me. That's good, I thought. No more violent jerks to my already damaged rotator cuff.

Later that night, I hooked Mahri's nice new purple lead to her collar to take her out for a pre-bedtime stroll. Mahri trotted by my side down the garden. Just as we reached the back paddock, I thought I heard something run across our path very quickly but, in the blackness of the night, one could barely see Mahri, let alone a fast-moving garden visitor. It was most probably a cat, but could equally have been a fox or a rat. Mahri immediately launched herself in its direction. The new lead was stretching.

"Mahri!" I shouted, as the lead stretched. "Mahri, stop!" I shouted again; the lead was still stretching. "Mahreee!" The lead was now exerting a greater pull on me than the dog. I had visions of my feet leaving the ground and me being catapulted through the air into the *Leylandii* hedge.

I dug in my heels in an effort to stand my ground and I was about to use two hands to haul Mahri back in my direction when something whistled past my ear. It took a split second between my hearing the whistle and understanding the nature of the sound. Unfortunately, that split second was just too long. The sudden release of tension sent me reeling across the grass like a child's spinning top.

"Mahreeeeeeeee!" I wailed, while trying to maintain some sense of balance and direction. She came back, but only because she thought this thing – me, bouncing along the drive – was the original object of her chase. I grabbed her collar to hold her while I struggled to my feet.

Mahri always wore two collars in case she slipped out of one. Airedales have a cunning trait. They appear to be choked by a tight collar one minute, and the next minute that same collar easily slips right past their ears. When I tried to clip the lead back on to her collar, I could only find one collar, her second collar; the nice leather one was still attached to the end of the lead. It dawned on me that I'd had three lucky escapes. First, not to have been whipped by the returning lead; second, not to have had an eye removed by the buckle on the collar; and, finally, not to have lost Mahri in the dark.

Mistakenly, but not disastrously, I'd grossly underestimated the pulling power of a young Airedale, and the vulnerability of quick-release plastic buckles. I made a mental note to replace all the dog collars with the type that had a proper old-fashioned metal buckle. They had the propensity to do more damage, but were less likely to open under stress.

Luckily, the very nice people from the website said they would upgrade the lead to the next weight if I returned the 23kg one and paid the postage. All that was left was to look forward to trying the whole exercise again the following weekend.

Glutton for punishment? More than likely …

15 September 2007

The stronger lead arrived and I promptly attached it to Mahri's collar and took her for a walk round the garden. She walked very well, just like last time. Then I took Elle for a trot round the garden on her red lead, which still worked fine. It would be a long time before she got anywhere near its upper weight limit.

The final test for the leads was to get Mahri and Elle on their leads while Mr Mac was running free. He always tried to play chase with the pups by grabbing a back leg and tipping them over. Then he'd run to what he perceived to be the end of their leads to tease them.

"Surprise, surprise!" Mahri managed to grab Mr Mac's neck and tried to topple him over.

The heavier weight lead was good; I could hold Mahri and tug her back to the heel position. Because of the lead's extra weight factor, I had the added bonus of Mahri's lead not tying itself in knots with Elle's lead.

We decided to take the three dogs for a long walk. Len had Elle on her two leads, I had Mr Mac, who preferred to walk with me, and Sally, who was one of Len's carers, took Mahri. When we went for longer walks, I used head collars. They are a bit like horse bridles. I started to use them because Mahri, being young and a tad over-zealous, would leap at people or dogs for attention, and, quite often, it was not met with the friendship that had been offered. Being true to her breed, Mahri met any form of rebuke with equal opposition.

The label on these head collars stated, 'control the head and the dog will follow'. Once the stretchy lead had been added to the equation, walking a dog whose middle name should have been 'Ricochet' became a pleasure. Mahri could walk to the end of the lead, sniffing here and there, but, as soon as she tried to stretch it a bit further, a gentle pull was exerted on the lead, bringing her head round and focusing her attention on me.

Sally loved my dogs but was not used to walking them and was prone to wrapping leads round her hand or wrist. Every time I saw her do this, I pointed out that, if the dogs went off at a tangent, she could break her wrist. One of the bonus points of this lead was that it was bulky enough to discourage the user from wrapping it round his or her hands.

The lead worked really well when a young pheasant flew across Mahri's path. She looked up, but didn't lunge. When a field mouse or something of that ilk ran in front of her, she couldn't resist the urge to pounce. Although the sudden movement startled Sally, she was not pulled off her feet into the nearby ditch.

In summary, I would recommend these leads, but suggest that, unless you know you can exert a greater pull than your dog, buy the next weight up to the one you need, especially if it is to be used with a young bouncy Airedale. Alternatively, buy the shorter version and, if the dog is pulling too much, you can still reach his or her collar.

30 September 2007

Things have been quiet on the home-front for a while. The weather has been wet and windy and I have even experienced my first tornado, which was quite unusual here in the UK. It was not something to which I'd like to become accustomed, I might add!

As you might have guessed, all this enforced house-bound quietness was not going to last forever and, on Thursday night, Mahri had to have a mad turn or two … or even several. She started off the evening by provoking a fight with Mr Mac. He was waiting patiently to get his dinner when Mahri jumped on him, grabbing him by the back of his neck and trying to push him to the floor. He quickly told her off, which meant that Elle had to join in. It was like being back in the school playground. Fight, fight, fight, and all the kids gather round to join in the mêlée. I managed to distract them by rattling the dinner plate and I got two minutes' peace while they ate.

I've been told a million times not to exaggerate, but, just a micro-second after Mahri had inhaled her food, she decided to provoke Elle. It was easily done. Mahri scoffed her dinner really quickly; then, just as Elle was about to eat her last morsel, she shoved her out of the way to inspect the plate. Mahri was either wise enough or not brave enough to take that last morsel.

Of course, all of this greed meant that Elle was obliged to reprimand her with glass-breaking squeals, yelps and growls, to which Mahri normally responded by going off to her bed and the situation would calm down. Not so on this night. Mahri took off like the proverbial bat out of a hot place, with Elle hanging from her tail. If you can picture a

Tom and Jerry cartoon, you'd be more than half way there to imagining what this situation was like.

Mr Mac was next to join in the fun and it was no longer clear who was chasing whom. Round and round the house they ran, sometimes tripping over Elle or trampling her under foot, or sometimes even carrying her swinging from their tails, flanks or ears. Every now and then, Elle stopped to spit out lumps of black or tan fluff.

"Enough!" I shouted. "Do you think it's outside you're in?" I don't know where the expression came from, but the dogs know that it means outside is for running like the wind; inside is not.

Silence. They stared at me.

"Oops, we've upset her now ... better lie quiet for a while."

I finally got a cup of tea and a chance to sit down and watch Caesar Milan and tried to emulate him by projecting calmness. Unfortunately, I managed to achieve the opposite effect to the one Caesar was demonstrating and Mahri took this as a cue to resume her manic run-around. She ran past the table, past me, bounced on and off Len, into the kitchen, back through to the sitting room and then bounced on Len again. He was still vibrating like a tuning fork from her last pass. As she sped past me, I noticed she had something in her mouth.

"Thank you, Mahri," I said, as I walked towards her. She immediately adopted her not-guilty stance, keeping her back to me and head down, but watching me while trying to conceal the forbidden object in her mouth. I offered her a crumb from Len's plate and, as she approached, I grabbed her collar.

"Thankyooo!" I said, as I removed the foam radiator

pipe protector from her mouth.

Whoosh! She was off in a flash ... *oh no, how many more protectors do I have to rescue*? Back she came, rushing past, and I made a lunge for her, successfully grabbing her collar.

"Give it to me," I said, trying not to laugh. She, of course, resisted and attempted to swallow her prize. Fearing the consequences, I wrestled her mouth open and extracted the contents. "Yeugh!" It wasn't the foam pipe protector I was expecting. It was a piece of half-chewed courgette.

When I went into the kitchen to dispose of it, I found that every time she'd run into the kitchen, she'd swiped something off the worktops: magazines, gardening gloves, tea towels, you name it. If it had been on the worktop, it wasn't there any more. The place looked like the tornado had ripped through it. By this point, Mr Mac and Elle had recovered and were back in the chase again. "Oh well, if you can't beat them, join them." So there I was, running round the house with them, picking up their toys as I went. That soon spoiled all their fun and all three dogs took themselves off to their beds for a bit of peace and quiet.

4 October 2007

You may remember the story of Mahri – aka James Bond's stunt double – and Mr Gateman. Well, Len, in his infinite wisdom, decided that, although the new gate had been put in the same place as the old gate, it was a bad idea, as our rear ends – well, the cars, not ours – stuck out into the road when we stopped to open the gate, and, with the dark winter nights fast approaching, it could be an accident waiting to happen.

If you are wondering why it wasn't dangerous for the 14 or so years we had already been at the address, the answer is that we usually left the gates open. Development in the area has meant that many people had sold off bits of garden to builders and now, as a result, a large number of extra houses have been squeezed into the surrounding area. The consequence of all this multiplying of human habitation was an increased volume of traffic on our tiny country road. The abundance of houses now attracted many strangers to the area and probably some dubious itinerants as well. The old ways of total trust and leaving the shed unlocked were now unfortunately relegated to history books. The shed was just as likely to disappear along with the contents.

Len liked to have the gate closed at all times. The trespass laws made it very difficult to move somebody off private land. Sometimes it could take years. I was told, if you opened a gate, then you had effectively broken in or entered without permission. Quaint British law suggested that, if the gate was open, then you were invited in.

Anyway, I digress. Mr Gateman was coming back today while I was at work to move the gate ten feet into the drive and put two new bits of fence up from the new gate post to the old gate post. One of several concerns I had at this point was the line of five-foot-high *Salix* trees planted down either side of this part of drive that were pruned into little spheres. I wondered where they'd be when I arrived home or whether it was worth repositioning them under torch-light prior to Mr Gateman's arrival. Next, my thoughts drifted to the dogs and whether I'd be ringing the lost dogs' home asking if they had three new arrivals, fresh from their escape from the safe enclave our house offered them. I dreaded to think what surprises awaited me on my return. At least I only had seven hours to go till I found out.

The wild bunch: *"Can we watch* The Great Escape *tonight?"*

Jackie: "Thank goodness I sold my motorbike."

7 October 2007

You would think that, after owning Airedales for 20-plus years, I would have learned to always expect the unexpected. Much to my embarrassment, I have not, and Mahri managed to surprise me at the weekend ... although surprise was maybe not the best word to use ... shock, stun, mortify or nearly kill would be far more suitable.

Sunday started off as a normal day with an early walk for the dogs round the garden while we waited for the carer to turn up to look after Len while I walked the dogs off the property. Elle was walked first. She was on her lead, revved up and ready to go as soon as the carer arrived. First, we had to pass the mini-monster – a little dog in a nearby garden that hated all other four-legged creatures. It gave Elle a lot of verbal abuse every time we walked past the house. Elle hated not having the last word, so she responded with equal if not louder decibels. I didn't know a little dog could make so much noise. Eventually, I picked her up and carried her past the hooligan's garden. Silence reigned ... almost. Elle still emitted a few final grunts of displeasure.

Half a mile down the road, we had to pass a big house

Mahri and Mr Mac

with two huge Rottweilers and five Spaniel-Rottie crosses that hurled themselves at the eight-foot-high iron gates. I was glad the gates were so big, because the huge hinges should be able to withstand the combined weight of the canine battering rams. Elle had had enough and could no longer contain her anger.

"Bring it on then!" she screamed. *"I'll take care of them all before breakfast."*

Once I was past that house, the rest of the walk was more or less uneventful; but, taking the recent experience on board, I was careful to return home by another route.

The next trip out was for Mahri and Mr Mac. Usually, my friend took Elle and I had the other two, but she was in Australia for six weeks. As a result, I was doing the same walk twice, which should have be therapeutic ... one might even say healthy. I put the head collars on the dogs and off we went. As I passed the mini-monster for the second time, I opened and shut the Velcro on my treat bag. Mahri took the bait and looked at me for her treat, which she was going to get if we passed the garden quietly. Snatch! She grabbed the treat so quickly I had to count to make sure all my digits were still intact.

Next we approached the big iron gates.

"Stand up straight, breathe ... project calm and serenity," were my thoughts.

Mahri, though, had other ideas, and, by this time, was whining and pulling. She was torn between rushing past the gate that imprisoned several tons of canine flesh, or the biscuit in my hand she was about to receive. Snatch ... the treat was gone and Mahri was dragging me towards the road. All dog training rules went out the window at this point and, like a Gatling Gun, I delivered commands: "Here, sit, down, get back, leave, pack it in, dinner", and any other words that might have distracted her. Mr Mac, as always, walked calmly by my side, probably trying to pretend Mahri was not with us.

Eventually, I managed to slow Mahri down, get past the gates and resume the walk. It was a beautiful autumn morning with birds singing, trees laden with berries, and a rich blue sky. We walked past the horses grazing in the field and round a small housing estate which led on to a main road through the village. There was a designated dog walk through a field just off the main road that we sometimes walked round and then circle back to the house, with the whole walk taking about an hour.

Just as I approached the entrance to the dog walk, a man with two Dobermans, both off-lead, turned on to the path.

"Hmmm ... maybe I should just go home."

After giving it some consideration, I figured that I had no need to be frightened of them. My dogs were on leads and had got over their initial 'go for a walk' enthusiasm.

The man walked straight down the path; just to err on the side of safety, I took the longer route all the way round the field.

When I re-joined the path, I saw a lady in the distance and, half way between her and my dogs, was a little terrier-cross dog. I thought she'd call it back, but she didn't. I decided to make my pair sit by the edge of the path until she passed us. This was an exercise they did at obedience classes. Mr Mac complained bitterly because there was an abundance of jaggy plants, nettles, thistles and the like and he refused to adopt the sit position. I moved to the opposite side of the path and the edge of the ploughed field where the weeds had been cut down. Now the dogs could sit and wait.

I was a bit concerned and irritated that this woman had still not called her dog to heel and put it on a lead. The dog was now about ten feet from us and showed every intention of making unsolicited contact with one or both of my dogs. I turned to Mr Mac, because he was very protective of me and his demeanour suggested that he was the one to watch. Mahri was such a big lovable lump I was never overly concerned about her staying by my side. "You're a good boy, Mr Mac," I said, and patted his neck.

The next thing I knew, I was being catapulted through the air. Splat!! I was face down in the dirt. "Mahreeeeeeeeeeeeeeeeee!!!!!!" I squealed, as her lead slipped through my fingers.

While trying to prevent serious injury on landing, I'd also inadvertently let go of Mr Mac's lead. He, thinking I was in danger, turned into 'Superdale' and ran over the top of me to help Mahri who, without any warning whatsoever, had lunged forward to greet the little dog. The dog clearly wasn't impressed with Mahri's offer of friendship and had promptly launched an attack on her throat. Mahri, who normally was not aggressive in any way and usually walked away at the first sign of trouble, decided to meet the attacker with equal force.

In defence of this unusual behaviour, all I can say is she was severely provoked, the unknown dog was off-lead and attached to Mahri's throat without invitation. The owner suddenly became very motivated and was running towards me, screaming.

"Mr Mac, Mahri, get back here!" I called, and he immediately came to stand behind me; Mahri also joined him at my side, back to her smiling tail-wagging self.

She gave me her famous surprised look, *"Did I do something wrong there? ... Moi, the friendly pup?"*

"Lie down," I hissed, and she did so without question.

When I asked the woman if her dog was OK, she took this as her cue to launch a verbal attack on me. "You shouldn't have dogs if you can't control them, etc, etc ..." When she'd stopped yelling, I said, with as much dignity as possible since most of my dignity was lying in the field, "My dogs *were* on leads. They go to agility and obedience classes. If I'd thought they were aggressive, *or* out of control, they would not have been here. Furthermore, if I'd expected any trouble from them, I would not have been taken by surprise and tipped face first into the mud."

She huffed and puffed, picked her dog up, walked towards me and then changed her mind. She filled the whole path so I could not walk past her. I could have walked up the ploughed field but, if a farmer is kind enough to leave a path, then I prefer not to walk on his newly-sown field. She insisted on heading back to the gate ahead of me. Her dog was now on a lead and my two perfectly-behaved dogs trotted at my side as if nothing had happened.

What did I learn from this experience? Well, Mahri needed to go back to school. It was all very well controlling the dogs after a situation had occurred; but, in hindsight, I should have made sure it didn't happen in the first place. Mahri can be too friendly for her own good; she believes that everyone loves her and wants to be her friend, and this is not always the truth. People let their dogs run free because they think their dogs are friendly, but sometimes dogs, for reasons known only to themselves, find fault with their own species and an altercation usually ensues.

15 October 2007 − Mr Mac has the WOW factor

Because of my little sister's early demise and Len's ill health, Mr Mac had not been at agility for the past six weeks. The weather had turned cool and it was dark by 7.00pm, so this week the agility classes were moved back indoors. Mr Mac's restriction of privileges following last week's poor behaviour on his walk had been lifted and he was allowed to go to class.

There is nothing like withdrawing a privilege to focus the mind, and Mr Mac was determined to please. I took both pups out for a walk and put them in their crates for the hour we would be out of the house. Mr Mac was taken out for his walk round the garden, where he leapt in the air, rolled on the grass, pulled clumps up and threw them about. Such was his joy because he knew he was going out by himself and there would be no noisy pups to steal the limelight.

We arrived at the school where the classes took place and, because we were a bit early, we went for a stroll to enjoy the setting sun. This also ensured that Mr Mac had sprinkled everything that was stationary and I could be sure he would not disgrace himself by marking any of the jumps set up in the class. He nearly forgot he was supposed to be on his best behaviour and almost dragged me into a ditch, but a sharp word from me pulled him up short. *"Oops!"* He looked at me sheepishly. "Just as well for you, Mr Mac. If you'd put me in that ditch, it would be straight home and no class."

I'd seen the instructor arrive, so we headed up to the big hall and helped lay out seats. Mr Mac had listened to me and was once again on his best behaviour as the dogs started to arrive. There was a new face in town – a lovely whippet. Mr Mac shortened his back, head tipped to one side and wagged his tail fifty to the dozen.

"Helllo ... The name's Mac ... Mr Mac," giving his best Sean Connery impersonation. Smooth as liquid chocolate.

"I'm Maisy," the whippet answered. *"I used to be good at this till I injured my shoulder."* He watched her complete the first round and looked at me. *"Well, I'm much better than that."* And with a little toss of his head, we approached the start line.   In our six weeks' absence, they had decided to train the dogs to body language only. You could tell them the first move, and then it was silence.

"Are you ready, Mr Mac? Are you really ready?" I whispered at him. "OK, up," I said, as I pointed up the A-frame and ran forward. A he descended the A-frame, I pointed down to the floor, then through the tunnel, a right turn over a jump, straight over two more jumps, a sharp right over the last jump and then back to me. I was speechless. Just as well it was to be a silent night. I really didn't think he would do it and, even better, to everyone's amusement, he stopped right in front of me, plopped his beam end on the ground and extending a paw for his treat.

"Da da! Impressed?" his look appeared to say. I was very proud of him. He continued to do well all night, working left or right on the course.

"See you all next week," he grinned from ear to ear, as we swaggered towards the exit. He was indeed a happy Mac.

22 October 2007

Do dogs get headaches? Or do they utilize some sort of pain transfer so they don't have to have them? I used to have long, manicured nails, but now I have stubs because the dogs, well maybe not Elle, will have walked up to my side, given their head a shake, which is just at my hand height, and ping! one or more of my nails would disappear … and that's on the quieter days.

Mr Mac used to run towards me at full tilt, swerving at the very last minute; but Mahri's not mastered that swerve, so is more like Dino from the Flintstones. You put your hand down to save your shins and knees and ping! there goes the last of your nails.

Mahri's other favourite trick was lying on the ground, so, when we bent down to rub her belly, we'd get a paw or two in the face in the process. Then, Mr Mac would wade in to see what was occurring and, if we were lucky, we would reach our full standing height before two Airedale heads met ours.

Crossing the living room when a full-speed chase is on is the most dangerous place to be. Mahri would be at the front, running so fast her back legs passed her front legs, Mr Mac almost alongside, trying to catch her back leg to flip her over, and Elle trying to hang on to a tail or leg furnishings. If one hesitated for a second and couldn't decide whether to step left or right, it would be too late, as forty-seven kilograms of dogs' body slammed into the lower part of your body, usually at knee level, but it depended on your height. Mahri could do a hand-brake turn, but, as I said, my leg to her eye co-ordination needed a bit more practice. Mr Mac, as usual, would be more intent on the chase than looking where he was going. Whack! He'd sideswipe you as well on the way by. And wee Elle was like the last skater on a string being swung out by centrifugal forces so she 'body-slammed' you as well.   Sometimes I thought it would be safer crossing a six-lane motorway like the M25!

24 October 2007

Mahri had been on restricted privileges since her bad behaviour on our walk two weeks ago. This weekend, I relented and took her for her long walk by herself so I could re-enforce her training and good behaviour. She was Little Miss Perfection. She trotted by my side with no pulling, she sat when asked and didn't jump at people or dogs. Because she had been well behaved, she was allowed to go to the agility class with Mr Mac.

My friend, Amy, had returned from Australia, so I picked her up at 6.00pm to go to the training class. I'd had Mahri running round letting off steam so she would behave and Mr Mac was on his best behaviour because he loves to go to the agility class.

We arrived at the hall, parked the car, opened the back door a little and started to put Mr Mac's lead on while keeping Mahri in the car. He was very fidgety, which was unusual for him. Amy noticed the reason for his lack of desire to stay in the car; it was a big black and white cat with one eye. It was the resident RSPCA cat and a very bold one at that. Thank goodness the Shogun had side hinges on the back door and wasn't an estate with top hinges, because that cat decided my car was better than all the others in the car park and nonchalantly strolled over to sit by the back wheel.

I waited a bit, then, thinking the cat had walked away, I called Mahri to jump down by my side and handed her lead to Amy. Next, Mr Mac was allowed to jump down; but, when I turned to shut the door, the cat was now sitting at my side, waiting for the invitation to enter the car for a snooze. Both dogs spied the cat. Mahri was immediately in play mode.

"Let's play chase!" she howled. Mr Mac joined in, but this confident cat was strong on its territory and stood his ground. He let it be known that he would not be intimidated by any other animal.

I shut the car door and we made our way to the hall. For Mahri and Mr Mac, peace was no longer on the agenda. Mahri was pulling and looking round to see if the cat would play chase, while Mr Mac was looking for any damsel in distress that might need rescuing. Once inside the hall, Mr Mac trotted up to the desk. *"Hi, girls,"* he winked at the trainers. *"I'm back."* He put his paws on the desk and leaned forward for a nose rub … strange behaviour for Mr

Mac … but he was mellowing a bit.

We paid our class fee and took a seat. Mahri had gone into bounce mode, but I'd boxed a little clever and made her wear her head collar so I had a bit more control over her. "Sit down and behave," I hissed at her, while trying to see what the circuit was. She lay down with her head on her paws and sang her sad whale song, "Ouoo ouooo." It started quietly, and then began to build in length and volume. Everyone was looking and smiling. "Ouoooooooo ouooooooooooo!" It got louder and longer.

She was still lying where she was told to lie, with her nose on her paws, but her big expressive eyes had started to wander round the room. *"Is anyone looking at me? Is there the slightest excuse at all to jump up?"* Somebody started to laugh. That was the sign she'd been seeking. She jumped up, tail wagging, bouncing, and ready to play. Fortunately, it was her turn to strut her stuff round the course, so there was some pay-off to all the excitement she'd built up. She still worked well on lead and she was coming along nicely over the jumps and through the weave poles. Then the tunnel …hmm … she still seemed to think she should stop just short of the exit to get her biscuit before continuing. To her, though, it must have appeared like the right thing to do, because everyone laughed. That is all the encouragement an Airedale needs to learn to do the wrong thing; they love to act the clown and make people laugh. The class was over all too quickly and it was time to go home. I decided that if she behaved all week she could go back the following week.

30 October 2007

Every year one of my American friends holds a photo competition. The dogs had to be photographed in a Hallowe'en costume or setting and we paid a dollar to vote for the best picture or as many pictures as we choose to pay for. All the funds received went to help CRUSA (Cairn Rescue USA). The Wild Bunch were always conspicuous by their absence in these fancy dress picture contests. I did attempt to take photographs each year and this year was no exception; I try, but, unfortunately, the dogs do not. I asked Mr Mac to pose for me, to which he responded, *"No, I'm too grown up for trick or treat now."*

"Ok; well, how about you, Mahri? Will you sit nice and wear this witch's hat?" Mahri responded by bouncing round the kitchen: *"Treat, treat, treat ... feed me, just give me the treat ... I don't need festive adornments to eat treats."*

"How about you, Annie?" Her response was to continue sleeping: *"Zzzzzzz. I'm hibernating; don't wake me."*

There was no point asking Elle because she had PMT (PMS) and not by the strictest definition either. I think I found out what PMT really means − 'Pure Mental Terrier'. She decided to take the Hallowe'en theme a little too far:

"Who needs fancy dress? I can turn into a vampire and fly at you, taking blood from your leg ... well, I'm only twelve inches tall, after all ... hmm, didn't like that? So watch me morph into a werewolf ... how do you like that? Look at these teeth ... all the better to bite you with. Scared yet?" I walked away from her so she would calm down from her little temper tantrum.

Elle screamed at me, *"Do not! I said, do not turn your back on me when I'm talking to you."* At that point, she morphed into a pit-bull with a bad attitude and sank her teeth into the back of my thigh, refusing to let go. In the end, I had to pull her off, which meant she took the flesh with her that she'd been holding on to. Quickly, I put her into her crate, before she decided to morph into Freddie Kruger and kill all of us.

By now, poor Mr Mac was hovering at the opposite end of the kitchen, wondering if he should help; but I think he realized it was safer not to, as Elle had already been really nasty to him a couple of days earlier. Mahri thought that it might be a good opportunity to get rid of Elle while she was distracted, but, luckily, her self- preservation instinct prevailed and she was good enough to go to bed when told.

All this had happened about half past midnight, so I wondered whether I would survive the night − or was Elle going to turn into ectoplasm in order to escape the confines of her crate and get me while I was asleep?

I shut Mahri in her crate so I could let Elle out, to see if she had calmed down. Now she had turned into a little quivering pup that bore no resemblance to the monster she was thirty minutes earlier. She was fine, but I still happened to be missing a large lump of flesh that required medical attention. I'm sure she was possessed … or something.

9 November 2007

We had an eventful three weeks with Elle and her PMT, although the vet insisted there was nothing wrong with her but bad genes. He had sort of left us between a rock and a hard place. Our last resort was to call in a Dog Whisperer − not Caesar Milan − but a nice lady from a village near us.

We knew it was not going to be cheap, but we had to give Elle the best chance to get over her problem.

The lady whisperer arrived at 6.30pm as agreed. I had both pups in their crates so she could come in without being licked or trampled on. She asked loads of questions along the lines of whether we'd met the mother and father, what were they like, the age we got her, her behaviour as a young pup, how we fed her and the way she was trained and groomed. We listed the observations of pre-bad behaviour and post-bad behaviour and, throughout the hour-long discussion, Elle screamed in the background. I explained that this was her normal behaviour because she was not getting any attention. The lady whisperer looked at Elle's pedigree and I explained her daily routine for walking, feeding, playing, training, how she reacted and to what she reacted in the house and outside the house, as well her behaviour in the puppy training class.

Elle at last quietened down. The lady whisperer asked me to bring her into the room so she could have a look at her. I brought Elle in on her short puppy lead and she totally ignored the lady whisperer. Instead, she sniffed intently at her bag and snapped at Mr Mac because he came too close. Once Elle was satisfied she'd learned everything she could from the bag, she turned her attention to the lady by bouncing up and down at her knees. The lady whisperer was sitting on a tall chair by the breakfast bar so, from a standing start, Elle was bouncing at least three feet high.

The lady whisperer ignored her jumping for a while and then she sat on the floor and asked Elle to sit. She offered Elle a piece of cheese and asked her to lie down or give a paw first. Elle just stared at her. The lady whisperer was obviously talking a strange language. Elle looked at the ceiling, the floor, left, then right, at the lady's hand, but not at her face. Finally, the lady whisperer told me that Elle wanted the cheese, but she didn't know what to do to earn it.

"She does," I countered. "She doesn't get her dinner unless she sits, gives a paw and waits … although it has taken her 15 months to learn that lesson."

Elle eventually half proffered a paw and took the cheese. She was then allowed to jump up and get cuddles. "Yes, I think I know what the problem is," the whisperer said, "but let me see how she is when you introduce Mahri into the equation."

Mahri was invited to join us. She was so happy. She bounced and wiggled around the lady whisperer, ignoring her bag on the floor. This person could be a new friend, so Mahri had to make a fuss over her. Elle went into her mad frenzy, acting like nobody should bounce other than her. As soon as Mahri sat quiet, Elle settled and was quiet, but rigid with rage.

"Yes," the lady whisperer announced, "this proves my theory. Elle has low levels of serotonin and for that reason cannot regulate her inhibitions. This means she can spike from calm to raging bull in a nano-second, but could take hours to get back to a calm state."

I had been aware for some time that Elle was rarely in a calm state and clearly was a confused, unhappy little dog. She was the only pup I'd ever come across that slept on her side with her legs straight and rigid. We had been training Elle and doing all the right things, but she hadn't as yet been able to pick up any dog skills. However, the good news was that it was fixable. We were told to feed her breakfast as normal, and then, three hours later, two ounces of white pasta and a vitamin B6 10mg pill followed by a normal dinner and some pasta and a pill again three hours later.

This was to continue over a ten-day period and she said that we should start to see a difference in just seven days. We were to continue the Tellington Touch – a form of massage therapy that I found helped calm Elle a little – and continue to give her treats every time the other two dogs were in the room, especially if they started playing or running about. The idea was that the treats would teach her that she could feel good even though the Airedales were in the room bouncing and charging about. In seven days, we could begin teaching her things to do and I was to report back with the successes and failures. The lady whisperer that came to see Elle worked at shelters rehabilitating rescue dogs and came well recommended, so we just needed to see if there was an internal teddy bear hiding in Elle to match the external one that people saw when they looked at her cute wee face.

18 November 2007

The diet made a huge difference and Elle was a changed little dog. She had returned to almost normal dog behaviour, playing with a tug toy and running round the house. She started to learn 'fetch the toy'. Eventually, this little game would lead to me telling her to get a toy and we would have a game, or her bringing me a toy of her choice and asking to play by sitting in front of me or placing the toy at my feet.

5 December 2007

The dog training school was holding a Christmas party this week, and all the classes were invited to attend. There was doggy party games and festive fare for both bipeds and quadrupeds. My friend, Amy, and I took the girls. With Elle's recent history, we knew this was going to be quite a test. I hoped her special diet and new social skills would help her cope with lots of dogs dressed for the occasion, lots of noise and a lot of people into the bargain.

Elle was perfection personified. No screaming. No aggression. She sat at our feet, and walked at heel for musical chairs. When the music stopped, the owners had to sit with their dog on their knee, which got rid of all the big dogs quite quickly. Mahri was a hoot, because I could get her to jump on to my knee. All you could see was two denim-clad legs sticking out from under a hairy dog. It wasn't only my body that was obscured from view. Mahri had licked my glasses, preventing me from seeing anything at all. With my glasses all smeared, I could barely see the chairs, never mind find an unoccupied one when the music stopped.

After several games, there was the fancy dress parade. Mahri and Elle were sporting their best Christmas bandanas by a top designer called Andrea, or, to be more accurate, my special cyber-friend in Wisconsin. A tiny long-haired Jack Russell won: he was dressed as a pixie and had a red jumper with green breeches and the cutest little pointy green shoes.

The prizes had to be awarded and speeches had to be made before we got to sample the gastronomic delights of the buffet. I'd chosen to sit near the food, thinking the smell would keep Mahri distracted and she'd be good with other dogs. Elle's recent behaviour had made Mahri a tiny bit wary of dogs getting too close to her. The food smells worked for a while, but when Mahri didn't get her own way, she sang like a demented whale, "Oooooo! OOOOO! ooOOooOO!" This amused everyone until their ears broke. I was left feeling a bit embarrassed and more than a bit of a failure. Twelve months of training and I had one of the worst behaved dogs in the room!

Mahri dragged and tugged at the lead to get into eye contact with everyone she could. First, she batted her big eyes and drooled a thousand drools. *"Look at me, a poor starving wretch. Feeed meee, pleeease,"* she'd wail in minus 3-part harmony. Meanwhile, Elle sat on my friend's knee − the epitome of picture postcard cute.

Then it was time for Santa Paws to arrive and every dog got a toy. Elle got a pink elephant almost as big as her, and Mahri got a yellow duck, which she quickly gave to me so she could join the queue for a second toy or, better still, another biscuit. Elle was still Miss Perfection and the night soon disappeared. All in all, it had been a good night … until we got home.

Elle and Mahri decided to quarrel over the elephant like two five-year-olds.

"It's mine … grr!"
"No, it's not … grr!"
"Yes it is … gruff!"
"No … bark!"
"Yes … growl!"

"Cease forthwith!" I yelled. "It's my toy now!"; and it was put in the cupboard. Mahri sulked in her bed for five minutes, but she was such a happy girl. Back she came with her ball and proceeded to throw it around and play her own little game. Elle sat by my feet with feigned indifference. I was surprised by her toy possessiveness, because it was not something that had ever been an issue in the past. She really liked that pink elephant. She never even looked at the yellow duck.

Mr Mac: *"I'm too grown up for Santa Paws, but I'll steal the elephant if I can."*
Mahri: *"I'll swap you for a biscuit."*
Elle: *"Greedy guts."*
Annie: *"Zzzzz ... don't disturb ... zzz."*

6 December 2007

When I got home from work yesterday, Len had gone out with some of his friends, so I had the house to myself for a couple of hours, which was a rare treat. The pups had been good and were wandering round the house. All seemed calm and normal ... or maybe surreal is a better adjective. I'd brought a fish supper home with me to save cooking. I fed myself first so it didn't get cold, with the intention of feeding the dogs the leftovers.

Normally, the dogs are not allowed near when I'm eating, but it was treat night, so they all lay down by my feet while I enjoyed the meal in front of the TV. As soon as I put my cutlery down, they popped up like little meerkats. When I stood up to go to the kitchen, I felt like the Pied Piper, as dogs fell in behind me and silently followed. The leftover skin and batter were chopped, checked for bones and divided between four plates. Mr Mac and Annie got their dinner and then Elle.

Elle could be a bit picky and took a while to eat, so I always gave her a head-start while Mahri had to sit, lie down, sit, give a paw, and give the other paw. Most times, it turned into an Airedale 'hokey cokey' as she tried to do it all at once to get her dinner as fast as possible. Once given the go-ahead, Mahri downed the food in a nano-second; but, by this time, Elle was finished eating and I'd removed her plate because she hated Mahri licking her plate, even though it was empty. I think Elle thought that Mahri was stealing her DNA and might turn into a Welsh Terrier.

On this occasion, Elle had licked the bowl within an inch of its life and was sitting down, staring up at me: *"Yummy, yummy … is there any more?"* She licked her lips – a big, slow lick, making sure not a single crumb was stuck to her beard.

Mahri scampered off, coming back with the yellow duck, and proceeded to throw it around. Oh dear … as calm as Elle had been, I thought that this might be the straw that broke the camel's back. But surprise! Surprise! Elle followed me back to my seat in front of the TV and sat by my feet. I wondered whether she thought there might be more fish on offer.

Mr Mac and Mahri played chase and tug with the duck till one of them pulled its eye out. I had wondered how long it would take before they lost interest and discarded it. Little Elle got up, picked the duck up and sat it by my feet. We were watching *Bones*. It's her favourite TV programme and she doesn't like to be disturbed when it's on. Once the programme was finished, she carried the duck about, hoping someone would play chase, but Mr Mac and Mahri were already tired out from their earlier games and were now happy to doze, one in the hall and the other in the sitting room, looking like a couple of discarded rugs.

The pink elephant had to remain in the cupboard. Otherwise, World War III might start. The only time Elle could have the toy to play with was when she was left in the room with Len and the other two were out in the garden with me. The other option was to allow the Airedales to play with the elephant toy until they were bored. Then Elle could have what was left of it. Perhaps I should have thought about re-introducing the toy along with a fish supper … they were certainly nice and calm after the last one.

12 December 2007

We have had a few issues with Elle, but Mahri is not without blame. With Mahri it was more a case of her charging about and stepping on Elle, rather than actually choosing to argue with her. Last night, Elle, who had been on her special diet for five weeks and was greatly improved, decided that Mahri had her uses after all and decided to call a truce.

I'd washed some carrots and put them in the dish rack on the draining board to drip. Len called me through to help him on his computer for a minute. Ha! When a computer is involved it never takes a minute; but I digress. I heard Elle barking and rushed into the sitting room to see what was happening, half expecting to have to separate her and Mahri. I was very surprised to see Mahri sitting quietly beside Elle.

"What's occurring?" I asked, with a trace of suspicion

in my tone. Mahri turned and looked at me with her huge eyes – I'm sure she stole them from a giraffe; they are big, expressive eyes with what looks like eyeliner round them. Perhaps it was Cleopatra she stole them from! Her look said, *"What? Me? I did nothing."* She always managed to look more guilty when pleading innocence. Then I noticed that Elle was standing with one foot on a large carrot, chomping away at one end. Was this genuine collusion? Hmm, I knew immediately that Mahri had stolen the carrot because Elle couldn't reach the drawer line, never mind the worktop, and Mr Mac had been beside me. The look on her face was such a picture I couldn't tell her off, but I did wonder how Elle had managed to take the carrot from Mahri without fur flying.

Len came through to see what was going on and took the carrot away from Elle and offered it to Mahri, thinking she would bite a lump off; but he's not strong enough to hold a wet carrot, so Mahri just grabbed it and ran off round the dining room table. It was Elle's turn to look, first at me, then at Len. Her face said it all, *"I don't believe he just did that."*

Then Mr Mac ran over to Len with a similar expression, *"I don't believe it either ... all this carrot going about and none for me."*

We had to give them all a piece of carrot, which meant there was one left. That meant carrot soup was off the menu, so we shared the remaining carrot between the dogs as well!

14 January 2008

The Wild Bunch lose a friend

Annie, the grand old duchess, has joined her best pal MacIain now. The poor wee soul was torn between the two loves of her life, MacIain and Len. She wanted to stay with Len, but she was old and tired and missed MacIain.

Annie close-up

The vet came to our house to do the deed. It was kinder to Len and Annie that they should both be in a place where they were comfortable. I put Annie's basket on the grooming table, which I'd brought into the kitchen. This was so Len could reach her and hold her paw. The vet couldn't find a vein in order to administer the injection. He tried her other foreleg, then her back legs, but she had no blood pressure. The vet was perplexed: this dog should not be breathing; there was no blood pressure, so no blood was being pumped round her body. We could see that she was really trying to hang on – to have an extra hug from Len or a couple more tasty treats. After much discussion, it was decided that the vet would take her back to the surgery, which was only ten minutes up the road, anaesthetize her, then administer the drug and bring her back home to us. This was supposed to be better for us because we didn't have to see what they were about to do to Annie.

Our girl was one in a million. She should have died

when she was just twelve months old after she ran into a truck and smashed up her leg and bruised all her internal organs. At four months old, she broke a leg when she escaped from the garden and ran across a frozen ploughed field. The unyielding soil was too hard for her puppy bones and she fell over, twisting her leg. We rushed her to the vet and she was diagnosed with a green stick fracture and was in plaster for a few weeks.

None of this slowed her down and she was always ready for her next adventure. We always said that Annie had led an eventful life. When she was spayed, she was the very rare dog that was allergic to her stitches and ended up with gangrene. They had to cut away all the bad flesh and, when she had healed, her nipples were all out of alignment.

We have so many fond memories of Annie that she will never really be far from us. She lived her life in the fast lane, which complemented MacIain's almost Rastafarian take on life. The three hooligans were now without their doggy leader who, with one little bark, could silence them far quicker than any of my attempts.

I can now see the funny side of yesterday and the eloquence of the animal world. While we were waiting for the vet to arrive, we decided to put the hooligans in the day kennel because Elle would scream till she got some attention, Mahri would bark and bark and Mr Mac would run back and forth huffing and gruffing, worried by the presence of a stranger in the house.

I knew they'd still carry on in the kennel, but at least we'd not be deafened or knocked over. They bounded into the kennel, anxious to get their treat, and for the next two hours, an unexpected silence emanated from the day kennel. The vet came and went. Silence. He returned. Silence. He left. Silence. We put Annie in my car and slowly drove to the bottom of the garden. The silence continued. I put the digging equipment in the shed next door to the kennel. Still silence.

We put leads on the hooligans and took them into the house. The trio rushed to Annie's kitchen basket, sniffed it all over and then rushed to her sitting room basket, barking in unison, before visiting her hall basket. They were confused. Annie was nowhere to be seen. Mahri had a brainwave and went to the garage door, jumping up to look through the window to see if Annie was shut in there.

When it was time for their tea, Elle wouldn't eat and just kept looking at Annie's basket. She remembered that I'd always helped Annie to stand and walk to her bowl before Elle got fed. Mahri kept going to her bed, where she was often sent for knocking Annie over in her rush to get to her dinner place. After dinner, they were much more subdued than was normal and not one of them would go near Annie's bed or her dinner place.

Well, that was the eloquence. Now for the funny side. I was too sad yesterday, but today, as I recounted my story to work colleagues, I was smiling and laughing with them. I knew my sister would have laughed her socks off had she been standing beside me.

Eleven years ago, we rescued a little two-foot sapling Scots Pine tree growing wild on an old coal bing on Lanark moor near my sister's house. (The area where she lived was extensively mined, so there are lots of huge black hills made up of the spoil from the mines. We call them Bings in Scotland. It means to pile up. Some bings have national heritage status, like the Five Sisters in West Lothian.) We brought the little sapling home and planted it at the bottom of the garden, where it could grow as big as it wanted and, when McGregor died, we buried him behind it as he loved romping through forests with us. When it was MacIain's turn, he was buried on the south side of the tree and a little bush planted, but the wind and the weeds didn't allow the bush to grow, so his grave was not as clearly marked as it should have been.

I had taken the afternoon off work yesterday to do what had to be done, as it was easier to do in the daylight. I knew it would be heavy going as the clay soil was saturated from weeks of rain. I also knew it would have been Annie's last wish to be with MacIain.

Either the ground wasn't as bad as I'd expected, or maybe I'd found an inner strength. I began to think that perhaps I should stop and move one pace to my left and start again, but I was sad, it was teeming with rain and the howling winds made the rain sting any flesh it came into contact with. Then, shock horror. As I dug up a clod of earth, a skull rolled off the end of my spade. Oops! Or several words to that effect. I knew it was MacIain, or at least what was left of him. I quickly reburied the skull and started a new plot one pace to the left. Yep, this time I was definitely digging virgin soil – brick-hard, compacted soil.

Len arrived to see if I needed any help. I knew he couldn't really do anything, but I said he could keep me company and tell me if the sides were straight and the bottom level, which he duly did.

I never told him about the little mishap. I just said I'd tidied up MacIain's plot and put a new tree in. Luckily, we had several native trees in pots that Len was planning to turn into bonsai trees. He went off to pick a tree for Annie and returned with a mountain ash, which was very fitting, because a year before Len had his accident, Len and I had climbed Ben Nevis with Annie and MacIain – it was the highest mountain in Scotland at 4409 feet. When we were told it would take 8 hours for the round trip, Len, in true Sergeant-Major and Airedale fashion, said, "Rubbish! It will take about 5 hours." He marched us up to the top, where it was so misty we couldn't see a thing, and then he marched us home again in 5 hours.

1 March 2008

You might have thought life would have been getting a little quieter with the Wild Bunch as they could no longer be classed as puppies; but not so. It had been a very wet February, with the odd nice day here and there being a welcome rarity. The Wild Bunch had been in the house, growing bored and more boisterous by the hour.

Sally, the girl that helps Len while I'm at work, decided it would do both Len and her waistline some good if they were to get out for a bit of fresh air. They got his four-by-four wheelchair out, put the leads on Elle and Mahri and started off down the road.

Now, I've been telling Len, and anybody else that will listen to me, that I had to walk the dogs on the road, as the public footpaths had been destroyed by farm tractors and thirty or more horses from a local riding school leaving two-foot-deep ruts filled with mud. But did he listen? Len thought he knew best and turned down an overgrown grass-covered footpath. The grass and weeds neatly concealed ruts, lumps and pools of gloop. I wouldn't even take my off-road car down there because it would get stuck, so Len's wheelchair didn't stand a chance.

About halfway along the path, the front wheel of Len's chair slipped into a rut, nearly tipping him on to the ground. The sudden jolt made him let go of Elle's extending lead; Elle, sensing freedom, ran off as fast as she could. Unfortunately, the very nature of an extending lead meant that it chased Elle down the path. The faster Elle ran away, the faster the lead bounced ever closer to her rear end. You can just picture the Disney cartoon scene!

Sally lunged forward to catch Len and Elle, and hung on to Mahri, who thought this was a new game. Unfortunately for Sally, her foot sank into the mud and then suddenly freed itself. This action caused her to lose her shoe, which was still buried in the mud, and she lost her balance. As she tumbled to the ground, she released Mahri's lead. Now they had a problem: Mahri was bouncing around like a gazelle and heading east, Elle was heading west at a rapid rate, scared of the lump of plastic that was trying to attack her rear end. Len was finely balanced at a 45 degree angle and Sally was picking herself up out of the mud, searching for her sock and shoe.

Len told her to get the dogs first, as he wasn't going anywhere. Sally nearly caught Elle a few times, but missed at the last minute. Already covered in mud, her next thought was to just go for it. She made a flying rugby tackle leap and caught the plastic handle of the extending lead and managed to reel Elle back in. Next she went after Mahri, who was every bit as good at evading capture but was eventually caught when she found something so tasty she just couldn't leave it (probably something a horse left behind). Finally, she had to rescue Len from the rut and get him back on to terra firma.

I, fortunately, was not present to witness this, but had

returned home to find Sally dressed in Len's old tracksuit and the drive covered in lumps of mud, as well as two very muddy pups in the day kennel drying off, and a grinning Len, who was very damp because of the back-spray when Sally hosed down his wheelchair.

Len proceeded to tell me what had happened. I, of course, was very sympathetic and listened without the slightest sign of a smile until the point where Sally lost her shoe. From there on I was howling with such uncontrollable laughter I couldn't even muster the composure to utter the words, "I told you so!"

7 March 2008

The Wild Bunch have been very quiet since their stay in the local dog kennels. Oops! Did I say kennels? I meant luxury doggy accommodation. We had made the journey north again to stock up on gourmet essentials like plain bread, square sausages, and haggis. You just can't buy these things in the south of England. Maybe the Wild Bunch were just so laid back and relaxed, they could no longer be bothered to cause mischief; but, as they say, all good things must come to an end, or, in the case of the Wild Bunch, bad things. If they were quiet for any extended period, like five or more waking minutes, then I worried about health issues.

Elle had been the most clingy, often lying on my feet or sitting in a corner like a discarded toy. She had the 'forlorn look' so perfected that I half expect a visit from the RSPCA to see if we were looking after her properly.

Last night, the Wild Bunch had taken themselves off to their respective beds: Mr Mac was in the hall, Mahri in the kitchen and Elle in the utility room. Share is not in their vocabulary – that is, if they had one.

About 3.00am, Elle woke me with her barking. I assumed she wanted to be taken out, which was odd, as she would not normally need out during the night. I took her out, or rather she dragged me out of the door, barking and yapping. She dragged me straight over the wet grass towards a hedgehog happily chomping on some slugs. Fortunately for the hedgehog, I'd spotted it in time to guide her round in a circle to another part of the grass; but it was too late. She knew it was there. She stomped and gruffed and grunted and kicked up turf like a miniature bull.

"How did you know that was out here? I don't believe you could have heard it walking past the house or chomping on its dinner … and I don't think you could have picked up its scent until you were out of the house," I muttered at her all the way back to the house.

She was reluctant to go in. She'd done the hunt bit and her dander was up. She wanted to finish the job. As I tugged at her lead to make her come in the door, a huge moth swooped down low, over her head and into the house. All thoughts of the hedgehog were left on the doorstep as she lunged at the moth. I quickly shut the door to prevent further invasion by the winged monsters and dropped her lead in order to free both hands to protect myself from the threat the winged beast represented.

Elle was in her element – no pun intended – chasing and leaping and pouncing after the moth. I left her to get on with it and returned to bed. As I drifted off to sleep, I was aware of the odd thump as she banged into the wall or door, and the occasional screech of the kitchen chair across the tiles when she mistimed one of her pounces. I hoped she'd tire soon.

I was up again at 6.00am and went to the kitchen. There in the middle of the floor on its back was one very large dead moth. Legs in the air, wings spread-eagled. Elle must have left it for me as a trophy from her night's hunting. She, of course, was curled up in bed sound asleep. Mahri, who had slept through all the commotion, or pretended to, stretched and came to greet me.

"Ooh, what's that on the floor? Could it be food? A pre-breakfast snack, perhaps?" She looked at it, tilting her head from side to side. *"Hmm, not food. Someone clear it up please! I can't stand dead things before breakfast."*

Mr Mac entered the room, stared at the inert body for a moment and wondered how he could get past it, puffing his jaws in and out while he formulated his escape plan. This puffing his jaws in and out as though hyperventilating was something he did when he was unsure of anything. Decision made at last, he leapt across the inert body to safety in a single bound.

Some dogs and other mammals consider the moth to be a delectable delicacy, but not my dogs. At this point, I picked up a brush and shovel and very bravely retired the moth from its reign of terror on the kitchen floor. I did think about leaving it for Sally to clear away when she arrived but I didn't think Mr Mac would come back in the house while the corpse remained on my kitchen floor.

11 March 2008

It's been 'Crufts Week', and seeing all the well-groomed dogs has spurred me into action to get my hairy crew ready for spring. Each night, I've combed, stripped and clipped a little bit of one of the dogs. It's too big a job to do in one go. I could spend three or four hours on one and that wouldn't be for show standard. Airedales and most double-coated Terriers are hand-stripped for the show ring. This involves many hours of plucking out dead coat. The dogs don't seem to mind, but I end up with sore fingers and shoulders, so I do a bit of both: clip the difficult bits like faces, ears and rears, and hand strip their back and legs.

On Friday night, it was Mr Mac's turn; he got his ears clipped, his feet cleaned, claws clipped and a general comb-through to get his undercoat out. I planned to strip his top coat out on the Saturday because it looked about ready. On the Friday night, I'd noticed a little scab on his ear that wasn't there the day before. *Hmmm.* I thought that Mahri must have got a bit too rough with him and nipped him. I gave it a wash with some antiseptic and really didn't think much more about it.

On the Saturday evening, I had the pups on leads walking round the garden. Mr Mac was running around off-lead because I thought he was sensible enough not to leave the garden. Suddenly, Elle started her screaming, *"I'm gonna git you ... I'm gonna kill you."* She screamed like this at birds, leaves, fluff, and anything that passed her without her permission. I looked in the direction of her outburst, only to see Mr Mac, who was on the opposite side of the garden, jump back from whatever he was sniffing and give his head a shake. I thought he must have been sniffing a bee. There had been a couple of big ones about the garden this last week or so. Elle must have telescopic vision, spotting a bee from the far side of the garden.

Playtime over, we returned to the house. I encouraged Mahri on to the grooming table with a biscuit and spent an hour or so working on her coat. Next, it was Mr Mac's turn. He jumped on to the table with almost no effort. His face was now at my eye level and I immediately noticed two lines of blood dripping down his moustache. I cleaned it all with some antiseptic.

"Mr Mac, you've been bitten," I remarked. He had four puncture wounds, two on either side just above his big black nose. That must have been what Elle was squealing at. But what was it? A rat or a snake, perhaps? We live near a grain store and get the odd rat in the garden. I've also seen two-foot-long grass-snakes in the garden.

I carried on doing the rest of his coat. His face could be done another day. Later that night, I noticed the wound was still seeping blood. It seemed a little bit odd that it hadn't clotted, but I wasn't too worried and cleaned it again.

I was just about to retire for the night when I noticed that he'd chewed a bit on both of his hips. Now I was getting a bit worried. I got his Buster Collar, or lampshade as I call it, in from the garage. It was left over from his 'Mr to Miss' operation. I washed all the chewed bits again. I also gave him doses of Ledum and Arnica, two homeopathic medicines that I used for first aid treatments. I expected him to be fine in the morning and I went to bed.

On the Sunday morning, the puncture wounds were still open. They were looking clean and he was eating, drinking and wagging his tail, so I thought he would be fine; but, to be on the safe side, my friend was going to look after him while we went to Crufts Dog Show. We like to go each year as it gives us the chance to catch up on the dog show gossip and meet with old friends that we do not live close enough to visit on a regular basis. Mr Mac was still fine when we got home, although he did seem to be

Temptation

scratching a bit more. I decided that I would take him to the vet on Monday.

The vet listened to my suspicions about the perpetrator of the attack on Mr Mac and I told her I was 100% sure it was not Elle. She looked at the wound.

"Hmm … definitely not dog, too close … but not snake or rat, because they could not have bitten over the bridge of his nose. Do you have a cat?" she asked.

"No," I said, but the penny dropped. "Cat? Yes, there is a feral cat that hangs about the hedge and I know she was very pregnant the last time I saw her."

"That will be it. He's probably stuck his head in or under the hedge and found her kittens."

Apparently, a cat can attack three times in the same outburst that a rat or snake would have attacked once. The latter attacked in defence and made its escape. Not so a cat. It attacks and, before you recover, puts the boot in. What's even worse is that their mouths are so full of bacteria, the recipient of the attack always ends up with an infection. In Mr Mac's case, the infection had gone right through his system. This was why he had chewed at his hips and scratched his cut ear, which now looked as if it had a strawberry growing out of it and lots of little cysts growing on the end of his ear.

He was prescribed some antibiotics for 10 days and a very low dose of steroids to stop the itching. The vet said that, if I felt his body and he was hot to touch but not panting, this showed he was fighting an infection and a possible allergic reaction to cat bites.

Poor Mr Mac was feeling a little bit sorry for himself. He even chose to sleep in Annie's basket, which is something he'd never done in all the time we've had him, and, of course, after Annie's passing, Elle took ownership of the basket. It was a brave dog that chose to sleep in her bed. Airedales are supposed to be very intelligent, but I suspect Mr Mac was at the end of the queue when brains were being issued. He had not learned anything from this encounter. Even with his Buster Collar on, he ran out the door over to the hedge and was ready to stick his head in it again. Perhaps he couldn't believe it was a little cat that bit him.

26 March 2008

The agility class where I used to take Mr Mac closed at Christmas. The people that ran the class decided not to open in the January due to other work commitments. By chance, when walking the dogs today, I saw a sign for a new club that was only a twenty-minute walk from my house.

It seemed like a good idea and I thought that, by the time I walked down to the field on a Sunday morning, Mr Mac's muscles would be warmed up and he could have some fun. The class was to run from 10.00am to 11.30am for beginners and 12.00 noon to 2.00pm for advanced. I took Mr Mac down at 10.30 and because he was so good they said he would probably be better at the next level. I stayed, but he didn't do as well as was expected. I suggested that I bring Mahri down for 30 minutes and then Mr Mac could have 30 minutes of each class. That way I wouldn't hold up hardened competitors as I had no intention of entering any competition.

On the second week, all went well. Mahri even learned to go over the seesaw. By the third week, we seemed to hang around a lot. In three hours, Mahri and Mr Mac each had run only one circuit. Mr Mac was bored silly on the fourth week. I also got some vague call saying that Mr Mac's time slot was changed to 2.00pm. I thought this might be a mistake, as that was when the last class finished. I decided to call round by the exercise field when walking Mahri and Elle on the Sunday morning. When we got there at 8.30am, some people had arrived. The classes, as I'd mentioned earlier, didn't start till 10.00am. "Oh, that's good; we'll take Mahri in early," I suggested to my friend.

The people who had arrived early just happened to be the 'child-model super-brat' with her 'super-brat mum' and her sister, who, considering her immediate family, was actually quite nice. The girls had a Jack Russell each. One dog was quite nice, the other a snappy little thing that bit people. No guesses as to which girl owned the nice dog. When the super-brat was told not to let her dog bite people because it wasn't funny, her reply was very rude and conveyed the general message of, "Don't tell me what to do with my dog". Naturally, this sort of attitude defeated the purpose of attending the dog training classes. It appeared that both parent and child had misconstrued the idea of a dog training class.

Anyway, we wandered in and said hello and what a good idea it was to get there a bit earlier. The mother rather aggressively said, "We've been asked to come early so he [the trainer] can assess my girls and their dogs."

OK, I thought, we'll still be first here and get a couple of rounds in at 10.00am when the class was due to start. While I was waiting with my friend Amy and the aforementioned family, the trainer walked over to speak to me. I was suitably attired, or so I thought, in my wellies and tracksuit, so I was not quite sure why he had a rather stern look as he approached.

"New dog?" he barked at Elle, or was it me.

"This is Elle," I responded, picking her up to say hello.

"Well, she will have to be enrolled in the next intake and from now on you're not allowed on the field unless you have proper agility shoes. And all dogs will work off-lead."

"Mahri is not ready to work off-lead yet," I countered.

"Well, she'll work off-lead here," he growled at me.

Turning his back, he called one of the Jack Russells back into the training field. I was more than a little miffed. Then he called the other dog back in. By this time, another lady had arrived and said that it was a bit boring hanging about for so long. The trainer's comments were, "Watch and learn, watch and learn." He took the new arrival next and then the two Jack Russells again. That was it! I had a major 'sense of humour failure'; my dogs were called to attention and marched back home.

While Amy and I were stomping up the road, we realized that it was after 11.00am. We'd been watching and, dare I say, learning since 9.00am. What was the lesson of the day? I do not really know. All we had learned was that this man, for some reason, did not like me or my dogs. When I got home and had calmed down with a nice cup of tea, I gave Len the abridged version of our lesson for the day. I told him that I would not be going back to that class, and put the sorry fiasco out of my thoughts.

The next day, Len got a call from the trainer's wife asking why we had walked away from the class. She said they were very upset by our sudden departure. Len gave her a brief answer and told her she'd be better to speak to me. Later that day, she phoned me and I told her that I did not think the club agenda matched the description she'd given me when I asked about joining and I would not be returning.

The trainer's wife wanted a fuller explanation, so I pointed out the new shoe rule and how absurd it was to expect me to buy expensive shoes to walk round a field on a Sunday morning, twice if I was extremely lucky. Still she wanted more reasons, so I told her that I'd stood for over two hours watching the trainer concentrate on two dogs. I said that wasn't a problem if the club's agenda was to bring on young handlers. However, I could not agree with the trainer's idea of 'watch and learn'. If dogs could watch and learn, then they'd all be driving cars and operating computers.

At that moment, mine were watching a car programme in the hope they could save me some money should they crash my car on their way to PC World to buy the next gadget that could be operated without opposable thumbs. I think she got the idea that I was unhappy and would not be returning. After all, Sundays are for reading the paper and walking dogs ...

The Wild Bunch: *"... And eating sausages! Think we'll let you stick to the driving for now."*

1 April 2008

One of my email friends in Airedale Rescue Nevada makes the cutest little Airedale and other breed ornaments from pipe cleaner-type sticks. She makes up different themes for each batch and this month's theme was 'Have a Heart'. All the proceeds from the sale of these items would go to help Airedales in need. She sent me a couple as a gift. I really liked my little 'Have a Heart Airedales'. They had little pink hearts on their collars and were playing with tiny striped sugar cane sticks. They were about one inch high and two inches long. Included in the parcel was a third little Airedale dog dressed as an angel with gold filigree wings and a little halo. I left the tiny ornaments on the worktop near the back corner, well out of reach, or so I thought. I showed them to people when they came to visit. I never thought for a moment that they would not be safe. Welsh Terrier Elle couldn't reach, Mr Mac never counter-surfed and Mahri seemed to have grown out of it. She'd never even touched the slice of bread I'd left on the bread board when Len called for my assistance the other night; so imagine my shock when, after nipping out to put the car in the garage, I came back into the kitchen to see Elle scampering off with something. At first, I thought it was a bit of scrap paper, and then I took a second glance.

"What's that you've got, Elle?" I asked, not really expecting an answer or her to bring it to me. I did recognize it as something she shouldn't have, but couldn't think what it was or where she'd pinched it from. You can't make a lunge to grab Elle because she's so tiny and very fast. She can scoot under the table and away before you even take a step in her direction. Fortunately, Mr Mac decided to prance about because he thought he was going to be told off. On this occasion, he had done nothing wrong except get in my way as I tried to catch Elle. I shouted at him to get out of the way, Elle felt obliged to add her two-pence worth, so she dropped her prize and ran off to reprimand him. Elle always had to have the final word if I've had occasion to reprimand the Airedales. She would run up to them, stand on her back legs and look them straight in the eye. I don't know what this action implied, but the big dogs never move and clearly know they've been told off.

I retrieved the object. "WHOOO DID THIS? MAHRI, GET TO YOUR BED NOW!!!!!" I bellowed. "AND THAT WILL BE WITHOUT DINNER!" I added.

Mahri went straight to bed and Mr Mac paced back and forth, puffing his cheeks. *"Oh dear, you've really done it this time. She is beyond mad!"*

The object was my little 'Have a Heart' Airedale and it was all bent and twisted. I went back to the kitchen to check the others. The angel was all that was left and she must have been sleeping when Mahri sneaked up and stole the two little Airedale ornaments.

I went in search of the other one and found one leg and then another leg. I was a bit worried because they were made of pipe cleaner and I hoped Mahri or Elle hadn't eaten any part of them. Eventually, my search was fruitful and I found what was left of the other Airedale, except for its little cane. This prompted a further search and finally the little cane was found in the hall. They must have had a tug-of-war, but, like Humpty Dumpty, I don't think all the King's men or horses could put these two pipe-cleaner ornaments back together again.

Mahri sneaked out of her bed and offered me a paw.

"Get to your bed, brat!" I growled at her. She immediately tried to climb on Len's knee and pretend to be Elle, which made us laugh. That was it. She'd won. She knew it and became all bouncy and kissy. I relented and gave her dinner after all. I was never really going to make her go without her dinner; that would have been too cruel to a foodaholic like Mahri. It amazed me that Mahri reached the back of the worktop. I think Mahri must have borrowed one of Len's extendable grabbers in order to reach the ornaments. Mahri jumping on Len's knee reminded me of the day she jumped on his bed. Unfortunately for Len, he was still in bed at the time. I laughed so much when she jumped on the bed and sat on him. Mahri thought this was good, so she did little pirouettes on his chest and licked his face, because she knew he couldn't push her off. When I tried to push or pull her off, she resisted so much that Elle – aka the cavalry – came to Len's rescue, which made it worse. Instead of a heroic rescue, Len was trampled by the stampede and deafened by the noise of Elle barking in his ear. There was nothing that could be described as subtle about that girl.

You just about heard his plaintiff cry, "Get them off of me!" in the cacophony of noise created by one very small dog. Have you ever tried to lift a fifty-pound Airedale with a fifteen-pound Welsh attached to one of her appendages off a bed, when laughing uncontrollably? You'd soon realize that it was not that easy. I couldn't lift them at all I was laughing so much. Luckily, Mr Mac didn't join in any of this; he was an ex-show dog and far too posh to join in this rabble.

17 April 2008

I don't think I need worry about Mahri looking fat any more. She shoved past me on Friday and got out of the house, minus her lead. Off she went like a Whippet, running down the road. The first stop was the garden where two Westies lived. Mahri jumped up to look in the window and surprised the owner, who came to the door just in time to see Mahri racing off, with me hot on her heels, to visit the Jack Russells' house on the opposite side of the road.

I just missed catching her as she vaulted the low hedge and ran off down the road to the Spaniel's house, with me still in pursuit. I had planned to trap her in the corner near the gate before she could dart past me again. Suddenly, with her nose twitching, she stopped in her tracks; then she homed in on an interesting odour. This was my chance – her nose was so busy she wouldn't hear me sneak up and grab her collar. Mahri headed for the drain in the road, as it seemed to be the place where the odour was most concentrated.

I couldn't even begin to tell you what it was that was creating this interesting diversion to Mahri's little marathon. I was far too busy inhaling any air that I could before I collapsed with hypoxia. One thing I'm definitely not is a sprinter. Mahri's single moment of hesitation meant

I could catch her and march her back home.

On Saturday, I attached an ordinary lead to her collar to take her for a walk. I thought (and exactly why I did this thinking thing I didn't know, silly me; I truly believe that 'thinking' should carry a government health warning) I'd try her without her Halti.[2] We got as far as the gate and she remembered the drain smell from Friday night. That was it! She was up on two legs, bouncing down the street like a marsupial, with me trying to dig my heels in, but continuing to progress down the road faster than safety permitted. I don't know if me tugging on the collar and screeching at her finally alerted her to my plight, or if she forgot where the drain was, or, perhaps, she might have smelt something more interesting altogether, but she dropped to all fours and made an effort to walk beside me. This was just as well, because I'd managed to trap my little finger in a fold in the lead and it was now giving me a great deal of pain. I was convinced she'd broken it. Sure enough, three days later, I was sporting a nice yellow bruise on my knuckle.

Today was extremely cold and windy, so long walks were not the order of the day and Mahri was volunteered for a grooming session. I had a new CD for company, so off we went out in the garage – music up loud, Mahri on the grooming table.

Comb and strip and comb and strip. Eventually, this very nice looking little Airedale appeared on the grooming table. No wide posterior, short leg or Westie head. I stood back and admired my handiwork. Her coat verged on mousy brown with not a lot of black; she had two pale

2   Head collar designed to promote maximum steering efficiency with comfort (of the dog) when walking.

beige heels and a soft coat. It was almost as if a soft-coated Wheaten sneaked in when I was distracted. Just to be sure, I offered her a biscuit. Drool, drool, snatch. No, this was not an imposter. It was definitely, my little foodaholic Mahri.

Next up for a good comb through was Mr Mac, and then it was Elle's turn. She was always four times more work than any Airedale, but I persevered and, once again, I was pleased with my handiwork. Even Len thought I'd made a good job this time and that was a big compliment coming from 'Mr Perfection'. In case the new music had anything to do with my creative success, I made a note to use that CD again for grooming. "And what was it?" I hear you ask. 'The Dance of the Seven Veils' and similar stuff from Arabian Nights! I used to use some blues or rock & roll music, but I've achieved better grooming results with this orchestral piece.

Elle seemed to be training for the Olympics, or maybe she was trying to run away to join the circus. Perhaps she heard me talking about my friend, Maureen, who always referred to her motley crew of Airedales as the Circus; it always sounded like such fun over there in Canada.

Len had Elle on her lead in the garden but, because he has limited feeling in his hands, he didn't realize he'd let the lead slip through his fingers. Elle had conjured a new cunning escape plan; instead of forging ahead all the time, she trotted by his side, lulling him into a false sense of security. When the tension on the lead slackened, Elle slowly walked away till she knew she was out of reach. Then, whoosh! and she was off.

As soon as I heard Len shout at her, I knew she'd escaped, so I headed for the corner of the garden where she generally sneaked under the hedge and fence; *hmm, propels would probably be a better verb.* I got under the hedge a nano-second too late and had to follow her into a neighbouring garden, where she was running round and round the two cars parked on the drive.

Now bear in mind that this was the scary neighbour that we avoid where possible. The fact that she had led us to believe she hated dogs didn't really make trying to retrieve my dog from her garden any easier or less frightening. I let Elle see me. Then I turned and ran in the opposite direction, hoping the dog would follow me. Everything was going just swimmingly and Elle was heading to the gate at a steady trot when the next minute – whoosh! – she dived past me and ran over the road to the Jack Russells' residence.

Len had joined me by this point, but only succeeded in chasing her further down the road. We managed to corner her again and Len insisted on trying to grab her, but couldn't hold on and she scooted off towards the geese in a nearby field.

Elle gave the geese a wide berth and headed for another field, which was surrounded by an electric fence. The fence was high enough for Elle to duck under. I, on the other hand, had to crawl under it. Then I was in the field with a beautiful big hunter stallion staring at me. Being city bred, I feel much more confident round horses when I'm on the other side of the fence and not in the same paddock. The horse looked at me and then at Elle, who was charging up and down his field.

"Look at me! Look at how fast I can run!"

I tried to call her quietly so I didn't startle the horse, but Elle had other ideas. The horse was now heading in her

Happy Elle

direction.

"How dare this young strumpet enter MY field?" it seemed to say.

Elle stood her ground. I wish I'd had a camera. She stood in a wide-legged, stompy stance.

"Yes? Your problem is?"

She visibly challenged the horse.

"Bring it on then. You don't scare me ... here I am ... there's no cage round me."

She skipped a bit nearer to the horse, who was still giving her a menacing stare.

"Yeah, whatever," she seemed to say, moving her tail very slowly from side to side, as if challenging the horse to catch her if it dared.

The horse was moving closer and snorting at Elle, and

I had visions of her orbiting the earth from a swift back-heel flick from one of the horse's hoofs. Elle still refused to budge. Fortunately, the horse's owner appeared and saved the day by calling Elle, who went to her immediately. Once again, I was apologizing for running round a stranger's garden attempting to catch this silly dog that will do everything it can to avoid me. Len suggested that we get a ball and chain attached to her collar – one that is big enough to get jammed under the hedge.

27 May 2008

The Wild Bunch had been fairly quiet recently, until yesterday … well, Saturday actually. The pups had to go to the vet's for their boosters and Mr Mac needed his kennel cough vaccine, so my friend, Amy, came with me and looked after Elle while I had, or thought I had, control of the other two.

When we entered the waiting room at the clinic, the vet was running a bit late and, as a result, there were quite a few people in the waiting room. I thought that the wait might prove interesting, as most people seemed to have cats or, to a dog's eye view, noisy boxes. Most dog owners know that any box that made a noise must be investigated by the dog. This commonly upset the occupant of the box, who then would make even more noise!

We started with the weigh-in and Mr Mac was first. "OK, son, on the scales … sit … good boy! And off. Now you, Mahri." Mahri was not so compliant and she had an audience to entertain who encouraged her by laughing at her antics.

"How about you only weigh one leg and multiply the answer by 4? No, well just weigh my front end and double the answer. No? OK, how about if I jump on and off real quick? Oh dear, you missed it. Try again. On, off. Off, on. Half and half? One foot, my nose and my tail ... OK, I'm bored now ... where's the parrot? It used to be in this corner."

By this time, everyone was smirking or trying to suppress a fit of giggles. "OK, Elle, your turn." She tried to show Mahri how it was done, but Mahri's mind had gone walk-about.

We took a seat as far away from the others as possible and all was calm. Elle was on Amy's knee and Mahri and Mr Mac were lying at my feet. While I was chatting with Amy, I heard footsteps on the other side of the reception desk, so I knew someone was about to leave. Just as I was tightening my grip on the two leads, a Staffordshire Terrier's face appeared round the side of the reception desk and it was smiling, almost grinning like a Cheshire cat. I didn't know what it said or who it insulted – had it suggested that Mahri had a big bum? All I knew was that, amid the sudden cacophony of barking Airedales and a squealing Welsh Terrier, I was projected from my seat in a horizontal direction and propelled across the floor. Fortunately, I had rubber-soled boots on and managed to halt my slide and return to my seat with my two dogs. Apart from the assault on our ears, everyone was unscathed. It was only when I sat down that I spotted the claw marks and skid marks from my boots on the lino. I sat there wondering wryly whether I should have stuck with tropical fish.

The vet examined Mr Mac first.

"I do like working with show dogs," she said. "They are so good." And he was, bless him, even when she squirted the vaccine up his nose.

Next it was Mahri's turn. I could not make her sit or stand. She just wriggled and wriggled and wriggled, although not in a nasty way. She was just totally excited.

"Let me see! Let me sniff! Look at me bounce! I can bounce higher than a Tigger!"

Eventually, we persuaded her to stay still long enough to get the injection and vaccine and the treat which we thought she been eagerly awaiting; but, instead, for the first time ever, I saw her refuse food. She took the tasty morsel from the vet, then spat it out. I offered it to her and she turned her head. I showed her the offering one more time and she still turned away.

"Oh well, Mr Mac, looks like you get double treats."

Last but not least, Elle was offered to the vet for examination. Now, I had been expecting trouble from Elle as she can be a bit of a nipper if she is prodded against her will. Elle was 'Miss Perfection': she took all the poking and prodding, the injections and nasal spray without a murmur and then daintily accepted her biscuit like the diva she hoped people would believe she is.

Later that night, the house a few doors down had a wild teenage party; they had one every year about the same time and it usually ended with the public phone being smashed up, bins thrown across the road and other mindless vandalism.

I took the dogs out, one at a time, because I knew they would take umbrage at the noise and influx of alien beings. Mahri barked ferociously at them and Elle barked and squealed. Mr Mac said nothing. I went back out by myself, moving the bins and locking the drive gate, hoping it would all end soon so I could finally get some sleep. There was no chance of that happening. Elle barked and growled the whole night. She was on guard at the door and no-one was going to get past her! She was very tired by daybreak, but then the whole household was very tired, having been kept awake by the external goings on and Elle's attempts to keep the party-goers from entering the house.

When I took Mr Mac for his morning walk, I noticed that the safety poles warning of the open drain outside our house had been smashed. Our neighbour from across the road, Sam, walked very purposely towards us, coming to a halt right in front of me. He was a tad deaf and as a result shouted a bit. As he started to speak, he pointed at the party house. Without any warning whatsoever, Mr Mac grabbed his wrist and held him. We were both really surprised, because Mr Mac was frightened of most men and ran and hid under the table if a strange man came into the house. The fact that he knew Sam made it all the more remarkable. We often exchanged greetings when walking at weekends.

We laughed and I told Mr Mac to let go. I pulled him back as he reluctantly released Sam's sleeve, inch by inch, till the very last bit twanged out of his teeth. As soon as Sam spoke to him, he was fine. There was no damage done to Sam, not even a wet mark on his jacket, but I suspected he might have had a bruise the following day.

5 August 2008

We had a couple of really bad thunderstorms during the last few days. When I left the office, the surface water on the street was so deep I had to take my shoes off and run to the car in my bare feet because the water would have ruined them.

By the time I'd driven 20 miles home from work, the weather had changed and everywhere appeared to be sunny and dry. I quickly changed into my tracksuit and my wellies so I could let the dogs out for a run in the garden; but, just as I reached the far end of the garden, the heavens opened and we were completely soaked before we could retreat to the house.

I dried the dogs while the thunder boomed and banged and lightning flashed. The Wild Bunch never flinched. There was not even so much as a nose twitch or an ear flick. Because my plans to do any outside activity had been scuppered, I decided to make a cup of tea. I picked the kettle up and turned the tap on to fill it. The view from the kitchen sink looked out on to the drive and across some fields. Just as I was contemplating the beauty of the stormy sky, a huge flash right in front of the window made me jump back.

"Oh dear!!" I said. "That was a bit close for comfort." The lightning must have hit the ground right outside the window. I felt really lucky that it had missed the house.

All the dogs went straight to red alert. Elle stood her ground in the middle of the kitchen, her little stompy legs braced against a would-be threat. Nobody would get by her! Like a spider in a web, she could charge in any direction. Mahri went immediately to the back door, barking enough to frighten the dead; and Mr Mac, the man of the house, of course shot under the table in one bound. He was not being a woose, he protested, and pointed out that he was taking up a tactical position as the last line of defence. If the thunder bunnies got past me and the girls, he would leap out and scare them away!

11 August 2008

Mahri came into season a couple of weeks ago. It was the first one we'd noticed. Although she was two in June, the vet assured us that she had been in season before and we'd just missed it. 'Silent seasons', she termed them.

Well, we certainly noticed this one. Mahri is normally the kindest of dogs. She did play a little rough at times, but never meant any harm. However, this past week, she had tried the patience of everyone. Even Elle, who had an evil temper, avoided Mahri and chose to sit on Len's knee rather than be trampled on.

Mahri had been barking incessantly at imaginary intruders, stomping on anything and anyone that got between her and the door or her food bowl. She head-butted my brother, bringing him to his knees on more than one occasion. As a consequence, he began to enter the house backwards. Her ears appeared to be no longer connected to her apparently intelligent Airedale brain. It was as if she was sharing the brain with an ostrich this month.

During the weekend, she surpassed herself with naughtiness. My friend Amy and I took the dogs out for a walk; Amy was holding Elle and I took charge of the force that was Mr Mac and Mahri. We walked the same route we always walk at weekends; but, for Mahri, it was as though it had turned into the movies: *Friday the Thirteenth* or *Hallowe'en*. Nothing was above suspicion. A leaf flew by in the wind and Mahrri rose up on her hind legs, barking and screaming at it. This was only the beginning of the torrent of abuse she was about to embark on. On the hit list to get the sharp side of her tongue was a fly and then a bird. A big hairy caterpillar that was walking up the road minding its own business became the next victim. Elle had walked past it and never even noticed – but it was spotted by Mahri at 50 paces. She screamed and barked and dragged me towards this creature. Mr Mac was on serious alert from all the fuss she was making, so he felt obliged to join in. Eventually, I managed to drag them past the creepy-crawly and continued with our walk.

You might have thought that would have been the last eventful moment of the walk – but no. A suicidal rabbit darted out in front of us and I only just managed to hang on to Mahri.

"That's it! Enough, the pair of you! You've spoiled a nice walk, so we're going home … and no toast for either of you!"

Mahri realized that I was dishing out serious punishment now. No toast! Her weekend treat for which she'd waited all week was off the menu. We walked halfway home with some reasonably good behaviour; but then, as we approached the house where the barking Pointer-type dog lived, things changed. Mahri had never forgotten that this dog ran at her and tried to attack her when she was young and she had promised to settle the issue one day.

I remembered that I hadn't seen it on the outward walk, but it was there now. Although it could not be seen through the gate or fence, it was making its presence known and was probably heard a mile away. All thoughts of toast were discarded. Mahri simultaneously rose up on to her hind legs and lunged forward towards the gate. Mr Mac's reactions were almost as quick and the combined force was more than I could hold. It was as if I had Huskies in the snow, only without the sled and without the snow to break my fall. They dragged me across the pavement as if I was on skis. I couldn't get a foothold and, to save myself from polishing the road surface with my face and body, I was forced to let the leads go.

There was an almighty bang as three dogs hit the big gates: one on the inside, two on the outside. I ran over and grabbed Mr Mac by the collar and tried to grab Mahri. However, she'd found the only space in the fence and was now hoping to grab the Pointer dog and drag him through the gap! I got hold of her collar and dragged the pair of them away from the gate, and marched them up the road a bit before pausing to berate them for their bad behaviour.

I was furious – first, because I didn't have the strength to hold them when taken by surprise and second, because the Pointer's owner had stood at the gate the whole time shouting at me to get my dogs under control and how disgraceful their behaviour was and so forth. I should add that not once on that occasion or any other has he called his dog to order.

On reflection, the vet was probably right about Mahri's season going unnoticed, because the last time Mahri behaved like this was around February/March, so she was probably in season then. I made arrangements to take her back to the vet's in a couple of months for a little surgery. That will sort out her hormone issues and in turn probably save me from sharing my skin with the road surface.

Mahri was sent to bed with no toast. Mr Mac was made to sit in the hall with no toast and Elle, the only time in her life that she never joined in the melee, got toast and extra games of tug. I think she was shocked into silence.

17 August 2008

This past Sunday, when I was walking the same route as last week, I felt Mr Mac and Mahri's leads tensing as we got close to the house where the Pointer lived. I was expecting them to lunge forward as we neared the gate. Sure enough, the dog behind the fence started barking like mad, but I had already shortened the leads and had a tight hold of my dogs, so we walked smartly past the house. Feeling slightly smug because my dogs were behaving, I shouted quite loudly, "Get your barking dog under control!" as I strolled past their driveway with my silent Airedales. My friend was laughing at me.

"He probably never heard you," she said.

"I know, but it made me feel better," I replied.

On the way back, the dog started barking again before we were level with the gate. Mine, *of course*, were quiet, even Elle. As we passed the gate, we heard a male voice shouting at the dog to be quiet, so I think he must have heard my earlier comment. I felt pretty good, because it was not my dogs that instigated the fracas last week. They were responding. It's true what they say about Airedales: they won't pick a fight, but they won't walk away from one either.

28 September 2008

Elle had been very good just recently, so my friend Amy thought she'd like to try taking her for a walk without the head collar. Elle hated that very fashionable item passionately. Instead, we clipped a big fat bungee-type lead meant for a 60-pound dog to her collar. Amy liked this lead because it was really comfortable to hold and, although Elle could pull quite a bit, the bungee effect meant there was less stress on Amy's arm and shoulder joint.

Off we went down the road, Elle as far ahead as the lead allowed, sniffing under hedges and in the grass verges. All of a sudden the lead went limp.

"Oh, noooo!" Amy exclaimed, holding the lead in the air, minus a dog. Elle was disappearing round the bend at a rapid trot. I handed Mahri and Mr Mac's leads to Amy and walked smartly to the bend. I would have loved to have given proper chase, but that was impossible while still in sight of the Airedales, because they would have dragged Amy off her feet trying to follow me.

I kept calling and, as soon as I rounded the bend and was out of sight of Mahri and Mr Mac, I sprinted to the end of the road, where it joined a very busy bypass. I couldn't see Elle anywhere. Fortunately, what I did see was a very large cat sitting by the road, basking in the early morning sun. This was a good sign; it showed that Elle had not gone in that direction. If she had, I'm sure I would have been deafened by either the squealing of the cat as it tried to leave or Elle screeching at the cat trying to prevent it from leaving without her permission.

As I walked back up the road to where I'd left Amy and the dogs, I scanned the hedgerows and the fields, but there was no sign of Elle. I asked Amy to take Mahri back and put her in the kennel and then return to meet me with a spare lead. I would keep searching for Elle and hoped that I would be able to stop her reaching the bypass. After asking Amy to watch out for Elle coming back her way, I walked back down the road with Mr Mac. Just as I turned and started to walk towards the bend where Elle was last seen, she popped out from the undergrowth, running towards me at full pelt.

She had a funny run; she would take four normal dog strides, followed by a gazelle-type leap and then returned to running normally again. I thought she was going to come to me but, just as she got within arm's reach, she scooted round me and headed for the bypass again. Mr Mac and I ran after her, but, most fortuitously, she saw a farm entrance and turned left into the driveway. In her haste to avoid capture, she never saw the cat by the gate post and ran right past it and its pal at the next gate.

I could see from the road that the gate was chained shut, so I dropped Mr Mac's lead over a concrete post, raced down the drive and climbed over the gate into the old farm road. I could see Elle sniffing about under the pine hedge and walked over, calling her name quietly so I didn't wake the sleeping farmer. Then I heard Elle barking.

"Please don't let a big farm dog be in here," I prayed out loud.

The next sound I heard was the chickens screeching. This was not a sound that I wanted to hear. According to the sign at his gate, this farmer sold fresh eggs, and, if Elle was in the chicken run, there was a chance they could be scrambled fresh eggs! I was creeping about, calling to Elle in stage whispers, praying that this dilemma would not end with a big dog or angry farmer or both chasing me or Elle off his land.

Then, all of a sudden, like a little time traveller, Elle popped out from under the fence and raced past me with what could only be described as a passing cheeky glance.

"Weeeeee! I'm freeeee ... catch me if you can!"

As she passed me, I followed her round to the old sheds further up the farm road and tried to corner her, but she outran and out-manoeuvred me every time. She headed back to the gate and I tried to cut her off again. My fear was that she would reach the busy main road. My strategy worked! She spun around and headed further into the farmer's fields. I ran back to the gate to check on Mr Mac, because I didn't want a passer-by to steal him or rescue him, thinking he'd been tied to a post and abandoned. While I was at the gate, I was also looking back up the road to see if there was any sign of Amy returning, and that was when I noticed that Elle was coming across the field.

Back over the gate I went, thinking that her growing fatigue might tip the balance in my favour. Was she puffed out? Had my chances of catching her got any better? NO CHANCE!!! This girl seemed to run on Duracell batteries and she was now scampering round the farmer's wife's flower garden. I decided to wait by the gate in case Amy arrived. Between the two of us, we could herd her into a corner. I half hoped that she might have grown tired of this game and would just come to me if I walked away from her. This ruse had not worked so far, but, ever the optimist, I walked back to the front entrance and stood by Mr Mac. Just as I reached the inner gate, I saw Amy arrive at the outer gate and, almost simultaneously, I saw Elle flying by me once again.

"Don't let her through the gate!" I yelled. "Just run at it and she'll turn round."

Amy did just that. Elle veered off to the right. Oh dear. She was heading back to the chickens; but, halfway to the hedge where earlier she'd found the chickens, she stopped.

She'd come across an old plastic dog bed and had to check out the interesting scents it contained. I slowly walked up to her, not even daring to breathe. Gotcha! I quickly got the lead on her, ran her down to the outer gate, and pushed her under the gate to Amy, who put a second lead on her just to be on the safe side till we got back home.

Elle went immediately to jail; she did not pass go or collect £200.00 or any other treat. Mr Mac and Mahri were rewarded with a very short walk, because I was puffed out after chasing Elle round the farm.

I told Len what had happened when he enquired why the dogs got a two-hour walk instead of the one-hour walk we usually do. He told me to bring Elle into his room, as he was going to give her a stern reprimand. I walked her in on her lead. She was trotting demurely as if butter wouldn't melt in her mouth.

Bounce! She jumped up on Len's bed, licked his head, and then bounced off on to the floor, showing him just how fast she could run out of the room, round the dining room and back in with a final bounce on the bed. She repeated this routine at least ten times.

We called these runs her 'zoomies'. She banked like a Super-Biker. Sometimes she'd lean so far over she was almost horizontal.

She never was scolded; but, on Sunday, she had a head collar with a safety lead linking it to her neck collar and a safety lead from the lead to her collar. It must have looked very strange: this tiny wee dog with so many controlling leads and the two big ones with a single lead each, walking perfectly in tandem.

14 October 2008 – Canadian Thanksgiving

I always thought these festivals were invented to encourage everyone to eat sprouts, but there was no encouragement needed in our house. They were my favourite vegetable and I always shared them raw with the Wild Bunch. Mr Mac got the first one and rushed off with his prize to eat it on the sitting room carpet. I don't know why, but it was the only place he would eat his greens. Mahri was next and it seemed like she was a bit unsure what they tasted like. Given Mahri's history, this was not really surprising. In fact, I don't think she knew what anything tasted like, as food only spent the smallest fraction of a second in her mouth. Elle sniffed the sprout at least twice and gently took it from my fingers, scampering off to Mr Mac's bed to enjoy the treat in peace. Mr Mac had eaten his treat and returned for a second helping.

Elle barked at the little green orb, growled at it, threw it in the air, and flicked it with her paw in a cat-and-mouse-style game, before delicately nibbling at it. The big guys got a couple more while Elle was busy playing with hers. I daren't give them too many, my main concern being that the house might resemble a nuclear fall-out zone with the amount of noxious gases that the dogs could produce after digesting several sprouts.

3 November 2008

There would be a lot of fireworks and bonfire parties, so I was thinking about all pets and pet owners over the weekend and hoped all would be well with them. There had been a few parties in our village and, for a while, the Wild Bunch ignored the bangs and screeches of fireworks exploding in the night sky. As the noise got louder and more frequent, Mr Mac gravitated towards me, puffing his cheeks a bit, the way he does when he's nervous. I concentrated on the TV murder mystery we were watching, hoping to calm them by ignoring everything that was going on.

At the very moment the TV went very quiet because the policeman was creeping round a murder scene, CrAsH! bAnG! WhIzZ echoed through the room! A huge firework exploded quite near the house and all the dogs sat up, sniffing the air. BANG! Another firework exploded nearby!

Mahri could stand it no longer and flew off to the back door, barking like mad. Mr Mac stayed right by my leg, but Elle followed Mahri to the back door, barking and squealing like a banshee.

"Turn the TV up and ignore them," I said to Len. He turned the volume up and, at that precise moment, the policeman who had been creeping around in the dark was confronted by a barking dog! "Quick! Turn the volume down!" I advised.

Too late. Back came Elle, flying straight at the TV to deal with the dog that was apparently hiding behind it. Bang! Whizz! Another firework exploded overhead and off went Elle to the kitchen. Then she ran back to the TV once more. She was very confused. She had no idea which threat to deal with first, so back and forth she ran, barking and squealing. Eventually, she worked it out and stood halfway between the door and the TV, apparently letting the threat come to her. At least, while her brain was in gear, her vocal chords and our ears got a rest. Meanwhile, Mahri gave up and went to bed. She would lose interest very quickly if there was no food forthcoming.

Soon the fireworks were done and all was quiet. It was time to break out the tea and treats.

4 November 2008

Mahri loved her food; in fact, she loved everybody's food if they were soft enough to let her have it. She would offer one a big sad-eyed, droopy-eared stare that begged, *"Please feed me, I'm starving"*, and one's heart would melt. It was so easy to feel sorry for her; but now I was beginning to see that she was not the size zero starving waif she made herself out to be, and I have adopted a stronger attitude to her eating habits. In fact, she was growing somewhat plump!

She didn't like agility very much, so I planned to exercise her to music aerobics. To help her, I sang a little song. It was like the one US soldiers sang when marching. I've seen it in the movies. I think it's called 'Sound-off', but I'm sure you will all know how it goes:

> We go jogging in the park,
> And we do it in the dark.
> Are we doing it just for fun?
> No, were trying to lose our bum!

> We go jogging in the park,
> And we do it after dark.
> We don't want anyone to see

Wobbly bits around our knees
We go jogging in the park,
And we do it in the dark.
We're not doing it for a run –
We'll be happy when it's done.

14 November 2008

Mahri loved to eat paper towels, tissues, envelopes, paper, cotton wool and cardboard. She raided the bins and stole any bits of papery material that had been discarded (no pun intended). Last night, as I put my cup on the breakfast bar, I spilt some tea, so I took a tissue from my pocket and laid it on the tea to soak it up. Mahri was there in a flash. She'd seen the tissue coming out of my pocket.

"Gimme! Gimme!" She pranced about, jumping on my knee and pawing at my arm.

I picked the wet tissue up and put it by the sink, meaning to dispose of it when I'd finished my tea. Still Mahri pranced and whinnied like a horse, jumping up by the sink. She put her head on one side so she could grab the tissue, but I kept pushing her down and repeating "no". The tissue's next destination was the dish along with the used teabags, ready to go out into the recycle bin. The dish had a lid, so I thought it would be safe from Mahri because it was now out of sight.

I finished my cup of tea, sorted my post, fed all the dogs and went through to play on the Wii with Len for 30 minutes. We had to shut the dogs in the kitchen or they'd try to join in and get bashed on the nose with the remotes.

After that session, I returned to the kitchen to prepare

our dinner and, as soon as I walked over to the sink, I knew Mahri had been there ahead of me because the dish had been moved. It wasn't much – just a few inches. The lid was a little squint. I looked inside and, as expected, the tissue was gone and the teabags and orange peel were untouched. I just couldn't believe that the little minx had even put the lid back!

Mahri, who knew I knew she'd had the tissue, brassed it out by sitting next to the sink, smiling and looking at the dish.

"Gimme! Gimme!" as she put her head from side to side, with her tail thwacking a beat on the cupboard door.

I didn't know why she loved tissues so much; we feed her – honest!

Given half a chance, she was quite the pickpocket and would remove a tissue from your pocket as quietly as a ninja. Sometimes you could catch the movement in the corner of your eye and she would stand very still, looking straight ahead, with the tissue still in her mouth. She appeared to think that, if she didn't look at you, then you couldn't see her. Then she scampered off to her bed with her prize before you could catch her. I've even seen her snatch a paper napkin from the picnic table and leave the sandwich on the plate, like a magician whipping a tablecloth and leaving the dishes still in their settings.

15 November 2008

Mahri was booked in to the vet's clinic to be spayed on Monday and it was suggested I take her in on Saturday for

Cake or napkin

a pre-op check-up. More like to help their Christmas fund, I thought, but better safe than sorry.

I arrived at the vet's with Mahri being as cute as a hippopotamus. She had been trained – not that you'd notice – in lady-like ways. She knew to sit while I opened doors and to wait until invited in. "Sit, Mahri," I ordered, and opened the door a little. Whoosh! Mahri barged through the gap.

"OK, folks, I'm here. See me now!! Things to do, busy, busy, busy!"

"On the scales, Mahri." To my amazement, she obeyed immediately, taking a running jump on to the platform and sitting as she landed.

"Whoa, there. Nearly skidded off the other end. I could try it again."

She smiled sweetly at everyone in the room, but I knew this was her Garfield smile and she was thinking up mischief. The reception desk was quite high and she could just rest her chin on it if she stood up on her hind legs and, if she stuck her tongue out like a chameleon, she could get the bit of paper just lying there waiting for her.

The vet called her name and she bounded towards him. He gave her biscuits on her last visit and she never forgot a kindness. In the examination room, she wriggled and pranced all over the place, making it very difficult for him to examine her. Sometimes it felt as if I could never win; she'd had the training and socialization, and attended all the classes. At home on the grooming table she was very good, but when she wanted to do it her way, she was all Terrier. There was no telling her or bribing her to make her do your bidding.

"Hmm," the vet said, making that sucking noise that mechanics make when they want lots of money to repair your car. "Yep," he announced. "Mahri is in the middle of a false pregnancy and is lactating." It wasn't very much, but the vet said it would be better to wait another two weeks before he did the operation. He offered some medicine to dry up her milk in the meantime. I booked the procedure for 1 December, picked up the meds and headed back to reception.

"That will be £64.00 [$96.00], please," the receptionist said. I gulped in some air, slightly shocked at the price.

"Is that for the operation as well?" I asked. It wasn't in jest either, even though I knew, deep down, the operation would be three figures. My brain had short-circuited and refused to do simple arithmetic.

"No," she replied with a straight face. "Just today's visit and the medication." I was dumbstruck. This tiny wee bottle of medicine cost over £50.00: 2mls a day for 6 days. I thought perhaps I should have let the false pregnancy run its course, but then she could have come into season again. It could have ended up being a vicious circle which could in turn lead to a more serious condition or an infection.

Jackie: "I think I'll be missing off the wish for a prosperous New Year on the vet's Christmas card this year."
The Wild Bunch: *"Yeah, miss it off. We could send that money to dogs in need."*

16 November 2008 − Mahri and the tissue, Part 2

Elle was barking furiously at something in the kitchen last night and, when I walked into the room, she had Mahri backed into a corner and wouldn't let her move. Mahri had that goofy look and was tilting her head from side to side. *"What? ... What have I done to upset you now?"* Elle stood her ground, though. Bark, bark, bark!

"What's all this noise for?" I asked, even though I knew I would not get a reply, or perhaps I would.

Mahri, on seeing me, spat out the paper towel that

241

she'd stolen and was trying to take to her bed. Elle stopped barking and stood aside to let her go to her bed without passing "Go" or using a "get out of jail" card. I didn't have to tell her any more; she knew when she'd been naughty and just went straight to bed, sometimes with a backward glance, just in case I might feel sorry for her (which I didn't). She'd been on the worktop and she knew it was off limits. Sometimes she could reach the corner of the towel roll if it had not been pushed far enough back. If it was within her reach, she pulled one sheet off, took it to her bed, ate it and then came back for another helping.

I put the offending and soggy article in the bin, while Elle trotted off to sit on Len's knee, all proud of herself that she'd thwarted the sneak-thief. I thought that Mahri might have learned a new lesson and she'd think twice about pilfering now that Elle was the household's self-appointed snitch.

Elle could be two-faced about telling tales, especially if Mahri stole some nice food and shared it. In these cases, Elle seemed to think that it was acceptable to eat the evidence first and then tell tales, but Elle couldn't eat as fast as Mahri. Mind you, neither could anything else. Elle usually felt obliged to warn everyone to stay away from her food. That always alerted me to the problem and, when she was reprimanded, denied all participation, vociferously nipping Mahri just for getting her into trouble. Mahri knew better, of course, and merely walked, head down, to her bed. She was so funny.

19 November 2008

Mahri had her medicine on Saturday night and Sunday

night and everything seemed to be fine. Nothing unusual noticed. On the Monday, I went off to work, leaving Anne and Len in charge of the dogs. When I got home, Len said that he thought Mahri had had her phantom pregnancy pups, because she'd dug up all her bedding and was surrounded by every soft toy she could find, including a rubber turkey, the only toy from her puppy days she'd never destroyed. She was darting out of her bed, snatching a treat, and rushing back to her bed again.

Elle was being a bit naughty. She was standing at Mahri's crate door, sticking her head in and sniffing. This encouraged Mahri to make a lot of squeaking noises, so we tied Elle to Len's chair to make sure she didn't escalate things.

After dinner, maybe in revenge, but perhaps not, Mahri chose to dig up Elle's bed. She was panting a lot and had now discarded all the soft toys, except for one little stripey cat that she'd stolen from the computer room and the turkey, which she'd hidden under a blanket with just the feet sticking out. I sat with her, rubbing her head and tummy to make her feel better. She was quite happy for me to do this. I handed her the turkey and she licked it all over, bit its tummy and pushed it under the blanket. Her appetite seemed to be the only thing that wasn't affected as she digested her dinner like a Hoover sucking up every single crumb and then rushed back to Elle's bed. When I took her out to the toilet, she was as quick as it took to do the necessary and dragged me back to the house.

On Tuesday, I returned home to find Mahri still in her bed, and Elle no longer curious. Maybe she thought Mahri had gone mad. Mahri would run up to greet you, all wiggly, and then would rush back to her bed, where she stayed and whined, but didn't seem to want anything. If any of the bedroom doors had been left open, she wandered round the rooms, sniffing the air. At least, that's what we thought she was doing. She was actually scanning all flat surfaces for any little stuffed toy that she hadn't already gathered. She had her eye on a white polar bear and 'Nono-leda'. Nono-leda is an Airedale toy made from recycled material in Alaska by Jan Williams. They earned their name because Jan's Airedale Leda kept stealing them and was told "No, No, Leda". They were made and sold to earn funds for Alaska Airedale Rescue.

This morning, she decided to try a new bed on Len's blanket box, but a rattle of the biscuit box and that bed was soon forgotten. We noticed that she moved the rubber turkey from bed to bed with her, where it was always hidden under a blanket with just its feet sticking out.

1 December 2008

I've found that all our Airedales will do something two or three times and then you get that stare that says, *"OK, I've shown I can do it; do we have to continue* ad infinitum*?"*

When Mr Mac used to do agility, he would go round the course three times and, on the fourth time, the course was reversed just to make him think about what he was doing, or he would just act the fool. It is the same with a game of fetch. After you threw a ball the third time, they seemed to get the message that the ball was to be discarded and would no longer bring it back. In fact, they wouldn't even look at the ball again for several days and then you would have to find it and initiate the game. It didn't work in reverse, though. How many times did I have to tell Mahri not to eat tissues? Did she get bored with that trick? NO! Maybe I should try to teach her to eat them on command. *Hmmmmmmmmmmm.*

Our dogs were not allowed on the furniture. Elle was permitted to lie on a cushion – to prevent pressure sores – on Len's knee every night at 9.00pm. She would put her paws on my knee and nod in Len's direction. This was my cue, or should I say her royal command, to be picked up and put on Len's knee. She'd get a fuss made of her and a cuddle, and then Len will say 'cushion', and she would sit up so I could put the cushion in place for her to lie on it like Cleopatra to watch the TV with Len.

On Saturday night, Len was going to have a late dinner, so he did not want Elle on his knee. The little diva took offence, got in a huff and promptly jumped up on the small couch behind Len. It was a leather couch and I heard her and got to her before she had a chance to sit down. I lifted her on to the floor with a sharp 'no' and went back to my seat by Len.

The next time I looked, she'd pulled her fleece all the way from the kitchen, placed it on the floor in front of the couch and was curled up with a pose that encapsulated the phrase 'nobody loves me'. She's got a masters degree in sympathy poses and pity eyes. We laughed at her and left her to sleep there till bed time.

The next day, the hooligans had been running amok in the house because it was so wet outside that they never got their walk and had plenty of energy to burn. I walked through the sitting room and, as I passed the little couch, there was Elle, curled up asleep as if on Len's knee. She'd been up on the little couch, pushed the pillow on to the floor, climbed on to it and gone to sleep. Well, at least, I thought to myself, she has learned that she is not allowed to sleep on the furniture now. I just had to teach her not to jump on it!

Later on that day, when the hooligans had their second wind and were playing chase and 'bitey-face' or, to be more accurate, 'bitey-body parts', I wandered into the sitting room just to make sure that they weren't playing tug with the dining chair cushions. They had already played that game when I was distracted with Len.

The first thing I saw was Elle standing on the big couch where nobody sits but me. I'm king of the big couch! And all creatures furry! I'm pretty sure about that because I make the rules. This is the rule, or at least I believed such to be the case. Pulling myself up to my full five foot zero, I shouted at Elle, "Get down!" To my surprise, she did not get down but defiantly stood her ground. I moved closer and shouted again, "Get down!"

I nearly fell over when Mahri's head popped up from under one of the cushions. Mahri was lying on the couch with her head under a big soft cushion and Elle was standing on her back. Mahri jumped down and scampered off to the kitchen, closely followed by Elle, who was mad at having been unceremoniously dumped on the floor by Mahri in her haste to pretend she'd been in her basket all day.

2 December 2008

Poor Mahri went to the vet's yesterday to be spayed. She was only just recovering from her phantom pregnancy and rubber turkey fixation when, to her horror, no food was on offer after 6.00pm on a Sunday night. Not in her wildest dreams did she believe that worse was to come, with no breakfast on Monday, and no 'guard the house' biscuit when I left for work.

Len delivered her and collected her in his car because it has a lift and is a lot lower than mine, so it meant she didn't have to jump in. When I got in from work, the wee soul was lying in the corner with her buster collar on, moaning away like an old World War II bomb siren. She started off low, *"ow ow ow"*, and got louder and longer.

She wasn't allowed any more pain-killers for the time being, so I gave her some Arnica. We considered taking her back to the vet; after all, she was an Airedale − a stoic Airedale, of the breed that pretended nothing could hurt.

An hour or so later, she seemed to perk up, so I offered her the special boiled chicken I'd carefully prepared for her. She sniffed it and turned her head away.

"Mahri, it's food. You love food! Have a sniff … no?" She turned her head from side to side to avoid it. I popped a piece in her mouth and she spat it out in disgust.

"Ptha! I don't want your STEENKING chicken ... I want my body parts back!"

Elle and Mr Mac had been watching all this fuss. *"We could taste a little bit chicken if you like ... just to make sure it doesn't taste bad ... snicker, drool, snicker, mmmmmm, tasty ... there's nothing wrong with that there chicken."*

Maybe she remembered the turkey and that's why she wouldn't eat the chicken. I encouraged her to lie by my feet on her side and she slept for a couple of hours. Then I made her up a nice comfy basket by the radiator and left her to sleep for the rest of the night. She was a lot better the next morning. No more moaning. She scoffed her normal breakfast and looked for more. We knew she was well on her way to recovery when she proceeded to terrify Mr Mac and Elle by running at them with her buster collar so she looked like something from *Jurassic Park*. No doubt my legs will be ravaged by that collar in the days to come.

7 December 2008

Mahri's had her buster collar on – well, maybe I should say 'busted collar' – since last Monday, when she was spayed. Apart from damage to soft human tissue as a result of an over-enthusiastic greeting or two, things have gone well. Her tummy healed very quickly and you would never have known she'd had fairly major surgery.

Yesterday, aided and abetted by the other two, she was playing up. They were bored being in the house all day, so the decision was taken to put them in the day kennel for a couple of hours in the afternoon while the sun was shining. *What harm could it do?* Anne went to bring them back into the house about 4.30pm, before it got too dark, and, when she walked round to the kennel, she saw Mahri and Elle were playing tug with something undefined. At first, she couldn't work out what it was. Then, as she went to clip Mahri's lead on, she realized what they were playing with. It was a bit of the buster collar. Somehow, Mahri was still wearing the other part of it, but it looked more like an old-fashioned bonnet tied under her chin, shielding her eyes from the sun.

When I got home, she bounded up to greet me, still wearing the redesigned collar. Anne thought it better to leave it on than risk Mahri chewing on her stitches. Did

Mahri care that the buster collar had been shredded? Not one bit and, with it, came a new go-faster zoom around the house, bashing and smashing anything that got in her way. Every time it made contact with the floor, furniture, body parts – canine or human – another bit snapped off. She was almost down to the blue collar that held it together. It's just as well Len was taking her to the vet soon to get the stitches removed, along with the diminishing self-designed bonnet.

8 December 2008

As far as I'm concerned, dogs communicate either by telepathy or vocally. We were usually aware of the telepathic ones when we sneaked one of the pack a little treat and the others appeared as if by magic for their share. On Friday night, we witnessed the vocal communication.

We had recently bought a Wii and usually play ten-pin bowling or golf for half an hour in the evening. This is Len's keep fit regime. I mentioned to Len that we could set up and design our own characters and make them look like caricatures of us. Absolutely loving the idea, he set straight to work and called up the relevant program. A couple of screens later, up popped a two-foot-high cartoon male that needed *important decisions* making for the eyes, nose and a few other things, a bit like a police identikit.

While all this was going on, Elle had been sitting by my feet, looking cute, watching the TV; but, as soon as Len put the beard on his computer character, she started to growl, low vibrating warning growls, with the merest twitch of her whiskers. From all my years of having dogs, I'm pretty sure this means, 'Back away now! Leave the room! Do not look back and you may live to tell the tale.'

We were laughing at her, but she was totally focused on the TV, and the growls increased in volume, with the whisker twitching becoming little snorts. She stood up and stomped towards the TV, placing herself halfway between Len and his look-alike alien. As the character just stood there with its silly grin, Elle barked and growled even louder, standing her ground against it. We thought she would realize it was a picture and ignore it. To our surprise, she turned her head towards the kitchen door and gave the tiniest of little puppy yelps, before turning back to face the TV, growling, snorting, barking, and then yelping again.

It seemed as though she was calling for Mahri to come and back her up. Elle repeated this process again, never once relinquishing an inch of ground. Upon the call of a double yelp, Mahri, who had been languishing in her big comfy bed, responded with a *"Woorurf – yeah, I'm right behind you ... call me if you need any help."* Elle, not satisfied with Mahri's response, again went through the growl, snort, bark and a double squeaky yelp routine.

This one did the trick. We heard Mahri getting up at super-fast speed, impeded slightly by the buster collar, and rocketing her way through the kitchen. Mr Mac, who'd been on his big comfy bed in the hall, decided that, if Mahri was up for it, then he'd better join her to save little 'Elle belly' from some monster. The two of them collided in the doorway like Laurel and Hardy as they both tried to enter the sitting room simultaneously. Mahri, out of control because of her lampshade-style collar, bashed everything she passed. The pair of them ran up to Len's chair and screeched to a halt.

"What's all the fuss about?"

They looked all around and whatever Elle had seen in Len's computer character was not apparent to Mahri or Mr Mac. Satisfied there was nothing afoot, they stomped off to their beds without so much as a backward glance. As soon as we moved on to setting up my character, Elle never bothered and went back to being a little toy dog at my feet.

My friend thought that, because the character looked quite like Len, it confused Elle, as she couldn't comprehend how Len could be in front of her and behind her at the same time; but I guess we'll never know what she found so threatening. She never chased the bowling ball or the golf ball on the games, so they must not have appeared real to her. She could get really grumpy if you tried to make her do something when a film was about to start. You could see her getting comfy on her cushion with her front legs crossed, ears alert, and eyes glued to the screen, taking it all in.

24 January 2009

A pack of Airedales is sanity; two Airedales and a Welsh is close to insanity. When I had only Airedales, my dogs were well behaved (with one or two notable exceptions). People would say that they were never aware we had a dog in the house, never mind two or three or, on occasion, four. Toss in a Welsh Terrier and things go rapidly downhill!

I used to laugh at people with outstretched arms walking a tiny dog; it would often be dragging them up the street, while my two Dales trotted perfectly by my side on loose leads. Well, not any more! Welsh Elle would not walk at heel and much preferred to impersonate a metal detector, zig-zagging left and right, on the end of an outstretched lead, stopping suddenly to trip me up at every opportunity. She squealed a high-pitched, ear-curdling screech at every opportunity. Her interest would be piqued by a bird, a leaf, the doorbell, the doorbell on TV, and lots of things on TV except, possibly, elephants, crocodiles and lions. The only thing I could figure was that perhaps she recognized she was no match for them.

Of course, one squeal from Elle would set Mahri off, and she would join in the chorus, and not with just a bark, but with a booming bark that could startle anyone and everything. Deafen them, too, so they couldn't hear her sneaking up on them with a view to whacking them in the shins with her head … or a little karate kick in the nether regions worked equally well. Once they'd doubled over from the initial take-down, she would give them a big wet beard-kiss. Mahri had honed this trick to perfection and could use her front or back legs equally well.

19 January 2009

Spring was in the air and Mahri was in the dog house. Actually, both Elle and Mahri were in the dog house.

It all started on Saturday morning. It was cool and crisp, at just a couple of degrees above freezing. When it came to dogs, dry is much better than wet, regardless of the cold. The gales and snow that were promised had never emerged, so off we went, out with the dogs. Amy with Elle and I took Mr Mac and Mahri.

Five minutes after leaving the house, Amy looked at the end of the lead where Elle should have been pulling with all her might and, oh dear … there she wasn't. No Elle. She was trotting along a few paces ahead of the lead, but now we knew, and she knew we knew. She stopped, looked us in the eye, then scampered off down the road. Oh dear, I had feelings of *déjà vu*. The last time Elle and her lead parted company, I spent ages trying to catch her in the nearby farmyard, and it looked like she was heading there again.

"Catch me if you can!" she squealed in delight.

"Don't chase her," I said to Amy, "and she might come back."

Not quite. She stayed a few paces ahead, pausing every few steps to taunt us. We tried turning back, even running back with Mahri and Mr Mac; but nope, she kept her distance, openly defying us, while all the time getting closer to the bypass.

I rounded the bend just in time to see her scampering up a farm entrance. I tied Mr Mac and Mahri to the gate post. Amy stayed by the gate to shepherd her towards me if she tried to get back to the road. By the time I'd followed her down past the farm house, I'd lost sight of her and was unsure whether she'd doubled back; so I ran back to where Amy was waiting and was in time to see Elle make a right turn across the fields. Just at that point, the farmer's wife appeared. I explained that the lead and Elle had parted company. We couldn't fathom how or why, but we were trying to catch her before she reached the bypass.

Elle had become curious and wandered back towards us, stopping about ten feet away. Advantage to Jackie and Amy? I think not. A bird moved in the trees and off she went, with me hot on her heels. Her luck ran out when we both discovered that there was chicken wire round the edge of the trees. After several near misses, I managed to corner her, pick her up and give her a belly rub, talking nicely to her while putting her lead on. Well, the farmer's wife was still listening. "Oh, Elle-belly, you are a little monkey, running off like that", is what I may have said. What I was trying to say was, "When I get you home, you evil little brat, you're going straight to your bed with no biscuits."

We completed our walk without further incident. On the way back, I said to Amy that, when we got home, I would leave Mahri's Gentle Leader on as I had a letter to deliver to a house in the village in the opposite direction from our walk. As Mahri has been a bit boisterous recently, I thought she'd benefit from the extra walk.

I left at a brisk pace, with Mahri walking to heel, down to the bypass, across the road, down to the village, turning right along to the house and, 25 minutes later, we'd arrived. I posted the letter and headed for home. Mahri had been good, so I relaxed the lead a little. A Cairn and a Yorkie romped past; she never even turned her head. "Good girl," I praised her.

By the time we got back to the main road, Mahri had started to get a bit bouncy again. I knew the reason, so I tightened my hold and shortened her lead. Two minibuses were parked just off the road on the grass verge and 24 miscreants assigned to community service instead of jail were milling about, waiting for some sort of instruction. I nodded, smiled a good morning and kept on walking. About 20 yards further up the road is the house with the Rotties and Spaniels. They were already barking and Mahri was getting to the skippy, prancy stage. I kept the Gentle Leader pulled down to make her look at the ground, rather that have her up on her back legs prancing like a bear. Just as we were opposite the gates, and without any warning, she did a backward corkscrew-somersault and body-slammed into my shins, collapsing me like a felon on to my knees. The pain was incredible, like nothing I'd ever felt before. I was convinced she'd shattered my kneecap.

The dogs continued to bark at Mahri, who was still bucking and leaping like a bull in a rodeo show. I managed to get into a sitting position and miraculously still kept my hold on Mahri's lead. She kicked and flipped from left to right, back and forth. At one point, she managed to kick me in the chest with both back feet, knocking me flat on my back on the muddy road. Like a true rodeo queen, I held on fast. Eventually, she stopped leaping and lay down. I was still sitting in the middle of the road when two of the young men from the minibus approached.

"Are you all right?" they asked.

"Yes, I'm fine, thank you. She's just being a bit playful."

I managed to stand up and, after assuring them again I was fine, marched off round the corner, dragging Mahri behind me. Once out of sight, though, the pain kicked back in and I limped home, feeling a little bit sorry for myself. Mahri went straight to the kennel and was denied all privileges for the rest of the day.

I changed out of my mud-covered clothes and had a reviving cup of tea and lots of Arnica. as my knee was cut and very blue. Miraculously, the Arnica worked, unlike much else so far that day, and I was able to spend the rest of the day pottering in the garden, amazed at the bulbs showing three inches through the soil. The carnations were in flower. Even the odd wallflower was smiling at the sun and this never really happened till late February.

Mahri was allowed into the house later in the day and

tried to make amends by sitting in front of me, offering paws and smiling her goofy smile. Her promise to behave was forgotten as soon as she'd eaten her dinner and she was up for a game of chase with Mr Mac.

Mr Mac had stolen a rug and was running through the house with it. Elle, dragging her fleece bed, was in hot pursuit; but because it impeded her progress, she soon discarded it in favour of one of Mr Mac's rear legs. She hung on for grim death as he raced round the table, having dropped the cumbersome rug. Mahri had been bouncing off and on the furniture, throwing the cushions about until Mr Mac grabbed her leg as he ran past. The three dogs, now led by Mahri, ran round the table into the hall and kitchen and back round the table.

It reminded me of a line of ice-skaters, with the littlest one on the end being thrown ever wider on the turns as the speed increases. Elle only let go when she was bounced off the side of the couch. She was none too impressed with this and gave Mr Mac such a scold. To calm the situation, he chose to stand behind me – well, that was his version. Elle was of the opinion that he was hiding.

Mahri started a new game of tag, which involved her vaulting over Elle and Mr Mac, and then bouncing on Len. Boing! And off Len. Boing! She managed several chest-high drop-kicks with her back legs on me and everyone else in the room, before trying it all in reverse. It really was as if I was winding a video back. It was so funny to watch.

Elle then decided to hang on to my leg wherever I went, like a clingy child or a koala bear on speed. It was quite strange walking everywhere with a ten-pound dog attached to one leg.

I wondered how they would entertain me tonight. The

prospect of a lot more snow at the weekend was certainly going to make my walks more fun. Perhaps I should just take one dog at a time and remember to wear some crampons.

23 February 2009

Are dogs reincarnated? Do they have memories of a previous life? If they do, then somewhere in Welsh Terrier Elle's past, I think she was a German Shepherd Dog or some other sort of police dog.

We were sitting watching a TV programme about salmon returning inland to spawn and trying to get past bears and so forth. She sat by my feet, watching the giant fish leaping out of the water, up through the rapids, to where the bears were sitting, waiting for their dinner. Mahri occasionally looked up at the TV and flopped her head back down again, as if the effort of lifting her head was not worth the view on offer. The seagulls swooped in to catch a fish and crows picked at a dead fish on the river bank. All the while, Elle just watched them all silently … until a wolf ambled by.

In a flash, Elle was up and in front of the TV, ready to send the wolf back from whence it came. Mahri joined her sidekick, poised and ready for action. Lucky for the wolf and my TV, it apparently sensed the danger and made a fast exit. Mahri lay down with a thump to continue her snooze, clearly irritated by the demands Elle had made. Elle returned to her warm place by my feet.

Next, the film showed how they filmed the bears catching fish in the deep-water pools. The camera man was dressed in a dry suit and a snorkel. Apparently, they had tried to use a remote camera, but the bears kept knocking it over. One in particular had found the cable and started to pull it. The camera man shouted at the bear to frighten it a little so it would drop the cable and move on. As soon as the bear looked at the man, Elle, in a flash, worked out that the bear was bad and needed to be taught right from wrong.

She flew at the TV – barking, snapping, and growling. Mahri, indifferent to Elle's belligerence, feigned sleep.

"It's a bear, Elle, ignore it." Mahri grumbled under her breath.

Elle, like a prize boxer, jumped from side to side, ducking and weaving. The bear turned and wandered back to the rocks to wait for more fish to pass and, once again, after a job well done, Elle returned to my side.

She seemed to be able to recognize when someone or something on the TV was a threat. If we watched a police programme, she barked and growled at the baddie. Even if the policeman was in plain clothes, she could tell the difference and knew policemen were not for chasing or to be chastised for shouting at you. Strangely, though, all animals that did not look dog-like, and this includes cartoons, were tolerated; but no dog or dog-like creature other than Mahri and Mr Mac was allowed in her house. If they tried to sneak in through the TV, like burglars in the night, she was ready for them from her vantage point on Len's knee.

I've been waiting to find out her views on police dogs, but we haven't seen them on TV yet. I'm sure she'll pipe up when the time arises.

Mr Mac: *"Elle could have been a policewoman, that's for sure."*

Mahri: *"Nah ... she was probably a postman ... why else*

would she not be keen on dogs?"
7 March 2009

Mr Mac came to our house three years ago as a retired show dog. He could be a bit grumpy in noisy halls where dog shows and the like take place; but, for the most part, he has been a gentle, loving dog. The odd rat might disagree and Elle when she's pushed her luck a bit too far. ...

Our weekend 'long walks' either take us past the Rottweiler's house (which means Elle barks and screams till she's sick, with Mahri having no other option but to join in) or a longer walk in the opposite direction along by a farm where the dogs could get quite muddy.

Some new people moved into one of the houses on the farm route and they had a large dog of indiscriminate background which has started to bark as we go by. Mahri played up a little, but our walks were usually uneventful. However, a couple of weeks ago, my friend who helped walk my dogs was away on holiday so, as a special treat, I walked each dog by itself on the farm route. As I approached the large dog's house, I noticed the gate was open, so assumed the dog would not be in the garden.

I relaxed Mr Mac's lead a little, but, as soon as we were level with the gate, the dog came flying out, all teeth and noise, right up to us. Mr Mac stopped in front of me and snapped his jaws shut, making the air crack. The dog, still snapping and snarling, backed up a pace or two. Mr Mac stood silently between it and me. I have to say I did not feel personally threatened by the dog, but, as a good dog mum, I would have had to protect my fur-kid, even though he had demonstrated that he was going to protect me.

All this happened in a split second and when I'd

recovered from the initial surprise I yelled at the dog to go home. We walked by slowly, with Mr Mac keeping his eye on the dog at all times and the dog still making a few threatening noises.

On the return journey, I was worried that this dog might be loose again. There was no other way back; but, fortunately, the gate was closed, although the dog was still barking. Mr Mac, superstar that he was, ignored it and we completed our walk without further incidents.

The next Sunday was a beautiful, bright, sunny morning, so my friend and I walked the three dogs to the farm road. Nearing the angry dog's house, my friend remarked that the gate was open, but she was able to pass by with Elle in silence. I shortened Mr Mac's and Mahri's leads so as not to be surprised and dragged off my feet should the dog appear.

Just as we got level with the gate, out came the dog. Mahri is only two-and-a-half years old and does not tolerate any form of threat. She's still finding her place in the pack, so is much more ready to defend her position, and Mr Mac will protect Mahri. So I was now between two Airedales snapping at each other. (Why do Airedales snap at each other in moments like this? Or is it just mine?) To make matters more interesting, a big set of teeth was heading in my direction, with the attached dog emitting very threatening growls.

"Get BACK," I yelled, and all three dogs stopped in their tracks.

Mr Mac stepped back to my side. Mahri tried to flip in the air and throw a few Kung Fu chest kicks at the dog as we walked by. The dog stood out of reach, making threatening noises. Oh dear. We had to return this way and

Mahri would remember that the dog had threatened her.

We took longer over our walk, feeding the swans before we wandered back. I planned to shorten the dog leads well before we reached the house, so they would not pick up our apprehension. By shorten I mean I would hold on to their Gentle Leaders like bridles, so I had total control of their heads.

The dog rushed out again, to be welcomed by much barking from Mahri. *"Let me at him. I'll show him ... I'm gonna get you one day,"* she screamed at him, as she was dragged kicking and spitting past the house.

So now my dilemma was between knocking on the door and asking the man to make sure his dog was not loose. If I chose this action, would the dog let me knock on the door? Or should I ask a friendly English bobby to knock on their door? I favoured the latter, as I felt anyone that leaves a gate open for a dog to run free will pay little heed to a polite request from a little not-so-young lady. I chose to wait and see if the dog owner would of his own volition apply some control or at least keep his gate shut.

15 March 2009

This weekend was the start of several big country shows in our area. The first was the Heavy Horse Show and, because it was a lovely spring day, we decided to visit the horse show and take Elle with us for a treat. We knew she wouldn't bark at the horses. Because she was so small, Len had her on his knee. She looked as if she was riding shotgun. Lots of people would come up and speak to Len and Elle, so both were in their element, being the centre of attention.

We had managed to find a space near the barrier so we could watch the best horse and cart or dray judging. The turnout was good and the display magnificent: all the manes and tails were plaited with ribbon, while the brasses were clinking and sparkling. You could see your face in the leather. The drivers were all in period costume and the wagons were pristine. There was a one-horse farm cart, a two-horse brewery dray and a three-horse fruit and vegetable cart. They all walked, trotted, then cantered round the ring.

While we were watching, a woman pushed in front of Len. He could still see, but she was blocking Elle's view, which annoyed her, so she groaned a little and loudly exhaled. The woman never moved. She tried again a little louder, which attracted the attention of everyone round us, but not that of the woman blocking her view. She edged to the left to see round her, then to the right. She stood up, still trying to look round the woman. She was now drawing more attention than the horses. Totally frustrated, she let out a long, exasperated whine. The woman turned and looked. Elle stared straight back at her and nodded her head in a clear off sort of fashion.

The woman, realizing her ignorance, gasped and apologised. "Oh, I'm so sorry," she said to Elle. As she backed away, I was worried that people would applaud, but they just laughed, because Elle had made it so clear that she was watching the horses and this woman had blocked her view.

Elle, unaffected by the whole scene, ignored them all and concentrated on picking her winner – the two-horse brewery dray with perfectly matched black shires sporting white front feet. Elle shared some of Len's lunch, had a walk about, then hopped back on Len's knee to get the best view.

When we got home, she went straight to her bed, puffed out by her day's activities. It was as if her batteries lasted long enough for her to reach her bed. She flopped on to it, groaning every time we walked by it because we were disturbing her.

6 April 2009

I've had three pairs of Airedales over the years and they have always been the best of friends; but at no time would they ever share a bed. I've seen MacIain take his biscuit, walk over and drop it in front of Annie, who promptly ate it; but he would never share the same sleeping space.

Our Bolshie little Welsh Terrier was no different; she had attitude by the bucket load and, for the most part, got on fine with the Airedales as long as they recognized that there are borders that should not be crossed. For example, Mahri must not lick Elle's food bowl or drink the clean water first because she drooled in it. She must not sleep in Elle's bed if Elle wanted to sleep in it; neither must she sleep in her own bed if Elle wanted to sleep in that one, too. She must surrender all toys on command, and growl or play with toys on command. Mr Mac just had to give up his bed and all treats, unless Mahri's were better.

So you can imagine my complete surprise when today I couldn't find Mahri to give her a biscuit before I left the house. Where food is concerned, Mahri is never very far from the source. I bent down to give a biscuit to Elle, who was curled up in the front of Mahri's big crate, and there was Mahri sitting behind her, waiting for her treat. I could hardly believe my eyes.

How cute is that? I thought. Then I began to wonder if perhaps Mahri had been curled up in the back of her crate asleep and Elle never saw her and plonked herself down at the front, trapping Mahri in the back. But she didn't seem unhappy about it. Elle liked to sleep in the warmest place, so maybe she had learned that it was warmer to share Mahri's bed.

Well, I should have gone with my instincts. Apparently, minutes after I left, Elle realized that Mahri was in the crate and squared up to her. Anne heard Mahri whimpering and, when she looked in the crate, Mahri was backed up against the wires. Elle was standing in the front of the crate with her eyes fixed on Mahri. I've been on the receiving end of Elle's withering stares myself and they really could turn milk sour.

Anne worried that it might escalate and felt sorry for Mahri, who was trying to make herself wafer-thin against the back of the crate. Anne tried luring Elle away with a biscuit, but this only made Elle worse, because Mahri – being food-driven every second of every day – moved her gaze to the biscuit. Like gunfighters at the 'OK Corral', you must never blink or look away. Elle stood her ground and growled.

Fortunately, Anne was quite dog-savvy or, at least, Elle-savvy, so she quickly grabbed the mop from the garage and pretended to wash the floor.

"Aghhh! Invaders from the garage!"

Elle immediately forgot about Mahri and pounced on the mop, because it represented a greater threat to her serene little world. Mahri made good her escape and the dead mop was returned to the garage. Biscuits were passed around and peace reigned once more.

The next morning, Mahri was lying in Elle's bed, waiting for her treat; she's a bit big for that bed, but at least

Mahri waiting for treats

265

everyone can see where she is.

22 April 2009

Andrea, my American friend, wrote to tell me that they have a PetCo where she lives and you can bring in your dogs to shop. There is a note stating: 'Loose treats are shelved at dog-nose levels – your dog eats it, you buy it!'

I could never have taken Mahri into a store like that. She walked fine on a lead; however, all small dogs would be in danger of disappearing as she walked past the open containers. She would inhale and it would be like a super vacuum sucking up all in its path. People would be hanging on to the shop fixtures and loose clothing would be sucked down, along with chews and biscuits. And that would be before she'd even got to the dog toys. There would be a trail of destroyed and broken toys. Her party trick is the ability to strip a tennis ball in 30 seconds without it ever having to leave her mouth.

Last night, Elle choked a little on her dinner and, as she walked away a few paces while she coughed the offending morsel out of her throat, Mahri, in a flash, nipped over, gobbled up the food in Elle's bowl, and nipped back to continue licking her own bowl, just in case she'd missed a bit. Poor Elle went back to her bowl and stared at its shiny surface, devoid of all food particles, then she looked at me and then at Mahri; her face was a picture. Mahri trotted off nonchalantly as if nothing was amiss and sat by the kitchen sink, in case any food fell on the floor while on its way to the bin or cooker.

Once Elle had got over her shock, she walked right up to Mahri, stood on her back legs, put her face up really close to Mahri's ear and screamed. It was an awful screeching sound – the kind that could break glass. It certainly hurt my ears. Mahri went straight to her bed and Elle sat down like a little cat and washed her face, satisfied that Mahri knew she'd been reprimanded for stealing her dinner.

Elle: *"She's such a pig. I, of course, am above all that behaviour, or below it, depending on whether I'm on Len's knee or not ... either way, I can't reach in the containers and help myself the way she can."*

5 May 2009

It was May bank holiday weekend and I had four days to spend at home with my dogs and Len. The forecast was good, so I planned to walk the dogs and groom one of them each day. We even considered taking Elle to the Truckfest on the Sunday if Len could drag himself away from the snooker. There's nothing more boring in the world than having to watch snooker, especially when you're colour blind, as all the balls except for the black and white balls are purple or they are brown.

Friday went as planned and I walked each dog individually. The sun was shining in a bright blue sky. The birds were singing and all was well with the world. Later, I met a friend in town for a coffee and a bit of shopping and then went home to potter in the garden while the dogs relaxed in the sun.

Then came Saturday. Everything was about to change. It was morning and the sun was still shining and the grass was wet with dew, so I donned my wellies to take Elle and Mahri out for their early morning walk round the garden. They were always lead–walked, as Elle-proofing the garden is just too expensive and Mahri was not to be trusted because she got herself stuck in the gate trying to escape.

Just as I stepped on to the wet grass, a tiny wee bird landed at the bottom of the paddock. It was the merest speck, but the budding guardians of our little estate decided it should leave and simultaneously charged at it – Elle screaming, Mahri barking. I was in mid-step and had one foot off the ground, stepping forward just as 70 pounds of dogs lunged, pulling me off balance or, to be more precise, flat on my back.

"Stop pulling!" I yelled.

Hanging on to the lead was my first rule of dog walking. NEVER, NEVER, NEVER let go of the leads, unless you were unconscious, and even then hope that some autonomic reflex kept your hand in a fist.

I was now sliding along the grass on my back, heading for the tree line near the end of the garden at a rate of speed that would have challenged the Iditarod winners. With a supreme effort, I managed to halt the dogs and sit up.

"Now look what you've done!" I hissed at Mahri. "I'm soaked."

Mahri, bless her, was full of remorse and immediately jumped all over me, giving me lots of healing kisses. Elle, the antithesis of caring, was still bouncing around squealing, despite the bird being long gone.

Later that day, I planned to give Elle a good grooming, strip her coat out and do her feet; but Elle had other ideas and hadn't forgotten about her impending score to settle with the bird. When I eventually let her down from the grooming table, she looked very smart, except for one shoulder which looked a little rough. It was the last bit to do, but she'd had enough and was pretty quick to inform me of this. Unluckily for her, I was equally determined that the job would be done. Eventually, we agreed to differ on the understanding that I place the following advert on eBay: 'Swap offer: one Welsh Terrier for one wild crocodile, a bear with toothache, a bull elephant with attitude and a pack of hyenas'. I'm sure that mix of pets would be much easier to handle than Elle, even on a good day.

23 May 2009

A few weeks ago, someone wrote about this new harness that discourages pulling, so I decided to get one for Welsh Elle, since she pulls until she just about makes herself sick, and nothing has been able to make her walk at heel. I've tried various harnesses: a Halti, a Gentle Leader head-collar, and a Canny head-collar. None of them have worked. I've spent every walk with my arm outstretched and Elle – aka thunder-thighs – powering her way forward. If a bird or rabbit should come into view, she prances forward on her hind legs, squealing like a banshee, trying to rip the nose band off. This is bad on three accounts: first, it's very painful on my ears; second, she might do herself serious damage; finally, it's very embarrassing.

Although convinced I'd wasted more money on yet another harness, I tried it out on Friday. It was really easy to fit. I just had to slip it over her head, place the coloured band under her chest just behind her front legs and clip the lead on to the D ring in front of her chest. Off we went.

We reached the gate, Elle at my side. We got to the

county lane, Elle still at my side. We walked along narrow ridges caused by the tractors; Elle was *behind* me. I had to keep checking she was there, because there was no tension in the lead.

Next, a rabbit crossed our path. Elle lunged at it. I held the lead at my side. She stopped, sat down and squealed at the rabbit. If you were listening and not seeing what was happening, you would think I was beating her to within an inch of her life. Nothing could make her stop screaming at the rabbit.

That was it. Walk over. We did an about-turn and headed for home. As she turned and trotted after me, she kept looking back over her shoulder, apparently hoping to give that pesky rabbit one more scolding – just in case it hadn't heard her the first forty-two times. Apart from the rabbit incident, the harness was a huge success and I would definitely recommend them for little dogs. I've yet to try one on Mahri, though.

24 May 2009

The girls were three years old on Friday. They were also due their vaccinations and vet check; so, because I know they can be a bit … how shall I put this? … enthusiastic, I took each dog for a long walk on Friday morning. I picked my friend up and drove into the local town where the vet's office is located, but parked in the centre car park to walk the girls about a mile along the river; it took about an hour round trip. By that time, I expected the girls to be tired.

We walked back through the town en route to the vet's and, as we came out of the car park, just ahead of us was a huge Rottie with a big, tattooed, punk-haired owner. Worse still, her husband was even bigger and scarier. I told Anne to cross over the road as Elle hates Rotties because of the two that hurl themselves at the metal gate at the house not far from ours. We'd no sooner crossed the road than the couple with the dog crossed right in front of us. 'Sugar', or words to that effect. ....

Elle immediately started to scream, so we returned to the side of the road we'd just left, only to be verbally abused by this couple for reasons best known only to themselves.

I ignored them and continued on to the vet's office. By now, Elle was in a right state, screaming and barking, but not pulling, thanks to her new Easy Walker harness. In the vet's office, Elle calmed down, thanks to all the attention she got. People petting you and saying how cute you are far from warrants any obscene screaming behaviour. She weighed 7.2kg and Mahri, who had been quite well behaved, all thing considered, was 22.2kg. We were asked to take a seat.

All was going well. Both dogs sat at our feet, looking cute and lovable, until a Yorkie walked in on the end of a lead. Elle launched herself at it, screaming at the top of her voice. Mahri felt obliged to join in with her deep, rough bark. The more Elle screamed, the more Mahri barked. The Yorkie was quickly taken through to an examination room but, as Elle was still making a fuss, the nurse asked us if we would like to wait in one of the other examination rooms.

"Yes, please," was my short, yet grateful response.

Elle stopped screaming in the room, but stood guard, facing the door, eyes fixed in total concentration, tail ramrod straight and quivering, legs slightly back and all muscles pumped up. *"Go on, just try and get in ... try it!"*

Anne said you could almost hear her heart pounding in

readiness for an unknown foe. The door on the opposite wall opened and the nurse walked in. Elle leapt in the air and came down to face that door.

"How did that happen? How did you sneak in here?"

You could almost see the text bubbles above her head. Elle was really quite intelligent. Realizing her dilemma, she backed up so she could watch both doors. I could imagine that all that staring would nearly be burning a hole in her eyes. It must certainly have hurt to keep them fixed in opposite directions for so long.

The vet came in and we put Elle on the table and he checked her joints, teeth, heart, and skin. She was announced 'fit and well-looked-after', as always. I could almost feel my chest swelling with pride. It wouldn't last long. What is it they say about pride coming before a fall?

She got her jab and some drops in her nose, which she didn't like, and shook her head and sneezed, but never complained.

Now it was Mahri's turn. The vet asked if I could put her on the table, as it would be easier. I doubted this very much. It had a shiny surface. Still, though, I managed to lift a 50-pound, recalcitrant dog on to a four-foot-high table. Now, Mahri sometimes came across as a bit thick, although lovable; but where food is concerned, she was not stupid. She had seen what happened to Elle and she noticed that no biscuit was proffered at the end of the ordeal, so she was not about to co-operate until the rules of combat had been established. She was eventually checked and jabbed. The drops in her nose were swiftly returned to the vet with a violent snort, so I'm not really sure they were in contact with her nasal linings long enough to provide the desirable protection, but the vet assured me they were.

After that, all I had to do was empty my bank account on the way out and get me and the hooligans home to a nice safe environment. I told them that there would be no cake because they were naughty, but, weakened by their shenanigans and glad to be home, I sneaked them some Scottish smoked salmon as a treat.

I had thought of using both a halter and the harness with a double-ended lead. That way, I could control the head and the body. I'm probably just kidding myself ... my chances of ever controlling Mahri, who can be like a cross between Isadora Duncan and a mule, were about as good as a three-legged horse's in a race.

At the weekend, I was walking Mahri down a path which has had some vigorous growth of jaggy plants. We came up to a clump of them and, understandably, Mahri refused to walk over them. She stood still, pulling back a little on the lead, while she formulated a plan, and then kicked her back legs up in the air and over at a ninety-degree angle, bringing them down in the centre of the path. She was now sort of L-shaped, so she stood up on her hind legs, twisted her torso to realign it, brought it parallel to the clump of weeds, then nonchalantly trotted by them. I took one step to the side and continued walking, wondering why the simple manoeuvre had not been her first choice.

10 June 2009

Things have been ticking over quietly for the last few months. The Wild Bunch have been concentrating on chasing birds out of the garden, eating and sleeping, except for Elle, who sat up with us and watched TV. A true couch

I'll chase you

potato ... .

We had a nice 36-inch plasma TV, but Len decided he wanted a bigger TV in order to appreciate the finer points of football, rugby, tennis, cycling and so forth − basically all the justifications a man usually comes up with in order to rationalize the purchase of a technology upgrade. Thus, he bought a 50-inch full HD TV, which is wasted on me as I can't tell the difference between men chasing a ball, HD or not; but there must be a difference, because Elle, who has always shown an interest in TV, found more things that could be a threat to her environment.

First, it was a 50-inch Westie staring out of the screen at her. She covered the length of the lounge in two bounds. *"Arghhhhh, get out of my house!* Grrrr! Bark! Arghhhhhh!"* Elle screamed. We scolded her and made her sit down. Worse was to come when a 50-inch man's head started talking at her. She was so spooked after that event that it took a couple of weeks for her 'kill anything that moves reaction' to go back down to normal … well, normal for Elle, that is. We have also noticed that Elle doesn't have to see the TV to know that there may be a dog or other threat about to enter the room. She actually recognizes the tune or the people speaking in the adverts and will come rushing in from the kitchen as soon as she hears the advert start.

On Tuesday night, Len decided to watch a horror movie. It was a low-budget movie with no special effects or scary bits. It featured a man running up and down city streets through clouds of steam or fog, giving terrified glances over his shoulder at whatever was chasing him. Len eventually gave up on the movie and went to bed, while I took Elle out for her midnight toilet break.

It was pitch black and silent. Not a breath of wind stirred in the trees. As I passed the end of the house, I noticed that the movement-sensitive security light was on at the back of the house and guessed an animal must have wandered by, setting it off. As I watched, expecting to see a fox or something else emerge from the lighted area, Elle lunged forward, growling fiercely at something on my right. I stared into the darkness, but could see nothing. I scanned the limited horizons. Nothing.

I told Elle there was nothing there, but she stood on guard, muscles pumped up, ready to take on any creature of the night brave enough to approach. I listened for noises in the silence broken only by Elle's low growl. I could almost feel my ears acting like radars, scanning back and forth, synchronized with my eyes and Elle's biological surveillance tools, which were far superior to mine.

Then, all of a sudden, I heard it breathing. I listened harder and peered into the darkness. "Hmm … this is starting to get scary now; let's go in."

Elle spent the next hour or so patrolling the kitchen and giving a bark or growl at two-minute intervals. Despite not feeling as threatened as Elle, I hardly slept a wink as my ears could not block out Elle's protestations, while scanning for weird noises at the same time.

I eventually decided that the strange breathing sound I'd heard was probably me or maybe it was Elle.

Last night, I took Elle out at the same time and she was still on high alert. Reminded of the previous evening's affair, I had to convince myself that all was safe in the garden. Just when I'd decided it was not spooky or scary, the burglar alarm on a nearby factory broke the silence … maybe Elle did know something was out there … maybe she told it that she already had back-up indoors. Of course, if any mysterious strangers had called her bluff, they could not know that the back-up was actually sleeping soundly in their beds on both nights, happy in the knowledge that Elle and Jackie would be keeping a watchful eye out for any would-be intruders.

Jackie and Elle: "Halt! Who goes there? Friend or foe?"
Mr Mac and Mahri: *"Zzzzzz … do not disturb … zzzz."*

1 July 2009

We were leaving for a Mediterranean cruise today; my brother had arranged to be married by the captain, so I was looking forward to a nice break. The Wild Bunch was booked into a doggy hotel for the next couple of weeks. I had made arrangements to deliver them at 8.00am on my way to work. The kennel staff were very good and always came out to my car to show the normally rambunctious dogs to their holiday accommodation.

Mahri and Mr Mac were eager to be off on their adventure – new smells, sights and sounds. They didn't even bother to look back to see if I was following. Elle had been over-eager to get into the car and start the journey, but she'd had time to think about the destination and now remembered the truth about holiday hotels: there was no Sky TV, no Len's knee or comfy cushion to perch on, no carpets to roll around on or scratch her face or dry her chin on. This would not do; not do at all. She decided she would cancel the trip and return home with me. When the kennel maid came to lift her out of the car, she backed into the furthermost corner.

"I'll just stay here, thank you." She gave her sweetest look, tilting her head from side to side.

"Come on, Elle. Mr Mac and Mahri are waiting for you."

"It's fine. On you go, thanks. I'm staying put."

The car had a very large boot indeed. It was so large you could chase Elle around for quite some time before she tired enough to let you catch her. Like a superhero smelling trouble in the air, I'd been smart and had her special car safety lead on that let her reach the back of the seats, but no further. This certainly prevented her from making a quick getaway when I opened the door to take the dogs out. With a gentle tug on the lead, she was encouraged into the arms of the kennel maid.

"Hmmm ... well, if you're going to give me cuddles, it might not be so bad after all," she beamed at the girls, as they headed for the kennel block.

"Bye all, see you when I get back; have fun, be good, missing you already."

20 July 2009

I returned from my adventure on the high seas, where the winds were gale force seven in the Bay of Biscay and gale force six from Gibraltar to the Bay of Biscay. The wedding went well. Fortunately, it was held the day before we reached Gibraltar, when the weather was calm and very hot.

It was great to see the Wild Bunch. I really missed them and I think they were a bit wild in the kennels ... at least, the girls were. The kennel owner, when asked if they had been OK in my absence, said, "Hmmm, Elle can scream, can't she? ... And Mahri − well, she is so bouncy; I mean she is ..."

He was searching for the right adjective. "Exuberant," I offered.

"Yes that's it. She barks because she thinks she should and Elle tells her off, so she responds with minimum force, and Elle then responds with maximum decibels and force."

"Yep, that's my girls."

Actually, Elle had been on her best behaviour since she entered the house. I'm not sure whether it is because she was in a huff with us or if she was merely making sure we didn't send her back to the kennels. Mr Mac, the star of the Wild Bunch, was so laid back he'd been no problem whatsoever.

10 August 2009

It had been raining for months – actually six days, but it felt like months! The rain then retreated and there was blue sky and sunshine. Regardless of their ever-improving good behaviour traits, I had to walk each dog individually, as they were now all too strong for me to cope with, especially when they chose to simultaneously run in opposite directions. I walked about six miles, with each dog getting about a one-hour walk, which is approximately two miles. Mr Mac had the first walk and the next was Elle's. Then it was Mahri's turn.

We walked past the barking mad Terrier-cross; she ignored it. Past the Rotties and Spaniels; she never even looked in their direction. And past the German Shepherd dogs; not even a flicker of the ears. Was this girl sickening for something or had my three-and-a-half-year-old pup suddenly grown up and was doing everything she was taught at dog school?

In a sense, I was quite pleased she was behaving so well. After we passed the German Shepherd dogs, we turned along a narrow footpath that ran between two fields and connected two small housing estates.

Mahri insisted upon trotting along at my side. It would have been easier if she'd adopted her usual position, forging ahead or dragging behind, as there is not really enough room for our two voluptuous rumps side by side on the path. I was in danger of sliding down into the drainage ditch on my right, whereas Mahri had chosen the safer position by the fence.

We crossed the little bridge over the ditch and walked

along a wider path, bordered by trees and gardens on both sides. A pigeon flew out of the hedgerow, nearly crashing into Mahri's head. Good behaviour was soon forgotten and suddenly she was the wild child again, leaping with glee after the pigeon; all thoughts of me on the other end of the lead were gone. She jumped and bounced, but the pigeon made good its escape. Next, a dragon-fly as big as a helicopter was the focus of her attention. Then a bee, a ladybird, and a blackbird.

As we neared the end of the path, a furry quadruped of the feline variety sneaked out of the undergrowth. It stood still, staring at us in a semi-crouch position, tail swishing slowly from side to side. Mahri responded. Head down, legs slightly bent, tail ram-rod straight, with the tiny twitch that probably only an Airedale owner would notice. Her eyes were totally focused, staring back. There was a moment of impasse when both of them considered the size and speed of the other and I braced myself for Mahri's decision.

Patience is not one of Mahri's virtues and she'd decided that she could not hang about to play this stare-each-other-out game any longer. There were bugs to chase and smells to follow. With all her legs leaving the ground in one single leap like a gazelle, she sprang forward. With a degree more elegance, the cat did the same; it was almost like a mirror image scene from a Tom and Jerry cartoon. Mahri landed on her back legs, ready to power forward again. An image of the big dog in Tom and Jerry cartoons sprang to mind.

The cat, as it landed, looked left and right, but had not made up its mind whether to cross in front of us and jump over the fence or turn left and outrun us to the end of the path, where it opened up into the little housing estate. It decided to go left.

Mahri had only ever seen the next door neighbour's cats that wandered through the garden when she was in the day kennel. They teased her because they knew she could not get out. Mocking her further, they usually sat on the Perspex roof and stared at her with an insolent grin.

I don't think she meant any malice towards *this* cat. It clearly invited her to play chase and she happily obliged. I held on to her lead, pulled her back to heel and made her sit. The path was still slippery from all the rain and I had visions of me turning into a dog sled and clearing the path of all debris before I got a chance to put the brakes on Mahri. To my great relief, she did as she was told and we walked home with only the odd leap at a passing bug or lunge under a parked car, just in case the cat was planning another ambush.

10 September 2009

On Wednesday night, I was convinced that Mahri and my friend's Airedale, Molly, a notorious insomniac, had been emailing each other for tips on how to keep the humans awake for the longest possible time. Every two hours, we heard Bark! Bark! Bark! at the door. The exterior motion-controlled lights were on, so I assumed a cat or hedgehog or some other critter had wandered by the house.

I took Mahri out because she *so* politely asked. Mahri barked once and sat by the door. If you didn't let her out, it would be two barks, then three barks, so you'd think to yourself, "OK, it's not a critter and she wants to be out." I would normally take her out on one bark, but if I've already had her out, I would decide it was an untimely critter, so I'd wait to see if she would tell me again.

By 5.00am, I was very tired and becoming concerned because even Elle was refusing to get out of her bed and go out with us. Usually, it was compulsory that Elle supervised every sortie. Mr Mac had stopped responding to Mahri's barks round about midnight; he did manage to nod at me when I walked past his bed, as if to say, 'Shout if you need me'.

I asked Betty, who was on duty yesterday, to keep an eye on Mahri, as I was concerned and, when I got home, she reported that Mahri had been the same all day, so I immediately phoned the vet.

"Can you see Mahri if I bring her up right away? I think she might have cystitis." While grinning, I asked, "Do dogs get that?"

"Yes, bring her right up."

When I got to the vet's, there was one dog waiting, a big German Shepherd wearing a muzzle. I sat down at the opposite end of the room behind the dog treat stand, so Mahri would be distracted. The German Shepherd ignored Mahri, who was happily sniffing the dog treats on the stand. Next, a woman entered the waiting room with a little Jack Russell Terrier, which appeared to be quite old and quite slow. She sat near the German Shepherd, who again never made a sound or moved. I started to wonder why he was wearing the big muzzle. Next, a man came in with a cat in a crate. He paused, looking at the German Shepherd, then the Jack Russell Terrier, who was now sitting on its owner's knee, and then at Mahri, who was sitting very nicely at my side.

"I think I'll sit over there," he said to the other two owners and pointing at me.

Mahri, who had been sitting so quietly, showed the nosey side of her character as she began pulling and scrambling to get closer to the crate. She wanted to inspect the contents. Meanwhile, the other two dogs sat quietly waiting their turn.

After ten minutes of Mahri hauling and pulling and the man trying to hide the crate from her – which made her worse – the German Shepherd was called through to the treatment room. It was like a scene from Betty Boop. The vet called "Max, please", and the dog jumped up and ran in his direction, with the woman being jerked off the chair and following as best she could. She was about five feet tall and a size ten – a UK size ten = skinny – with high-heels, an oversize bag and a shopping bag. The lead was four feet of chain with a leather hand-hold. She held everything with her left hand, as her right was in constant use, flicking her long blonde hair about.

The man now decided that sitting next to the Jack Russell would be much better and moved. Mahri sat down to contemplate the treats on the stand again. When the Betty Boop Lady came out, it was just as funny. The dog kept walking round her, so she was tied up in the chain. Trying to unwind the chain, she kept whirling round, flicking her hair.

She had no control of the dog at all, which, although funny to watch, was not really funny at all, and I can only hope that if something scared the dogs she would act like an anchor on the chain and hook round the nearest lamp-post.

Eventually, it was Mahri's turn and, yes, she did have cystitis. Two injections and five days of antibiotics would put her right.

"Oh … and on Sunday, please collect a sample so we

can check it's all cleared up."

"Hmm, that will be fun … I think not!"

I made her some barley water to help her feel better and she managed to go four hours before needing out.

17 September 2009

The critters, all warm and full-bellied, were dozing. The sun had set and all was well with the world. Suddenly, the 'greater sous-sofa monster' – aka common house or hobo spider – scuttled almost silently across the room. I say almost silently, because it was not quite soundless enough to avert the attentions of the three sets of ears that pricked up almost simultaneously. I followed their gaze.

"Eeek!! Look at the size of that," I screamed. "Save me, save me, Mr Mac," I cried in my best *Gone with the Wind* accent, and promptly jumped on the couch to get away from the spider.

Mr Mac was stretched out on the rug, fast asleep, but he lifted his head to see what all the commotion was about. *"It's only a spider, woman. Nowt to be scared of,"* he grumbled, and went back to sleep. Mahri, who had also been curled up asleep, sat up for a closer look, agreed with Mr Mac and flopped back down to continue her snooze. The spider, meanwhile, had been darting hither and thither like a commando sneaking up on the enemy.

Elle had also been awoken from her slumber by my shrieks and came charging to my rescue from the kitchen. *"I'm here! Where's the fight? Let me at him!"*

She rushed right up and nosed the spider. It stopped in its tracks. It backed up a few paces. Both were locked in a stare that would have made the gun fighters at the OK Corral look like sissies. The spider reared up on its back legs, about to jump at Elle. Whack! Her paw, with the speed of lightning, came down, trapping the spider by its back legs. She studied it carefully, tilting her head from side to side, sniffing it all over, taking in every nuance of its personal odour.

Frozen by the irrational terror, I could only sit and watch, unable to move, but also unable to avert my eyes. I hate spiders. Having to look at one for this length of time would usually make me sick.

To my utter amazement, she pulled one of its legs off and let it go. It hobbled off under the TV and she trotted back to her comfy bed with the jaunty wiggle of one who knows it was a job well executed – maimed perhaps, but not terminated.

The following night, same time, same place, the now lesser-limbed 'sous-sofa monster' emerged from under the couch at a much more sedate speed. The events of the previous night were apparently not forgotten, as it took the most direct route from couch to TV to ensure that Elle could not make it from the kitchen in time for another confrontation.

I combed the web – no pun intended – to see what sort of spider it was. I was right to be scared of it. They are nasty, aggressive solitary creatures who can't get on with their own type, never mind anything else. As so many unsocial creatures often are, they are also ferocious fighters.

This one met its match when it decided to cross swords with a diminutive Welsh Terrier with attitude. Elle knew it was about and still had seven legs. She peered under the couch a few times and under the TV.

"Come out, come out wherever you are," she taunted it.

One day they will meet again and she may not be in one of her more benevolent moods, such as she was the other night.

Elle: *"Why is it always left to me to do the dirty work around here?"*

> There was a wee Elle that swallowed a fly.
> I don't know why she swallowed a fly;
> Perhaps she's sly.
>
> There was a wee Elle that swallowed a spider
> That wriggled and tickled about inside her;
> She swallowed the spider to catch the fly,
> So now we know that Elle is sly.

18 September 2009

Most nights at 9.00pm, Elle tiptoed up to Len's chair and put her front feet on his, which was the signal that she wanted up on his knee. Once there, she has always sniffed his ears and eyes. I never knew why she did it, but it was her little ritual. She would sit down to await the arrival of the 'diva cushion' – a big cushion we put on Len's knee to prevent pressure sores. She'd then lie down to watch the TV with him.

Last night, she went through her little ritual, but stopped short of lying down. She sat there like the queen of the castle surveying her territory. Her head tilted a bit to the left, then to the right. You could almost see the daggers flying out of her eyes. There he was again, boldly hobbling across the carpet! The 'seven-legged sous-sofa monster' had returned.

I was poised, ready to grab her in case she took a flying leap off Len's lap; but no, she merely stared daggers at it. After what seemed like five or ten minutes, or an eternity if you are poised on the edge of a sofa betwixt spider and a would-be 'flying ace' named Elle, the spider backed up slowly and retreated under the TV. Elle watched it depart, tilting her head to make sure she saw exactly where it went.

"If I wasn't so busy keeping Len company, I would have had another of your legs," she mumbled, as she lay down to watch the lions and tigers and dream of fights (or do I mean hunts?) to come.

While Elle had assigned herself the job of controlling the local spider population, the Airedales, sensible creatures, had taken to sleeping at the opposite end of the room, out of harm's way.

21 September 2009

I failed the sanity test, which is probably why I get on so well with my Airedales. All year I've been saving a hedgehog from Mr Mac. He thought his only task in life was to search, find and bring a hedgehog to me. He crawled under the jaggy hedges to retrieve the little critter, raced towards me and would then throw it in my direction. He did not appear to hurt it, but I don't like to think of any creature being scared, and I would be scared if I was rudely awakened from my nap and moved to a new location by an unequivocally large Airedale.

McGregor, our previous Airedale, used to do the same with birds; he would take them out of the bushes near the house and move them to the bushes by the gate. He never harmed them, other than giving them a nasty scare. I actually ran along behind him once, telling him to drop it. I could see the wings of the bird flapping as his mouth was only closed enough to prevent escape. As soon as he got to the trees, he would put the bird down and run back to get another one.

Anyway, I digress. Due to his obsession with the hedgehog, Mr Mac was lead-walked in the garden first thing in the morning before the sun was quite up and as soon as it was dusk, when hedgehogs are likely to be around searching for food. Thus, you can imagine how mad I was when I arrived home from work on Friday, drove towards my gate and saw this half-flat, brown, spiky lump in the middle of the road.

"Arrrggggghhhh!" I shouted at it, "you stupid, stupid hedgehog!"

I parked my car in the drive and stomped back up the road. I was still shaking my head and ranting, "How could you be so stupid? After my efforts to keep you safe all summer and you go and run out in front of a car in broad daylight."

I reached the little spiky brown lump and stared at it as if I was hoping for an answer to my questions about its stupidity. Then a big smile spread across my face and I looked round sheepishly, hoping that no-one had witnessed or heard my outburst. The little spiky brown lump was left on the road by a horse.

I breathed a sigh of relief, turned and headed for the house. Len told me he'd stopped in the road as well, thinking it was our hedgehog. Later that night, I saw our little hedgehog snuffling about in the big paddock, quite safe and happy.

20 October 2009 – Mahri's Self-Prescribed Diet: Paper

As stated previously, Mahri had a penchant for paper. She just couldn't resist it, so we were generally careful not to leave any within her reach. One day last week, the doctor had called in to see Len, who was unwell. Vera, the carer, contacted me to come straight home as the doctor had left a prescription for some medication and I would need to take it to the chemist before it closed at 6.00pm. This was going to be tight, as I didn't usually get home till 5.40pm at the earliest.

On this occasion, I'd be dishonest if I didn't tell you that the way I made sure I got to the house on time was to partake in a little speeding. Just a little bit, though, and I arrived home by 5.30pm. The prescription was not on the shelf where it should be.

"Where's the prescription?" I shouted to Nita.

"On the breakfast bar," she replied.

"No, it's *NOT*," I responded.

Vera stopped what she was doing and searched the empty flat surface that is the breakfast bar.

"Have you put it in your bag or coat pocket? Could Mahri have eaten it?" I asked.

Mahri was dozing in her bed and looked up with her big eyes full of innocence. *"Moi, steal the prescription! That's outrageous."*

She looked away from my questioning stare. I had no time to search any more if I was to get to the surgery for a copy and then get to the chemist before it closed. I made it to the surgery and explained to the receptionist that the doctor had called in to see Len and left a prescription for some new medication starting that night. Unfortunately, we could not find the prescription and we thought the dog had eaten it. Then I asked if I could have another before the chemist closed in ten minutes.

"The doctor's in surgery at the moment," the receptionist said with a condescending sneer.

"Yes, I'm aware of that, but couldn't you nip in between patients and ask her to sign another? I wouldn't ask if I didn't think it was important." I gave her my most winning smile. It never fails when Mahri does it to me and I've learnt from the best.

"Have a seat and I'll see what I can do."

With two minutes to go till closing time, I rushed into the chemist, waving the new prescription. Fifteen minutes

The Wild Bunch

later, after it was filled and they unlocked the doors, I was out. I rushed home with the sealed bag and gave it to Vera. She opened it to inspect the contents.

A course of antibiotics and drinks!

The same pills as the emergency ones kept in the medicine drawer that we had been given to take with us on our summer holiday; and some re-hydrating drinks, the same as the ones I took on holiday. Arrgggggh!

We were going to train Mahri to be Len's assistance dog, but she clearly didn't have the mental agility required for the role. In fact, the only thing she usually assisted in achieving was chaos.

At the weekend, I walked into the kitchen just in time to see Mahri with her feet on the breakfast bar, breathing out forcefully so that a post-it note containing a telephone number would float off the table on to the floor. I leapt forward, arm outstretched, and managed to grab the note as it fluttered floorward. Mahri just kicked her heels and wandered off in search of more paper.

I think she must have been an accountant in a past life, because the only trail this dog will follow is a paper trail.

12 November 2009

In many a multiple-dog household, when you called one dog, they all arrived. When I call Elle, the two Airedales appear. I don't think there has ever been a time the Welsh came when called. If Mr Mac and Mahri are having a hard-of-hearing day, the word cheese usually cured it, or opening the fridge door and looking at the cheese will have the pair of them break all land speed records to get as close to me – and the cheese – as possible; but not Elle. If it was absolutely necessary to get her to come to me in the house, I had to ring the doorbell; then she arrived faster than the speed of light. Outside, she couldn't be let off-lead because of this little quirk in her nature – we called it her feline quirk. Often when I was eating my dinner and the dogs were lying round the room like scatter rugs, I just needed to think I might leave a crust for them and they started to migrate toward me, except for Elle, who feigned indifference. As soon as my cutlery was laid on the plate and the plate pushed away, two Airedales arrived at my side, sitting nicely and looking from the table to me.

"C'mon, hand it over. We know it's for us," they seemed to say.

If I cleared my plate, they never even lifted their heads from their recumbent position; they just knew that there were no left-overs for them that night. Elle let them do all the work, because she knew we will always treat them the same. Either everybody received treats or nobody received treats. Elle had even taught Mahri to bark at us to let us know when Elle wanted a toilet break. This was no ordinary bark and had been developed especially for times when Elle wanted out. Mahri would give her funny squeaky bark and sit by the door, and Elle would wander through to the kitchen and sit by Mahri. Every time I picked up Elle's lead, Mahri retired to her bed, I'd take Elle out and everyone was happy. I often thought that I'd got the only dumb Airedales in the world, but maybe I'm the one that's too dumb to evaluate their IQ.

18 December 2009

My little Wild Bunch experienced their first-ever blizzard last night, with gale force winds, driving snow that stabbed at your eyes and gave frostbite to your corneas. Six inches of snow blasted down upon us in just an hour. The wind had lifted the lid off the hot tub, so I battled with that and then I went flying with the drive-wide five-bar iron gate. As I tried to shut it, the wind took it and left me no choice but to hang on to it for a short flight. Eventually, the weather conditions got the better of me and I gave up and anchored it open.

All night the wind howled round the house like a ghostly wolf pack and things frequently went bump in the night. Mahri curled up into the smallest ball at the back of her crate. *"I'll hold till morning,"* she glowered at me, when offered a midnight walk in the garden.

Elle was up for it. *"I'll go. I'll eat all the snowflakes and bark at the wind till it goes away."*

There were no tiny pawprints in the snow from Elle for me to admire; just huge scrambled areas where she hauled and stretched to get at anything that moved. Mr Mac bounded over to the nearest tree and back in as few moves as possible so he would not get snow on his feet. Once all were safely tucked up in their beds, it was my turn to curl up and drift off to sleep …

Wrong! After 30 minutes of trying to ignore the bumps and bangs, I gave in and went to investigate. Worse! Just as I stepped into the hallway, the power went off. I headed for the fuse box in pitch black, shuffling my feet so that I avoided tripping over any discarded dog toys. Suddenly, my foot banged into something large. I screamed and leapt in the air. Mr Mac, at that precise moment, also screamed and leapt in the air. I knew this because he tried to occupy the exact same airspace as me. We landed in a muddled heap. Poor Mr Mac could not understand why I'd been so mean to him, or why he'd been jolted out of his peaceful slumber.

I eventually got the power back on and checked poor Mr Mac, who was still a quivering wreck. *"How could you treat me so badly?"* he seemed to say, as he looked at me with his ears still turned inside out. The storm must have scared him and he probably felt safer if he lay in the middle of the floor, rather than in his bed. I'd thought it was safe to walk in the middle because he usually went to sleep with his back against a wall.

"Oops, sorry, Mr Mac. We'll go build a snowman this afternoon."

25 January 2010

There must be something in the air. Could it be spring? Mahri, our lovable, big, bouncy three-and-a-half-year-old girl, who normally acted more like a Labrador than an Airedale, pushed me out of the way as I was trying to leave the house and escaped into the garden. She saw the gate open. I'd opened it as I was about to drive into town. I called her. She stopped, turned her head and looked me straight in the eye. *"Not today, thanks,"* she appeared to say, and, turning away from me, she bolted out the gate.

I followed her and, fortunately, she'd met a neighbour with her two little Westies. We often pass each other and

Mahri is always good, so I wasn't too worried. She was standing nose to nose with one of the Westies when I walked up to her. I was just about to grab her collar when she turned and was about to run off down the road. The lady with the Westies quickly grabbed her and I escorted Mahri unceremoniously back to the house and into her crate. I told Mahri that she would be on restricted privileges for a month and all her treat money is going to benefit senior Airedales, which she is unlikely to become if she continued running out of the gate.

When I got back from shopping, I took Elle and Mahri out on leads round the garden. Mr Mac, who could usually be trusted not to run off, was allowed to run free. He ran round the perimeter of the garden and then into the middle to meet us. On this day, he didn't arrive as quickly as usual, so I figured he'd be raiding the bird table. I started to call him and called and called, eventually concluding that he was not at the bird table.

I quickly put the girls back indoors and went in search of the errant Mr Mac. I heard my other neighbour shout in response to my calls for Mr Mac to come. Mr Mac had found a hole in our hedge, and one in the neighbour's fence, crawled through and found their bird table, which was much better stocked than mine. He then proceeded to avail himself of the tasty morsels as if he was some poor unloved stray.

Elle was next to join in the bad behaviour lark by nipping knees and ankles of anyone who dared move at a pace quicker than that of a mollusc with a limp.

As a result, they will not be getting any treats for at least a few days and none while I'm out of the house. No long walks to follow random scents either. It would be back to basic training for them. All walks would now be punctuated with lots of sit, lie down and stand orders till they agreed that I was the one in charge and I knew best and I *would be* obeyed.

27 January 2010

Elle had come a long way from the distant little pup we brought home in June 2006. Had she been human, she would have been labelled autistic. I could now tell her to 'get me a toy' and I would play with her, but she wouldn't always be interested. If she was in the mood to play, she would trot very slowly and nonchalantly, with tiny deliberate cat-like footfalls and with the merest hint of a wiggle, to pick up a discarded stuffed toy – actually de-stuffed would be a more suitable adjective – and then would rush back to me, growling like mad. This was her cue for 'catch it if you can' and 'wrestle it from me if you dare'. If you dared instigate it, the game was on until *she* tired, not you. And she ran on long-life batteries, so one should be prepared to play till one dropped.

If there were no toys near, she would go to the toy box or to the nearest bed and drag a blanket over with which to play tug. Once or twice, she had gone to Mr Mac's bed, a large basket-shaped concoction of corduroy and fleece, and tried to drag it over for a game of tug. On one occasion when it would not be dragged over the carpet, she jumped in and tried to push it. While funny to watch, and impressive from a problem-solving perspective, there was definitely some sort of flawed logic being displayed.

Last night she was pestering us to play, so she was told,

"Get me a toy then." She trotted over to Mr Mac's bed and started to wrestle it in my direction. For a cheap giggle, and, yes, I knew it was cruel, I tipped the bed over her like a giant tortoise shell. What happened next I didn't really expect: she reared up on her hind legs a couple of times to tip the bed back on to the carpet, but that didn't work. She ran to the left, ran to the right. Like a blind tortoise, she moved around lost.

We were all laughing at her so much, Mr Mac and Mahri came to see what all the commotion was. The look on Mahri's face as Mr Mac's bed staggered towards her was an absolute picture, or would have been if my camera had been to hand.

Suddenly, a tiny black nose appeared. Then a bit of brown muzzle, followed by two eyes and an ear. Elle had managed to find a gap in the stitching that joined the base of the bed to the sides and pushed her head through, so she could see what was amusing everyone. This didn't really stop anybody laughing at all. In fact, quite the opposite, as she looked even more like a tortoise carrying its home on its back.

She kept turning from left to right to try to get the best view.

Mahri couldn't believe her eyes and barked at the object of our mirth while looking at us to see what we would do. We did all we were capable of doing and just laughed some more, so she lay down to plan her next move. Mr Mac had retreated under the table until things returned to normal. In the end, I composed myself and lifted the bed off Elle and put it back in its rightful place. What happened next... the little minx casually walked over to get the bed to play the game again. I think she

297

must have found it funny too.
15 February 2010

When considering getting a small dog I suggested a Jack Russell, but Len said they were too snappy and yappy. Then he chose a Welsh!

I walked Elle, the Welsh, for two miles on Saturday and thought I'd puffed her out, as she was dragging her heels a little on the last 100 yards or so. Mahri and Mr Mac had already walked the same route. Soon after a little sip of water and a shake, Elle was ready for action again. The two Airedales had already recovered from their walks and all of them had started screaming round the house like Honda 250s at a race meet.

"Hoy! Do you think it's outside you're in?" I yelled at them.

The response was that Mahri came running towards me at full speed, veered left under the breakfast bar that I was leaning on, circled round the back of me and performed a perfect drop-kick in the ribs. This knocked the wind right out of me, and then she proceeded back on course and grabbed Mr Mac's ear on the way past him. I'm sure I could hear her laughing as she whizzed by. It's great to watch them having such fun, but all good things must be in moderation.

"Toast anyone?" I shouted. This time all three dogs came screeching to a halt at my side. "That's unanimous then." They sat in silence, eyes fixed on the toaster, willing it to cook faster so they could have their Saturday treat.

23 February 2010

The other night, Elle was playing tug with me. We'd just bought her a new rope tug toy and she loved it. I'd let her pull the rope for a while, but then I would pull it back and forth for her to tussle with. We play this game most nights before dinner. She was busy pulling away, when suddenly she changed direction and ran towards me, her bottom teeth colliding with my finger.

"Ouch!!!" I squealed, and clamped my hand tightly round my finger, as if I was holding together two separated parts, hoping it would ease the pain. I was too frightened to look because I wasn't sure if she'd bitten my finger or just put her teeth through the nail. The poor wee soul froze to the spot for a minute and then slunk away to sit beside Mr Mac, who, on hearing my squeal, hid behind the couch in case whatever it was came after him.

After I recovered my composure enough, I limped through to the kitchen, not because she'd hurt my leg in any way, but I now had pins and needles in it from kneeling on the floor. I took three Arnica, followed five minutes later by another two, and repeated that in another five minutes. The huge pain had subsided, so I plucked up the courage to inspect the damage. She had managed to catch my nail, bending it back to the point where it snapped. About two-thirds of the way down, it was only attached by one corner, so, gritting my teeth and summoning up my Airedale spirit, I clipped the nail free. I put some padding over the nail bed to protect it and taped it all up to keep it clean.

Subsequently, as a result of this incident, I have only been able to type with one finger for the last two days and, to add insult to injury, I'd just given myself a full manicure on Sunday and reduced the length of all my nails to almost stubby. The funny thing was that I had only told Len a couple of days previous that I'd better reduce them before the dogs did it for me. Ha! Look at how that worked out!

I couldn't play tug with her now in case she banged my finger; so, to make amends, I bought her a new soft toy to play with till my finger healed and we could play again. The new toy was a grey elephant; she absolutely loved it and carried it everywhere with her. She did let Mahri and Mr Mac have a little play with it, but then changed her mind. *"This toy is not for sharing."* The last time she was like that was with a yellow duck and we had to put it in the bin because it caused too many fights every time one of the other two went near it.

24 February 2010

"Are your ears ornamental? Am I shouting at you for the good of my health? Hoy! Cloth ears, are you deaf or something?" These are a few of the questions asked at high decibels in Mahri's direction, all of which were usually ignored.

I know that the words 'biscuit' or 'dinner', uttered in an almost inaudible whisper, would bring her racing to my side. However, when she was careering round the garden, chasing imaginary prey, Elle or Mr Mac, I always seemed to forget that important nugget of information.

Anyway, the reason I have been muttering about Mahri and her auditory inadequacies is that last night I found out the answer to these questions. It appeared that Mahri was aware that she had a hearing deficiency and, in order to rectify it, she borrowed one of Len's rather expensive hide-in-ear hearing aids. Fortunately, he was not wearing it at that moment in time. As we know, dogs do not have a prehensile thumb or any other means of pinch grip, so Mahri, who always tried to solve her own problems, decided that, if she couldn't put the hearing aid in her ear, any other internal organ would work just as well.

My suspicions were first aroused when I saw Mahri running for her bed, her head held high, and with a very deliberate, prancing gait. This usually alerted me that she had stolen or found a prize and was taking it to her bed to savour without the interference or a request to share from the other two. I was preparing dinner, so called Mahri over for a tasty treat, with the plan being to check her bed while she checked the floor. In the past I've found, when I've attempted to crawl on to her bed, that Mahri will barge past me into her crate, grab her prize and scarper while I'm still trying to stand up. The solution to this conundrum was to throw a handful of shelled peas over the kitchen floor to keep her occupied for a few minutes.

What I hadn't realized was that Mr Mac had sneaked into Mahri's bed as soon as she vacated it, grabbed her prize and was about to make off with it when he came face to face, or rather, face to knee, with me. Mr Mac was the biggest wimp you'd ever be likely to meet and he immediately dropped the prize on the floor. I still wasn't really aware of the problem, but I was aware that they were acting rather strangely.

Mahri, by now, had hoovered up the peas and ran over to grab what Mr Mac had dropped.

"Leave it!!" I shouted, and then stared at a sort of rectangular black object that made me wonder whether it was a large beetle. ... I could see teeth marks in the hard shell, but the dogs usually only puncture them and not kill them, because they probably don't taste very nice, despite being a delicacy in certain countries. I looked closer. No legs could be seen so I tentatively put my hand out to pick up this object, only because I was now sure that it had always been an inanimate one, or at least part of one. As I picked it up, I sighed with relief as it was indeed a hard plastic object. Then I turned it over. Eeeeek! It was Len's hearing aid.

This was just the start of the panic. First, I had to tell Len, who surveyed the damage in silence. "It looks like we're in luck," I said. Only the little plastic cone covering the bit that goes in his ear appeared to be missing. "How did she get the hearing aid? Did it drop out of your ear?" I asked Len. "No," he replied. "I took it out and left it on the computer desk because it was whistling."

I searched all the carpet from the desk area and the tiled floor in the kitchen, following the route she would have taken to her bed. I found two tiny crystals, but no bit of white plastic. I carefully checked each layer of bedding as I emptied her basket inside her crate. She had several layers of dog fleeces to make sure she was well protected from the hard tiled floor and any drafts. Two layers down, I spied a tiny silver object. "Oh, sugar" and "Thank Dog" were uttered simultaneously. The silver object was the battery from the hearing aid. I also found the tiny piece of black plastic that was the door that kept the battery in place. I went to tell Len the second lot of bad news, but advised him that it was in fact good news, because she hadn't swallowed the battery.

I still hadn't found the white plastic bit and I checked my jewellery and could not find any with a missing stone or an entire missing piece of jewellery, so the owner of the two crystals that I found remains a mystery. The dinner, which was going to be mince, potatoes and brussels sprouts was now mince, potato soup and brussels sprout mash; but, as I hate waste, we ate it anyway ... and Mahri got none!

Len was off to the city the following day to see if the hearing aid could be repaired and Mahri was waiting to find out how many days' RPs (restriction of privileges) she would get.

21 April 2010

The weather was getting warmer now, so the dogs got to play in the day kennel. Last night, I put the leads on Elle and Mahri and walked them round to the big paddock. It was only a short walk between the house and the day kennel, but it was to teach them that they don't run out of the kennel and they don't run free till they are on the grass. I used to let Mr Mac run free from the kennel, but he and Mahri messed about in the alleyway and bounced me off the wall, so now he has to wait until I come back for him.

Last night, I followed the routine and on reaching the grass I let the two girls run free. I watched them as they ran down the side of the paddock, then I ran back round to release Mr Mac. He charged off to join the girls in a game of tag and I followed him to join in a game of chase and hand out the treats. As I rounded the corner of the stable block, I saw Mahri leaping into the air to catch something, then throw it and leap to catch it again. It was at that point I realized it was a bird. "Nooooooo!" I yelled, as I ran towards her.

For the first time ever, she stopped and looked at me, as did the other two. When I reached the dogs, they were standing in a circle, necks outstretched towards the bird, which was now lying, feet up, in the grass. Elle was trying to inch a bit closer on account of her neck being half the size of an Airedale neck.

I looked at the bird. Oh dear. It was still breathing. I didn't know what to do. I couldn't tell whether it would stop breathing soon or if it would be OK, get up and fly away, hopefully trying not to impersonate a Frisbee in the future.

I managed to get hold of Elle's lead; it was a light puppy lead that she wore all the time so we could catch her when necessary. I got Mahri's lead slipped over her head and started to pull the girls away. Mr Mac bounced about just out of my reach, but still managed to follow me away from the bird.

I turned round to watch the bird, hoping it would fly away to safety, for two reasons. First, I, ever the optimist, wanted the bird to be OK after being mauled by an Airedale; and second, I now had to get three hairy beasts, whose prey drive was at fever pitch, back to the house without consuming the bird, dead or on the way to being dead.

My prayers were answered. The bird rolled over on to its feet and started to fly off. Its flight was somewhat impeded by some dodgy looking feathers on one of its wings. It landed near Len's log cabin and quickly ran under it to recover from its death-defying ordeal.

Mahri and Mr Mac scampered off to play tag and chase, the bird now forgotten; but Elle had also been watching the bird to see what it was going to do. Elle had the prey drive of a hungry wolf and the patience of a bear with a sore head, as well as the memory of an elephant.

She dragged me up to the log cabin, screeching like a banshee. She went straight to the spot where the bird ran under the cabin. I could see that Elle would get under the cabin by fair means or foul. She tilted her head and pushed it under the flooring. She could definitely get in, but probably not out. Len would have been less than impressed if I had to lift the floor to rescue her. "Why," I hear you ask, "did you let her go up to the cabin?" Well, Elle had a tiny wee neck and, when she pulled, I tended to follow rather than risk damaging her windpipe. She had a harness for out-of-garden walks, and when Elle was in one of her 'I'm gonna get you' moods, you do not attempt to pick her up unless you have arms that are five foot long and galvanized.

I did eventually manage to coax her away from the cabin for her dinner; but every time I took her out thereafter, she headed back to that same spot. She would not go to the toilet while that bird might still be under the cabin. Now, she had patience in abundance. I could only hope the bird made good its escape during the night and that Elle would find a new smell to chase.

5 May 2010

I have had six Airedales in total; three of them would view a bone with disgust: *"Yeuch ... you don't expect me to put that in my mouth, do you?"* One would nibble on the corner, so you had to be sure to leave it where you wanted it chewed on; and Mr Mac chewed any meat off the bone, then ignored the rest of it.

That brought us to Airedale number six – aka Mahri; at

305

50 pounds of joy, she bounced and wiggled like a puppy Labrador and lived for food and paper napkins. The former she would take gently from your hand or ingest from her bowl in a micro-second; but the latter was to be snatched and swallowed before you could prise her jaws open to retrieve it. She had split a marrow bone into fragments on several occasions, so I won't buy them for her any more in case she swallowed a bit. I didn't think the postman needed to worry about losing any of his appendages, though, unless they were wrapped in kitchen towel.

Mahri preferred the eastern style of combat. Her favourite move was ippon seonagi or 'ippon seon Mahri', as I preferred to call it. You could be walking along the road admiring the view, when she noticed something you had not. A leaf twitching in the middle of a five-acre field, for instance. In what appeared to be one fluid movement, she could rise up on her hind legs, insert one leg between yours and flip you over into the gutter. My one big rule was never let go of the lead; so, while you were rolling around in the mud trying to return to the perpendicular, she would perform several other judo-type moves. Her other favourite was to stand on her front legs and drop-kick your chest or face with her back legs. She could do this in quick succession. Then, while you were lying there battered and bruised, she would do a drop-kick followed through by a twist, so she landed on her back legs with her front legs on your chest, pushing you back into the mud. She could pirouette like this several times in the hope that you would release the lead. If, after all this, she had failed to make you let go of the lead, her final move, which I am sometimes too exhausted to resist, was to sit on you and give you a big sloppy kiss.

Of course, this was usually played out with a group of young farm workers watching and they usually waited until she was sitting quietly before they approached to ask if you needed any assistance. My answer was always, "Oh, no thanks. She's just playing. Some days she can be a bit boisterous."

26 August 2010

The hot weather had come to an abrupt end with lots of rain, strong winds and falling temperatures; it was quite autumnal now. I had to take Len to meet his friends for a boys' day out, and took an early dinner break yesterday.

I left work at 11.00am, drove home, then left in Len's car at 12.30pm to drive to the club. I dropped Len off at about 1.30pm, then I had a one-hour drive back to work, where I stayed until my shift finished at 6.00pm. At this point, it was back to club to pick Len up at 7.00pm. All this was done in torrential rain with lots of surface water, so it was not a comfortable drive and I didn't get home till 9.00pm.

The Wild Bunch were in the day kennel where Anne had left them in the afternoon because I knew we might be late getting back. I hadn't had time for any lunch or dinner, so I made us a hot drink and me a sandwich. The Wild Bunch could wait; they'd had extra breakfast and tit-bits from Anne.

I sat down to enjoy my sandwich and three dogs, who all know they are not allowed to beg at the table, and that includes the coffee table, plonked themselves down in front of me. I stared at them. "Yes!" I said; this was my way of telling them to leave until I'd finished eating. This request had started with our very first Airedale, who was from Ireland. Let me explain.

Carrie, our first Airedale, would approach the table when we were eating and we would ask her, "Yes!!! What do you want?" It later got shortened to just 'yes' and has worked well with all our Airedales. All of them have come from the same breeder in Ireland. We always thought it was an Irish thing, but Welsh Elle knew and understood that yes means no … and she was from Lincoln.

After several 'yes' comments, the Airedales wandered off to the scatter rugs in the middle of the room and threw themselves down with a thud and a huge sigh. "I know," I told them. "You are usually fed at 7.00pm and I eat at 8.00pm but, if I don't eat first, I will expire and there will be nobody left to feed you."

Still they ignored me. Elle, on the other hand, decided that her wee tummy did not hold as much food as Mahri and Mr Mac's, so it needed to be topped up sooner. She sat in front of me and licked her lips, looked at my sandwich, then nodded towards the kitchen door. I ignored her so she put her paws on the seat and repeated the action in case I hadn't seen it the first time. She has a particular way of nodding sideways with her head that seemed almost human at times. You just knew that she wanted you to move in the direction of the nod … or perhaps I just watched too many episodes of *Skippy* when I was young.

"Yes!" I said to her, fully expecting her to comply with my wishes and retire to her bed till I was finished eating. She sat down and looked at the Airedales. *"A bit of back-up would be nice."* She glared at them. They ignored her. She walked to the side of my seat, gave a squeak to get my attention and nodded at the door. I ignored her, so she repeated the action with a louder squeak and a step closer to the door. She made it clear that I had changed the routine without consultation or permission from her and she was not happy.

I gave in and followed Elle to the kitchen, who went straight to her feeding station and sat down. The other two happily bounded into the kitchen for their dinner after letting Elle do all the work. Mr Mac and Mahri, now fed and happy, allowed me to drink my almost cold tea and eat my sandwich with only the smallest sideways glances, just in case I dropped a crumb or two. Elle, to prove a point, went to her basket in the kitchen and stayed there all night, instead of lounging over my feet as she did every other night; she too, could change the routine when she wanted.

5 September 2010

We had a wonderful warm sunny weekend. On Sunday, I walked Mahri and Elle with the minimum of fuss – no leaves blowing in the wind for Elle to scream at, or Mahri to lunge at – and had a nice gentle stroll with time to admire the harvested fields, blue skies, and swallows darting about, chirping to each other. To feel the warmth of the sun on your back was always nice.

I always took the girls first because they could be, hmm … shall we say, boisterous … and then Mr Mac got a walk with me. This was his special time when he had me all to himself. I decided to walk down by the grain store because it was dry and we would not be up to our elbows in mud.

I was strolling along, contemplating what I would do

if I ever won millions in the lottery, when *whooooosh*, Mr Mac made a ninety-degree turn, jumping into the recently harvested field to our right. I had no other option but to follow his lead, in both senses of the word. I was expecting at any moment to be pulled horizontally forward, both by speed from Mr Mac changing direction and the gravitational pull of the planet. Left and right, back and forth he scurried, his nose never more than an inch above the ground. I tried to remain upright and slow him down.

He ignored all my verbal commands because most Airedales cannot multi-task; when the nose was working, the ears did not. I was suddenly aware of several pairs of eyes watching me. I glanced towards the grain store, where a few of the workers who had heard me shouting at Mr Mac were now watching to see if I would indeed plough the field with my nose and any other appendage unfortunate enough to be at right angles to my body. As suddenly as Mr Mac had darted into the field, he stopped. This action also nearly caused me to collide with the ground, but I managed to regain my balance just in time, because Mr Mac pounced forward into the grass and grabbed the rat he'd been chasing. At least, I think he was chasing it; but, as he was not known for his bravery, it might have been it that was chasing him. A quick shake and the rat was quickly dispatched. Mr Mac did the shaking – not me, I might add. This was a case of 'you caught it Mr Mac, you deal with it'.

Mr Mac had decided it was his prize and it was going home with him. "Drop it!" I told him. "Drop it!" I asked him. "Drop!!!" I hissed at him through clenched teeth. "Put it down," I asked sweetly … "No, not lie down, put it down!" He stood his ground, ignoring me while the rat grimaced at me and the workers smiled, waiting for my next move. I patted Mr Mac on the head. "Good boy, Mr Mac. Good boy."

Eureka! It worked. He dropped the rat and we could go home without a backward glance. I was tempted to clean his teeth and face, not that there was any blood or anything on them, but I just thought they should be cleaned. He was having none of it and wanted to be off, boasting to the girls about the great battle he fought and won with the rat. Well, at least I hope it was the rat he was boasting of having fought and not me!

7 September 2010

We had a huge storm last night. Strong winds and horizontal rain. Elle could hear it bouncing off the garage door and wandered round the house growling and muttering. Just as she wandered through the kitchen en route to her bed, the wind blew something into the side of the house with a bang. The object then proceeded to bounce across the patio. This was more than Elle could stand and she threw herself at the door, barking and screaming and growling, all at the same time.

If it wasn't so ear-splittingly loud, it would be funny. The only way to calm her down was to take her out on her lead so she could patrol the garden to prove nothing was amiss; or, more importantly, something was not there that shouldn't be.

I opened the door and stepped out into the driving rain with Elle and Mahri. More barking, yelling and growling from Elle as she dragged me across the drive. Mahri felt obliged to join in with her booming bark that vibrated through your chest. Simultaneously, they dragged me on to the grass. It was just as well the offending article was close to the edge of the drive, as 75 pounds of combined dog weight was too much to hold back in wet and slippery conditions.

As soon as they reached the green plastic watering-can, they stopped all pulling and noise.

"Oh yes, we know what that is ... but it should be by the tap, not here on the grass," Elle muttered, her embarrassment mounting.

"Ah, but it could have been a rat," Mahri suggested, as if to justify their outburst.

Finished causing a scene, they dragged me back inside, anxious to get out of the rain. Elle had apparently forgotten that she wanted to go out for a more personal reason, so, with no sign of the rain stopping, out she went again.

An hour or so later, when it was time for the last outing before bedtime, I rattled the leads. Elle glared at me from under her eyebrows. *"You are joking. Have you seen that rain?"* She buried her head under her fleece and went back to sleep. Mahri stood up, turned about and lay back down again, making it clear she agreed with Elle that *I* was some kind of maniac.

Mr Mac, who had not been part of the attack on the watering-can, came bouncing up, ready for an evening stroll. Mr Mac always pushed ahead to get out of the door first and I knew I should have stopped him, but it was easier not to. Elle always felt obliged to chastise him for being pushy and Mahri, who thought she might be missing out on a treat or something, joined in, and the poor soul got beaten up by the girls.

I opened the door and Mr Mac took one leap forward

and a bigger leap backwards.

"Whoa! What was that?" he said, shaking his head; it had taken the full pelt of driving rain. He looked at me with his lop-sided, quizzical look.

"Do you really want to go out in that? I'll go with you, but it's a very bad idea."

"No, Mr Mac, I do not want to go out, but neither do I want you asking out at 4.00am when it will probably be just as wet." He darted out to the nearest blade of grass, had a quick pee and darted back in again. Not one of them stirred till 7.00am, in case I took them out in the rain again.

8 September 2010

Poor little Elle picked one squabble too many with Mahri yesterday and is a bit battered and nibbled today. Len took her to the vet today for a check-up because she was still very subdued. She was eating and going to the toilet yesterday, so, apart from a small puncture wound to her ear, we thought she was OK; but, today, she was yelping when she put her weight on her right front leg. I thought it was a sympathy yelp. She usually did that when she'd been told off for bad behaviour, but, as I was at work when the altercation took place, I didn't know for certain.

Amy, the new carer, did her best to stop the scrap, but she told me that Mahri was actually very good and none of it was her fault. She'd only used the minimum of her considerable strength to stop Elle being foolish. Elle had flipped for some reason, got really mad and poor Mahri was on the receiving end of her bad temper. Mr Mac has always scarpered and was usually found howling in a corner when disputes like this arose. Mahri walked away as she always did, but Elle would not let the issue drop. Mahri grabbed her and held her till she calmed down. As soon as she was released, Elle kicked off again.

Apparently, Mahri repeated this a few times before Elle would give in and go to her bed to calm down. Mahri could have treated her like Mr Mac's rat but, instead, chose to hold her like a naughty pup. I would have waded right in to separate them and probably been mauled by Elle in my attempt to save her, so letting Mahri deal with it in her own way might have been for the best. Perhaps Elle may have learned her lesson. Mahri was still treating Elle as her pal but, as far as bruises go, Elle's pride was probably a bit more bruised than her physical self. It was always best to get her checked, of course. Len's wallet would now be battered and bruised like Elle herself after the vet was finished with it.

9 September 2010

After our vet visit last night, it appeared Welsh Elle is in need of a bit more healing than we had realized. We thought her collar was a bit tight on Tuesday night, so slackened it by one hole. We also thought she was a bit warm, which was one of the reasons Len took her to the vet yesterday. When Len explained what had happened and said that we could only find one little nip on her ear but it had bled quite a bit, the vet shaved her neck from chin to chest, so he could have a good look, and there were five pairs of puncture wounds. The other set are down the back of her head and neck, and they had become infected overnight.

The vet explained that puncture wounds always become infected, whereas cuts do not; but Len couldn't remember what the explanation was. He thought it was because of the close-up trapping of germs inside. She was given antibiotics and painkillers, but this did not stop her moping about, feeling very sorry for herself. All changed this morning, though. The pain had obviously subsided and she was feeling better and ready to finish the job she started. We thought it best to keep her apart from Mahri for the time being.

When I went to take them for their morning walk, Mahri was bouncing about saying 'hi' to Mr Mac and me. Elle was stretching and getting up, just starting to show signs of animosity towards Mahri. The first three or four times she growled, Mahri just bounced about, ignoring her. The next time, Mahri started to look back at her, as if to say, *"What's your problem?"* I distracted Mahri, but Elle persisted. Mahri stared her down again. *"Bring it on; do I look scared?"* she seemed to say to Elle.

I managed to keep them busy and distracted till after they had their breakfast. I put Elle back on her vitamin B6, as I think her serotonin levels might be low again. I was going to get her a DAP collar, which gives off mummy pheromones to keep her calm.

We've had her tested for all sorts of deficiencies, apart from the serotonin one, as it requires a lumbar puncture and she's too small to go through that. Her demeanour shows the classic symptoms and we know in the past she responded to the special diet. Now that we were sure she was OK, Len would give her lots of extra exercise, so she would be too puffed out to argue with anything but her pillow.

I should have picked up on her mood sooner because, when I arrived home from work, she would get a toy and ask me to play. I would play with her until she got bored or tired. She hadn't done that for a week or so. Bad me. I should have paid more attention, but she has had huge spiders to chase and flies and wasps to bark at, so she has been a bit too busy for boring games of fetch or tug.

14 September 2010

Little Elle-belly has fully recovered from her disagreement with Mahri. I have to say that, when I was told that she had bruised ribs as well as several puncture wounds, I started to laugh. I knew it was very mean of me, but this picture popped into my head of Mahri standing with Elle's head in her mouth, kneeing her in the ribs and throwing her against the wall like a scene from a *Rocky* or Jean-Claude Van Damme movie.

She was still showing a few signs of bearing a grudge towards Mahri. There was the odd growl now and again if Mahri bounced about like a Tigger, but, other than that, they have been running around in the garden together. Mahri would grab a lump of mulched grass and Elle would chase her till she dropped it, and then would run back to get another bit. Finding common ground, they then shared the grass, just because I've told them *not* to eat it.

Mr Mac was more cautious round Elle than Mahri was; but, then, he'd always been scared of her. Just to be on the safe side, we would not leave them alone together in the day kennel till we were sure Elle had got over her little tantrum. Every time Mahri spotted Elle, she was bum in the air, head down, ready to play; but Mahri was always like that. She thought she was a puppy Labrador that had endless energy and springs instead of legs. Boing! Boing!

Mahri bounced over Mr Mac once. That confused him. He couldn't work out where she went. Boing! Boing! *"Ha, ha! You can't catch me."* she laughed, as she charged round for another bounce.

But he could! He grabbed her by her tail, knocked her off balance and grabbed her back leg. It looked so funny as she continued to bounce on three legs like some Disney ballet scene. I suppose it could be called, in ballet terms, a 'pas de chien' or perhaps a 'pas de trois'. (The ballet term is Pas de chat, which is 'steps of a cat'.)

We called Elle a funnyoscity, which is a word we've made up especially for her. She's a cross between funny 'ha-ha' and funny 'hmm, that's odd' or 'curious (curiosity)' because we could not fathom her. We've met lots of other Welshes. In fact, we looked at them and chatted with the breeders, for it was three years before Len made up his mind to have one. I wanted a Poodle because they were kinder on the fingers for grooming, or a Wire Fox Terrier because they were kinder on the eye, being white. I'd see it in the dark. However, we got Elle – kinder on the vet's and dog trainer's bank accounts.

Elle was certainly not kind on the fingers, with her coarse wire wool-like coat, which gave hand stripping a whole new meaning. Her nips without warning to any parts of the anatomy she could reach were, by no means, friendly. That being said, the little minx wormed her way into our hearts and had us wrapped round her little paw. She would win a doggie Oscar one day. She knew just when to sit and look so cute or hold a paw up as if injured.

317

If she'd been really good, she knew to give us the tiniest of smiles. Like a true diva, she could milk every occasion for her own benefit, even after she picked a fight. She would pretend to be scared when Mahri approached, only to run at her snarling when her back was turned.

30 September 2010

I was out in the garden with the dogs last night; it was only 7.00pm, but it was already dark. Thick cloud obscured the moon and the slight drizzle made everything damp and smelly. All this reminded me that we were actually in the middle of our autumn season, although you'd never guess it was almost Hallowe'en. I have catkins on my hazel trees, some rosebuds and a single blossom on my apple tree.

I have been trying to get the dogs in party mood for the annual photo competition in aid of rescue Airedales. Mr Mac still insisted that, as an ex-show dog, he would not dress up or act the fool. Mahri reckoned she was more of an impersonator and her favourite character was a bull in a china shop, closely followed by her impersonation of an ostrich with its head in the sand. She had been working on her lion tamer act with Elle as the ringmaster, but it needed a few refinements yet before it was ready for her stage debut.

Elle, being the diva that she was, graciously allowed me to adorn her little body in a red devil cape, but when it came to the little horns, she protested vociferously.

"OK, how about Dracula, with these pearly white fangs?" I suggested, and offered a black cape. *"Pfiff."* She shook the cape off and walked away muttering. *"Black is so out this season, daarling."*

Her little tail was ramrod straight as she stomped out of the room. I tried to tempt her back with a little bit of chicken. *"Pfah."* She spat it out and went to her bed, throwing all her fleeces out, just in case I'd hidden a pea under them to make her bed uncomfortable … and to prove that she really was a princess.

I started to make dinner and generally ignored her for the next 15 minutes. When I turned round to get something from the fridge, there was Elle sitting in front of the fridge looking so cute … or was it contrite? She was bundled up in her fleece bedding.

"This, daarling, is this season's fashion. And 'this' is the only costume I will wear."

I grabbed my camera and got a picture before she changed her mind. She sat there for another 10 or 15 minutes and then went off to find Mahri for a game of chase.

In the Sunday supplement that week, the fashion pictures were all World War I pilot-type jackets lined with sheepskin. How did she know?

7 November 2010

The fireworks had more or less stopped now. The house next door had a big party for their grandchildren and it was like World War II outside our house. I suppose the DAP[3] thing did work, but perhaps not quite as well as I would have wanted. Mr Mac was a bit jittery and wanted to stay close by me. Mahri tried to sit close, but then couldn't decide what she wanted to do, so wandered off to sit in a corner, before moving to the middle of the room and

---

3   Dog Appeasing Pheromones diffuser.

This, daarling is this season

staring at the ceiling.

There was a particular group of really loud fireworks which set Elle off barking, yodelling and squealing. The fireworks also woke Len up, who had been dozing all day as he was not feeling too well. His waking transported us to the set of a *Carry On* film or wacky cartoon. Len woke with a start and pushed his table aside, tipping all the contents on to the floor. I jumped up to grab the table before it tipped over completely and smashed the glass-topped coffee table. Not realizing what was happening around him, Len nearly fell out of his chair with fright, but I managed to stop him.

I was trying to pull Len and his table back into an upright position and trying to grab his medicine pot before Mahri got to it. This was all too much for Elle, who was in an 'I want to kill something' mood, brought on by all the noise and commotion. She launched an attack on my leg, hauling and pulling at my trousers. For such a wee dog, she impeded my movement quite a bit. I think Elle may have seen my save attempt as an attack on Len. After she was unable to dissuade me from pulling him by pulling me, she jumped up and bit me in the back of my knee. "Yeowee!!" Believing she had resolved the issue, she trotted off to the kitchen without a backward glance to take on the world or her corner of it.

In 28 years and six Airedales, I've never been bitten. I had a few bangs and bruises from bone-heads coming up to greet me as I bent down, but only Elle with her tiny mouth and teeth had taken lumps out of me, little minx. I often told her that I'm trading her in for a rabid crocodile.

The table was OK and Len drifted off to sleep again, this time with Elle on his knee. The other two dogs had taken themselves off to bed, so I relaxed with a nice coffee and listened to Robert Plant's life story.

My knee still stung. I couldn't believe she drew blood but never ripped my trousers. All was well in my world again, though … better, in fact. I had been in charge of the remote control for the TV nearly all night … my idea of heaven!

I wish I'd got a video. It would have been worth a few

pence on one of these TV shows.

I spoke too soon. Len awoke again in a confused state. I went to his aid, and Elle's, in case he knocked her off his knee. I'd grabbed Elle and put her on the floor and then tried to help Len, who had turned into a cross between a dodgem car and a Sherman tank, bouncing off the wall as he flicked the joystick of his chair back and forth. Elle, once again with no thought to her own safety, ran to save her precious Len. This time my flesh remained intact but, alas, my trouser leg was severely lacerated. Fortunately, they were my scruff ones for working in the garden or with the dogs.

9 November 2010

Elle made me laugh. I had been teaching her to sit when we got near some houses with horrid dogs that bounced barking and growling off the fence. Her behaviour was improving, albeit at a snail's pace. Anyway, on Saturday, we were walking down the road near one of these houses, and Elle started to stiffen up, squeal and strain at the lead.

"Elle, sit!!" I commanded. In a split second she had plonked her rear end on the tarmac and then proceeded to hop down the road like a frog, but still maintaining the sit position. I couldn't tell her off. She was sitting – just not in the one place.

And some say dogs cannot think for themselves. ...

Epilogue

As the year 2010 was winding down, I was busy with plans to relocate to a warmer climate. The Wild Bunch were much quieter in their middle years, so I thought it would be an ideal place to end this chapter in their lives. I've always said I wanted the book to have a happy ending. Of course, this could leave the way open for a sequel. I might call it *Mad Woman and English Dogs Go Out in the Midday Sun*, and recount their antics on warm sunny beaches.

My profits from the sale of this book go to support my favourite charities listed below. Please visit their websites; there are many dogs looking for loving homes, and there are always interesting items for sale, which helps pay some of the medical bills for the rescued dogs.

Websites to visit:
http://www.cairnrescueusa.com
http://www.airecanada.com/index.php
http://www.aire-rescue.com
http://www.soar-airedale-rescue.com
http://www.airedalerescue.net
http://www.nc-airedalerescue.com
http://www.atrva.com
http://www.wirefoxrescue.org
http://www.animals-in-distress.eu/donate.html
http://www.poodlesinneed.com/Pages/default.aspx
http://www.dogstrust.org.uk
http://www.bluecross.org.uk
http://www.poodlerescueofhouston.com
http://www.airedalerescue.net
http://www.maryshouse.us

Elle and Mahri in the snow

Lightning Source UK Ltd.
Milton Keynes UK
UKHW020630101022
410232UK00015B/903